THE
LEAN
STRATEGY

THE
LEAN
STRATEGY

Using Lean to Create Competitive Advantage, Unleash Innovation, and Deliver Sustainable Growth

Michael BALLÉ | **Daniel JONES** | **Jacques CHAIZE** | **Orest FIUME**

New York Chicago San Francisco Athens London
Madrid Mexico City Milan New Delhi Singapore Sydney Toronto

3 4 5 6 7 8 9 LCR 22 21 20 19 18 17

ISBN 978-1-259-86042-3
MHID 1-259-86042-6

e-ISBN 978-1-259-86043-0
e-MHID 1-259-86043-4

Library of Congress Cataloging-in-Publication Data
Names: Ballé, Michael, 1965- author. | Jones, Daniel T., author.
Title: The lean strategy : using lean to create competitive advantage,
  unleash innovation, and deliver sustainable growth / by Michael Balle,
  Daniel Jones, Jacques Chaize, and Orest Fiume.
Description: 1 Edition. | New York : McGraw-Hill Education, 2017.
Identifiers: LCCN 2017005169 (print) | LCCN 2017021604 (ebook) | ISBN
  9781259860430 | ISBN 1259860434 | ISBN 9781259860423 (hardback) |
  ISBN 1259860426
Subjects: LCSH: Lean manufacturing. | Industrial management--Technological
  innovations. | Organizational effectiveness. | BISAC: BUSINESS & ECONOMICS
  / Production & Operations Management.
Classification: LCC HD58.9 (ebook) | LCC HD58.9 .B35 2017 (print) | DDC 6
  .4/0132 235
LC record available at https://lccn.loc.gov/2017005169

McGraw-Hill Education books are available at special quantity discounts to use as premiums and sales promotions or for use in corporate training programs. To contact a representative, please visit the Contact Us pages at www.mhprofessional.com.

To all of our sensei

CONTENTS

Preface ix
Acknowledgments xiii
Introduction: The Meaning of Lean xvii

CHAPTER 1 **Make Things Better** 1

CHAPTER 2 **Think Differently** 23

CHAPTER 3 **Lead from the Ground Up** 53

CHAPTER 4 **Framing for Learning** 71

CHAPTER 5 **Organize for Learning** 117

CHAPTER 6 **A New Formula for Growth** 141

CHAPTER 7 **Reusable Learning for Continuously Growing Value** 163

CHAPTER 8 **Accelerate the Gains** 195

CHAPTER 9 **From Kaizen to Innovation** 223

CHAPTER 10 **Change Your Mind** 237

Conclusion: Toward a Waste-Free Society 251
Notes. 259
Index. 263

PREFACE

This book is about *learning to compete in a fundamentally different way*. Today, the practice of management has narrowed increasingly into a finance-driven approach: reducing headcount, consolidating footprint by buying or selling companies, and replacing individual responsibility with IT systems. As we've all experienced, both as customers and employees, this generates ever larger bureaucratic companies with disappointing products or services and disengaged, distrustful employees. We know there is a better way to compete. We have been fortunate to witness how businesses can grow sustainably and profitably by focusing on customer value through developing the businesses' people.

This dynamic approach—a people-centric way of working together—delivers better business results, for the organization, for its employees, and for society at large. It does not treat employees as commodities to be replaced by robots, nor does it trap managers in bureaucratic systems inherently resistant to change, nor does it encourage short-term solutions at the expense of the environment. At companies that practice this way of working, employees are involved in improving their work, and overall, the conditions for continuous innovation are created day to day without wasting precious resources. In the process, the changes needed to compete in turbulent markets are based on the talent and passion of the people creating the value themselves as they seek a better way to do their work.

Nearly 30 years ago we discovered that a people-centric management system lay behind the rise of the Japanese car makers, especially Toyota. Sharing this approach resonated with many people struggling to improve their own organizations, and it led to many experiments in every kind of sector, from start-ups to healthcare, from industry to services to IT, and to an ever-growing global Lean movement—called "Lean" to capture the agility, speed, flexibility, trimness, and robustness that distinguishes it from traditional management.

Common practices in this system, which were codified as Lean tools as a means of teaching the core principles, were originally seen as the key to eliminating waste and designing more efficient processes. However, because these tools challenge conventional thinking, they have to be learned by doing, rather than in a training classroom. In fact, we now know that the Toyota Production System is a *learning* framework for helping employees to improve their work and to work together to create the value customers are paying for. While many still interpret Lean as simply a management system, there is much more to it.

This insight, in turn, called for a very different way of managing the learning process at the front line and in supporting activities. To do so, we learned another set of management tools, including A3 problem solving, daily management, value stream analysis, and Hoshin planning. It became clear that a different way of *thinking* was needed for these tools to deliver results, that they had to become the responsibility of line management, and that they needed active leadership involvement to be sustained and spread across the organization.

Indeed, much of what has been written on Lean takes an organizational perspective, rather than a business one. With this book, we look at how the leaders of successful Lean transformations—the very executives who run the company—adopt Lean thinking, change their own ways of managing, and spread this knowledge throughout their business. To understand these leadership challenges, we turned to the initial pioneers who used Lean as an integral part of their strategy from the start. This was the starting point for this book, and it brought this unique team together, a pioneering CEO and a CFO who both had personal experience of leading Lean plus two authors with many years' experience in coaching leaders.

As this book came into focus, we learned three lessons. First, adopting Lean thinking is a complete business strategy. Lean thinking redefines the traditional notion of strategy: attacking markets with proprietary technology and standardized processes, and managing operations through capacity investments and relentless cost cutting. Lean strategy represents a fundamentally different approach: seeking the right problems to solve, framing the improvement directions such that every person understands how he or she can contribute, and supporting learning through change after change at the value-adding level in order to avoid wasteful decisions. Sustaining an improvement direction toward a North Star and supporting daily improvement to solve global challenges make up a strategy, and a winning one.

Second, leading a people-centric organization is all about learning—how to think differently about management so that improvement becomes an integral aspect of doing the job. Humans deliver the greatest performance when they are engaged in improving, when their efforts in doing so are supported and recognized, and when they see their own progress—in short, when they see the *meaning* in what they do. The highest-performing teams have the latitude to hold their own opinions about how they fare, the incentive to think of better ways of doing things, and the control and autonomy to enact changes that will make them better at what they do. The Lean learning system offers a structured way to support all the teams in their own learning efforts—and beyond each team's ingenuity, it enables leaders to learn how to better compete in their field by learning from their operational improvements.

Third, Lean learning can improve the bottom line: improving quality supports sales and margin (by reducing the cost of nonquality), while accelerating flows leads to better use of capacity and cash, and daily kaizen supports cost controls at each team's level. At the business level, a Lean view of profitability for today and tomorrow (and how to finance it) radically changes where leaders choose to invest and how. By investing in people's competencies and understanding how step-by-step improvement can open up new capabilities, leaders create the conditions for real, sustainable innovation, financed mostly by cash improvements from accelerating operational flows. This radical rethinking of what makes a business profitable distinguishes Lean leaders from traditional financial managers who break down sales, operational costs, and capacity investments into separate silos and, as we can see all around us, continue to destroy true value for the sake of short-term accounting gains. Mutual trust as confidence in leaders, in teams, and in oneself is the bedrock of sustainable profitability.

It is commonly said of Lean efforts that "CEO involvement" is the key to success. This book takes the perspective of CEOs who have successfully transformed their businesses with Lean, showing how they transformed their own thinking as the first step in changing others:

• Lean thinking is a different form of workplace-based reasoning where we learn to find the right problems to solve from daily work experience, face them and create the right metrics, frame them in a way everyone in the organization can understand and adhere to, and solve them by forming new solutions step by step, involving the teams themselves in practical controlled experiments and changes.

- Lean is a learning system that each Lean leader can develop in his or her own company starting with an understanding of how the template of the Toyota Production System can be used to establish a North Star for customer satisfaction and profitability. Lean supports individual learning through stopping and investigating rather than living with defects and errors, encourages cross-functional learning by using the tools of just-in-time to reduce all lead times, and grows employee satisfaction and mutual trust by creating a different work environment in which problems are seen as the fundamental material for improvement and problem solving is at the heart of the firm's culture.

- A Lean understanding of how the various financial elements of the business really generate the bottom line and how Lean leaders use greater wisdom in their financial management to support the ingenuity of their teams and sustain genuine innovations from improving capabilities and developing individual competencies. In the Lean approach to finance, the success of the company starts with the personal success of each employee, and management supports a positive relationship between each person and his or her work and customer satisfaction.

- Lean provides insight into continuous innovation by using the learning system to discover value analysis and value engineering opportunities to concurrently develop engineering, production, and supply chain capabilities to deliver breakthrough (and industry-changing) innovation from team-based kaizen.

We hope that this book will inspire readers to begin their own experiments in searching for a better way of managing as if people matter. Join us on this journey to make the world a better place.

ACKNOWLEDGMENTS

From Michael: My gratitude first goes to my parents. My father, Freddy, first got me to the gemba to see the experiments he was running with Toyota 25 years ago, and he has been teaching me "learning by doing" ever since, helping me to learn, step by step, how to see with the eyes of an area supervisor, production management, site director, and ultimately CEO. My thanks also to my mother who taught me what writing was really about and who patiently read and corrected my many texts, leading me to hopefully become, over the years, a better craftsman of my own trade.

Gratitude to Tom Ehrenfeld, the "chief engineer" of so many great Lean books (and eight Shingo prizes)—we couldn't have done this without his guidance on the argument and deft touch on the page.

Thanks to my many senseis for being so patient with my sometimes too-quick conclusions and ideas and for always bringing me back to the core of the matter: Dan Jones, Jeff Liker, John Shook, Orry Fiume, Art Smalley, Marcus Chao, Art Byrne, Durward Sobek, Jim Morgan, and Jim Womack; and Toyota veterans Tracey Richardson, Peter Handlinger, Hugues Pichon, François Papin, and Gilberto Kosaka. Special thanks to Sandrine Olivencia for her thoughtful inputs on Lean and agile and the design of www.TheLeanStrategy.com. Thanks to Kelly Singer and her groundbreaking work on Lean and green on her LeanGreenInstitute .com blog. Special thanks to Joe Lee, TPS sensei in Taiwan, for challenging me about concrete and abstract thinking—a conversation that started on the gemba and continued over several months, which later led to writing this book!

I am also deeply indebted to the executives I've had the privilege to work with. They've helped me experience this set of ideas firsthand in real-life situations. I am now fortunate to call many of them friends as well as colleagues: Stéphane André, Klaus Beulker, Jean-Claude Bihr, Laurent Bordier, Jean-Baptiste Bouthillon, Steve Boyd, Jacques Chaize, Fabiano Clerico, Furio Clerico, Cyril Dané, Patrick De Coster, Norbert Dubost, Boris Evesque, Frédéric Fiancette, Christophe Frachet, Benjamin

Garel, Nicolas Guillemet, Evrard Guelton, Michael Kightley, Christophe Riboulet, Thierry Rosa, Mike Schembri, and Pierre Vareille, as well as the Lean officers who have made these changes possible by their inventiveness and dedication: Ariane Bouzette, Paul Evans, Florent Letellier, Michel Marissal, Marc Mercier, Yves Mérel, Eric Prévot, Alain Prioul, Philippe Pull, and Cécile Roche.

Gratitude also to my colleagues at the Institut Lean France for their support and initiative in spreading these beautiful ideas—Godefroy Beauvallet, Yves Caseau, Catherine Chabiron, Marie-Pia Ignace, Richard Kaminski, Fabien Leroy, James Liefer, Olivier Soulié, and Aurore Xemar.

Finally, I would like to thank deeply Florence, Roman, and Alexandre for putting up with me while I write at my desk and, although physically present, I am very, very far away. I love you.

From Orry: There are too many people who have helped me to grow in my thinking about Lean to list them all here. That said, I would like to acknowledge the influence of Dr. Edwards Deming, Thomas Johnson, and Robert Kaplan, on my initial foray during the late 1980s into questioning what I had previously been taught, and I had practiced, about management and accounting. Listening to Dr. Deming for four days and reading Johnson and Kaplan's pioneering 1987 book *Relevance Lost: The Rise and Fall of Management Accounting*[1] turned my world upside down. I would also like to express my appreciation to all of my teammates at The Wiremold Company, especially between the years 1991 and 2002. This team, led by Art Byrne, our CEO, understood that Lean was the strategy that would allow us to serve all of our stakeholders better. This did not come without some initial difficulty, but as soon as people began acting differently and seeing the enormous benefits of doing so, the team came together to successfully implement our Lean strategy. I would also like to pay tribute to all those who read this book and finally abandon traditional strategy thinking and adopt Lean strategic thinking.

In the spirit of "life-long learning" (or as one of my professors called it "rust proofing") I would like to acknowledge how much I have learned from my coauthors. Lots of things that I thought I knew have become much clearer because of their collective contributions to this book. Thank you to each of you.

Last, I would like to acknowledge my wife, Claire, our combined five children and ten, soon to be eleven grandchildren. Even though I am "officially" retired, your support of this project and my other Lean endeavors has been wonderful.

From Jacques: This book is a learning journey that started 10 years ago when Michael Ballé helped me and my teams transform ourselves and turn around our company. Thank you, Michael, for this incredible gift.

My gratitude goes to the Socla and Danfoss teams, who shared this fruitful journey, particularly Frédéric Fiancette, Eric Prévot, Lionel Repellin, Christian Amblard, and Mathias Fumex. Thank you for having never given up!

My thanks to the worldwide Society for Organizational Learning (SOL) community and its organizational learning approach that helped me enter Lean through the right door: Peter Senge, Arie de Geus, Irène Dupoux-Couturier, Heidi Guber, Odile Schmutz, Alain Gauthier, and Gilles Gambin.

Many thanks to my friends at APM, a unique management network, for sharing their own Lean journeys: Frank Flipo, Stéphane André, Alain Genet, Philippe Counet, and Stéphane Lequin.

My gratitude to these great entrepreneurs, friends, and real Lean strategists: Pierre Bellon, founder of Sodexo, Jean Chagnon at Lallemand, Jorgen Vig Knudstorp at Lego, and Niels Bjorn Christiensen at Danfoss.

Finally, to Chloé, Quentin, Henri, Clément, and Hugo, our five grandchildren, may this book be, in a few years, a useful read for their future entreprises!

From Dan: I would like to start by acknowledging Tom Ehrenfeld: without your help and patience, this book would not have happened! Then all the folks on the many gembas we visited—and the many Toyota senseis who patiently answered our questions—with more questions for us to think about! They opened our eyes to really being able to see what is going on in the gemba. We learned so much from them—both about what worked and what did not, challenging us to dig deeper to understand what might work in our next experiment.

Then colleagues in the Lean movement who have shared a lot of these questions over the years—including Jim Womack, John Shook, Dave

Brunt, Rene Aernoudts, Wiebe Nijdam, Oriol Cuatrecases, Steve Bell, Alice Lee, Eric Buhrens, and the leaders of the LGN Institutes—dedicating their efforts to spreading Lean across the world.

Then all the Lean authors who have contributed to our discussions on the Lean Edge (www.theLeanedge.org), Planet Lean (www.planet-Lean .com), and the Lean Post (www.Lean.org/LeanPost/).

Also the following for taking the time to review this manuscript and giving us valuable feedback: Art Byrne, John Shook, Jeff Liker, Torbjorn Netland, Arnaldo Camuffo, Pierre Masai, Cliff Ransom, Ed Miller, Gary Brooks, and Jyrki Perttunen.

My warmest thanks to my wife Pat for surviving "another book."

Also Michael's father, Freddy Ballé, one of the earliest true Lean pioneers in Europe, without whom this book would not have happened.

Thanks as well to our McGraw-Hill editors Knox Huston and Donya Dickerson.

And finally, thanks to my fellow authors who have made this book writing process such a rich experience—I am really proud to have been part of such a unique team.

INTRODUCTION

The Meaning of Lean

Rarely do any of us have the opportunity to change the story of our lives—the way that we see and respond to problems, the choices that we make as individuals and organizations trying to produce things and deliver the services that address our needs and, ideally, make the world a better place.

We all want to live well; we all want to succeed. The promise of ever better and smarter products, fulfilling careers, stable and caring communities in which to bring up kids, and even some free time for personal fulfillment is still very much alive. However, the side effects of the system we've built up to deliver well-being—financial stress, environmental anxieties, disengaging jobs, overcommercialized escapism, growing feelings of unfairness and inequality—are increasingly threatening the system's ability to deliver. In short, the prevailing industrial model of work, production, and thinking about work has fallen short of its promise.

Markets today are saturated; financiers have hijacked the economy as the source of profits. The value of manufacturers, or anyone creating new products and services, has become discounted at a time when somebody, somewhere in the world, can quickly copy the product (through cheaper labor or other means) or digitally disrupt its usage. Jobs are increasingly seen as short-term gigs without loyalty, benefits, ownership, or growth. It seems that only those creating new "platforms" (the Googles and Facebooks of the world with gated digital markets) have enduring value. So how can companies grow and prosper in this age?

We believe the answer lies in changing their story. And not just the easy tale about who they are and what they do or make—but something deeper.

Today Lean is known to many but truly understood by few. Between us we have many collective decades of working with Lean, and we have come to believe that the real meaning of Lean is about changing the story of how your organization and industry create value for users and society at large. The Lean strategy is about using your company to change the story of your industry.

Consider Toyota, the primary source of what today is known as Lean. For many years Toyota has been changing the story of mobility. Planned obsolescence was a mainstay feature of the automotive business until Toyota changed the game by offering top quality cars in the low range of the market at affordable prices. Quality became free. Today the slightest doubt about a new car model's quality dramatically damages its reputation. Gas guzzling and high emissions were once accepted as prices to pay for power (at a time when electric cars were seen as an unrealistic pipe dream for future generations to figure out) until Toyota learned how to succeed with hybrid fuel-electric models that started with the Prius and now extend across a wide range of models (8 million sold and counting). What were once seen as necessary trade-offs are now viewed as complementary parts of the total equation. And Toyota has in fact made its next impossible goal public—to produce a hydrogen-powered car whose exhaust is . . . water.

Toyota changed the story of the auto industry by learning to design and build high quality cars more effectively than its competitors well before it went on to pioneer alternative power train technologies. This fact belies the common assumption that technology is the only way that the story of an industry can be fundamentally changed. Many studies of technology show that user acceptance and legacy organizations and mindsets are the biggest constraints on realizing the opportunities opened up by new technology.[1] Toyota created the learning culture able to develop these breakthrough technologies *and* the ability to scale them quickly through several product generations as the market for them grew. In so doing, it created what the deep thinker Takahiro Fujimoto has described as an "evolutionary learning capability."[2]

Toyota is far from a perfect organization, and any of its leaders would agree that it has just as many problems and flaws as any other automaker. The difference lies in the fact that its executives have learned to embrace these problems and face them with their frontline team. That doesn't make Toyota perfect, but it makes it visibly better than its competitors (as the world's sixth most valued brand in *Forbes*'s ranking, Toyota is the top industrial one, and it is way ahead of its competitors). Actually, Toyota does not seek to be perfect. It strives to be better today than it was yesterday and to be better tomorrow than today. Its leaders have discovered that sustainable performance is born out of dynamic progress, not static optimization, which is a crucial lesson for businesses beyond the automotive world.

Changing your story is about finding and solving the right problems—the ones that help your customers solve problems in their lives without wasting their time, effort, and resources on the wrong things. Doing so better than your competitors pressures them to do the same, which eventually changes the story of the entire industry. Cars, for example, are no longer seen today as unreliable—dangerous—things. They are now considered to be the most advanced product we use in terms of quality and safety. Yet changing the story of an industry is not an aim in itself; it simply makes for a better business case. By constantly challenging yourself to be better, you put pressure on your competitors, and you reframe the conditions of success in your industry to those which you do best.

Lean is a method to change the story of your business in order to change the story of your industry. Managers today seek profits primarily by exploiting external factors rather than looking for value by dramatically improving productivity and quality. As a result, many companies operate as a "black box" around the way value is constructed—by market monopolies, vendor bullying, customer lock-in, substitution threats, and so forth. This need not be so. You can shift from seeking value through financial gimmickry and instead create value from within. Such an approach challenges the conventional business school mindset: Lean is not a way to temporarily dress up your company's sale value but a way to boost enterprise value by radically improving its ability to deliver more and more value over time. This in turn creates a better, more sustainably profitable business case for your company in terms of better sales, better cash flow, better margins, and more efficient capital investments.

This Lean strategy helps people radically rethink the question of what they "need to do," and this approach helps individuals to create their own stories rather than have others imposing stories upon them. Beyond the personal strategy change in helping people build their own journey, it reverses other broader narratives. While making money is recognized as necessary to keep cash flowing through the business to nourish daily operations and fund new developments, the maximum profit is not seen as a goal in itself but a means to a greater end. The purpose of the firm—that is, the service it renders to its customers (and the benefits it provides to society as a whole)—is what markets reward in the midterm. Higher quality and better value improve sales. The organization's tale is the sum of all personal development stories aligned toward helping customers do something they want to do—which they reward us for.

But let us be clear: this story is firmly rooted not in a grand abstract perspective of how the world *should* be. Rather, we have built this argument from years of practice in which we have observed compelling results of people and organizations using this different approach to achieve remarkable results. By all measures and values, we have learned that Lean is simply a better way of enterprise today.

Dan is cofounder of the Lean movement (with Jim Womack); Orry was the CFO of one of the first truly Lean businesses out of Toyota (Wiremold, as chronicled in *Lean Thinking*[3]); Jacques is the retired CEO of Socla and led its Lean transformation firsthand; and Michael has been studying Lean for 25 years and has pioneered seeing Lean systems as learning systems. Together, we aim to share with you the excitement of the performance potential of Lean thinking for any business—and indeed, we've witnessed Lean transformations firsthand in every possible sector, from industry to services, from hospitals to start-ups. We've also learned about using Lean thinking from witnessing how business leaders have embraced Lean, made it their own, and led their companies to success and their employees to achieve their full potential. We hope to share the genuine fun of seeing things differently, coming to grips with one's hardest problems and solving them, shoulder to shoulder, with all in the company to build deep relationships of trust with customers, employees, and suppliers and, in doing so, move from improvement to true innovation.

Lean thinking's core insight, that of better coordinating people, equipment, and work to create more value while generating less waste, has been in many ways a countermeasure (or a series of countermeasures) to the problems that emerge at the most successful companies. As any company grows, it develops "big company disease," turning meaningful work into meaningless work and converting engaged employees into disposable and devalued assets. Bureaucracy grows while quality, productivity, and initiative inevitably decline in the face of symptoms such as these:

- *Robotic process focus over customer concerns:* Businesses become so obsessed with standardizing processes and driving down costs that they ignore the problems, preferences, and lifestyles of their individual customers (ever tried to resolve a problem through a call center?). Internally, imposing standard processes on employees (generally as a cost-containment exercise for the sake of organizational "efficiency") robs them of the latitude they need to learn and to help and support real, live customers. Providing extra value becomes constrained—prevented—by internal rules and regulations.

- *Silo thinking over collaborative teams and a systems approach:* Conventional management holds that if all individuals do their job as they should, everything will work out well in the end. They do work out, but at a completely ridiculous cost. Organizations today are too big, and interrelated, for any type of point-optimization approach to produce better overall outcomes. As long as each functional head is determined to solve his or her own problems regardless of the cost to others in the organization, then most efforts to improve something or achieve a specific goal come at the cost of someone else. The first step toward teamwork is understanding what colleagues are trying to do and recognizing the problems and challenges they face and how one's own work helps or hinders this, to develop better collaboration.

- *Devaluing rather than developing human capital:* In most companies, especially established bureaucratic ones, middle managers see their role as defenders of top management's orthodoxy. They enforce silent obedience from employees who are there to execute, not think. There is neither a premium put on meaningful individual thought or contribution nor a way to harvest this systematically. People are there to do their static job duties; their personal experience is rejected as a source of learning.

- *"Brown ocean" strategic thinking:* While most forward-thinking CEOs speak wistfully of pursuing "blue ocean strategies" (capturing new markets with new technologies and strategies), the vast majority of companies in this dynamic economy are far more focused on defending legacy technologies, legacy assets, and legacy transactions than on actually doing something new. They cling to antiquated technologies, and they coerce customers to remain, rather than trust in new value propositions. The constant pressure to squeeze economies of scale chokes the resources needed for new techniques and technologies while protecting legacy technologies to justify sunk costs. These are zombie ideas: dead but still walking around destroying people and innovation.

Lean thinking combats big company disease by spurring managerial thinking to provide meaningful work to people who work mindfully, in order to always deliver better value for customers. This new form of thinking rests on the fundamental intuition that as leaders, we do not need to tell others how to do better work. Instead, *we need to explore and discover with them what working better means* in their own situation.

Lean thinking hinges on a transformational change of leadership posture: we're not going to make people work better (after having decided what they should do differently). We're going to seek and explore with them what working better means. A Lean system, we learned from Toyota, is a set of interrelated learning activities to explore, at the workplace, answers to four deep questions:

- *How do we satisfy customers better?* We don't just want products and services people like; we want products and services they *love*. We want *completely* satisfied customers, which means understanding what we can do better right now to help them with their *individual* problems as well as figuring out how to evolve our offer to better satisfy them *collectively* in the future.

- *How do we make work easier?* People seek meaning in work just as they do in every aspect of their life. How do we involve all employees in improving their own work and their teams' work in eliminating all the obstacles that get in the way of doing the best work for customers? How do we make the work experience flow better? How do we make it richer and more fulfilling because anyone can pitch in, have her say, and be supported in trying her ideas? In addition to this, how do we make work safer as well?

- *How do we reduce total cost?* To remain competitive in fast moving markets, how do we continuously reduce our cost base, not by squeezing budgets line by line, but by sharing larger cost issues with the people in the processes themselves and involving them in helping us reduce the *total* cost of making products or delivering a service? How do we lighten the burden of cost on every product or service by eliminating the waste in the corporate, engineering, production, supply chain, and support systems? And how do we minimize the impact of what we are doing on the environment and the world we live in?

- *How do we learn faster together?* The breakthrough thinking that Lean offers is that of better individual competence and better teamwork. This means taking responsibility when things go wrong (as they do daily) and not explaining them away by blaming someone or something else—confronting the problems together without feelings of guilt or fault. We learn together when we learn to face our problems and support each other without denial or blame. We roll up our sleeves and think deeply about the situation and try various ways to improve, with everyone's input. True learning is not just about learning to do better what we already know how to do. It is also about discovering what we need to learn that we simply don't know. Learning faster together requires an underlying atmosphere of trust and effort, and it is nourished by quick feedback, even when it sounds on the spot like criticism (it is not). Learning needs open, curious minds, certainly, but also warm hearts.

This big company disease is deadly. As start-ups scale up, they usually do so by pursuing the success of a product or application, ignoring complexity costs as they boost capacity as fast as they can. As they fill their market demand, rapid growth tends to slow down and cross-functional costs increase, so that the entire cost structure starts to outpace revenue growth. At that stage, companies typically try to optimize their cost structures, and they do so by adding layers of bureaucratic controls, which compounds the problem and makes it less likely that they'll find an innovative way to attract a new swath of customers. When these optimization actions fail to either restart growth or slow the increase of operational costs, executives, often pressured by their boards, resort to taking cost-cutting measures such as restructuring and/or reducing the footprint and head count, which, in turn further damages service to customers and hastens the demise of the company. The curve in Figure I.1 shows the effect of unchecked big company disease. The Lean challenge is to fight big company disease in order to find new innovative ways to fuel further growth while keeping the

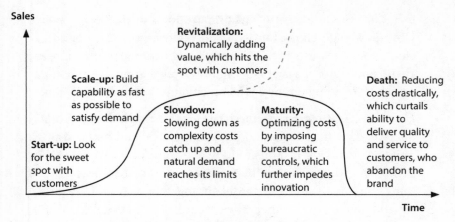

Figure I.1 Unchecked Big Company Disease

cost increases in check through more flexible and more frugal investments and less bureaucracy.

Over the past two decades Lean has been accused of being a means of squeezing more from a fixed asset by optimizing its resources through eliminating waste, improving processes, and eliminating resources—and above all people. This is simply wrong, and we hope to start a different conversation about Lean with this book.

Lean thinking is a cognitive revolution first, one that inevitably leads to an organizational one. It's about learning new thinking and doing skills (and indeed, learning by doing) to come to grips with business situations differently and look for new, innovative, not-thought-of-before ways of better solving our problems, with all employees, not against them.

It's about changing the story of your industry, your business, your work, and your self. For good.

CHAPTER 1

Make Things Better

Create more value by . . . creating and delivering more value.

Close to the end of his 30 years' tenure as CEO of Socla, a water valve manufacturer within a larger corporate group, one of us (Jacques) was faced with a severe crisis. The capital markets had dried up in the wake of the Lehman Brothers collapse and subsequent financial meltdown, halting most construction projects and threatening his company. Socla had thrived for years with a bold strategy. While most competitors had taken the low road, offering a reduced range of products sourced from low-cost producers in other countries, with correspondingly low quality, Socla had offered a wide catalog of top-range quality products that could be delivered next day.

This strategy had delivered a solid reputation and high profitability because customers were ready to pay top dollar for a top brand. But it was cash draining because of the massive inventories needed to deliver a large range of products from the catalog on the next day and because of the investments required to keep assembly and machining productive in a high-cost country. When the crisis hit, demand dropped radically, and cash became a live-or-die issue as the parent company found itself also unexpectedly strapped for cash—so much so that it decided to sell Socla, but it couldn't find a taker precisely because of the cash situation.

Jacques had in fact tried Lean at Socla prior to the crisis. He had always been open-minded toward progressive managerial experiments (he was in fact cofounder of the French chapter of the Society of Organizational Learning), and he had brought in a top-notch consultant for a spell. But after realizing some results through several productivity projects with Lean tools, Jacques and his COO Frédéric Fiancette abandoned the work. Post-project performance improvements were hard to maintain, and people were becoming increasingly negative and resistant to the idea of joining existing projects or initiating new ones. Always very sensitive to the work atmosphere in the company, Jacques and the COO took a step back. They both saw the promise of Lean—no hesitation there—but clearly, a list of "improvement" projects was not the way to do it.

The crisis imposed a new imperative to respond, and so Jacques and Fiancette decided to try Lean again. This time they followed the approach outlined in *Lean Thinking*, working with a Lean sensei. On the shop floor, the first contact with the sensei was confusing at best, vexing at worst. The sensei's position was that Jacques and Fiancette simply didn't understand their industrial problems, and neither did he, expert as he was, but that their goal should be to discover these problems together—this, to a management team who had successfully run the company for decades. Second, his proposed method to discover the deep problems was to fix the obvious operational issues where the company's promise for delivery to customers and safety to employees was visibly unfilled. Solve these practical problems, the sensei argued, and the rest will come. Start here, the sensei essentially said, and we will address the broader issues as we go along.

This was hard to swallow, but Jacques and Fiancette gave it a go and, to their surprise, found that, yes, the rest did follow. Over the following years the company radically transformed itself, maintained its sales in a down market, captured market share, and became cash positive. The parent group eventually sold the business for a double-digit multiple of the earnings before interest and taxes (EBIT), at a time when few such deals even happened. In retrospect, Jacques is still amazed at how they turned the company around without ever reorganizing, restructuring, or reengineering. They just made things better. And then better again. If they did anything, it was to learn the principles and techniques Toyota had pioneered to learn to make things better.

Can the thinking of a Japanese car manufacturer be relevant to today's issues? Fifteen years ago, the pioneers of "natural capitalism" sought to reconcile capitalism with environmental sustainability, and in doing so, they came across *Lean Thinking*, a bestselling book cowritten by Jim Womack and Dan, as a viable alternative. While the title could not have been clearer—Lean *thinking*—many readers (and those seeking to apply its lessons) have focused on the authors' arguments showing that any human activity is riddled with *waste* (human activities that absorb resources but create no value) generated by the run-of-the-mill way operations run, that this waste degrades performance and satisfaction, and, just as importantly, that this waste can be eliminated.

Paul Hawken, Amory Lovins, and Hunter Lovins envisioned an economy of service and flow, where companies don't own excess capacity but accomplish more by a constant search for efficiency, dematerialization, simplification, and Lean thinking at all stages. "For the first time," they claimed, "we can plausibly and practically imagine a more rewarding and less risky economy whose health, prospects, and metrics reverse age-old assumptions about growth: an economy where we grow by using less and less and become stronger by being leaner."[1]

Lean thinking was poised to step into this void and fill the need for a new form of capitalism, a better way of making things based on a fundamentally different approach. But, not surprisingly, it has taken many years and many false starts to learn how different this approach really is. Jacques's early experience was typical. Leaders were attracted to the promise of engaging employees in eliminating waste and cutting costs, and they would hire "experts" or consultants to solve problems for them. The consultants saw this as a new business opportunity, and they were watching very closely what these Japanese "consultants" were doing to see how they could fill this need.

In the early days these Japanese sensei consultants would visit their clients for a week every four to six weeks to teach western managers how to get started with *kaizen*: small-step improvements by the frontline teams themselves. To do so, they would conduct five-day demonstrative "breakthrough" kaizen events with teams to dramatically reconfigure their activities and demonstrate for top managers what Lean could do. (Real kaizen does not normally occur within an "event" but is part of the normal way of doing the job, with either suggestions or team-based quality circles, such as dedicating one hour a week to solving specific issues.) They would also conduct training sessions in Lean tools and assign homework for teams to complete before their next visit. They also watched how Toyota leaders developed their local suppliers by developing model lines. These became the building blocks of their consulting offerings, often wrapped in a maturity framework. Larger organizations also built internal Lean teams to assemble all the Lean and Six Sigma tools into their "production system" and roll this out across the organization in the same way as they had rolled out Six Sigma.

Dan and Jim observed many of these programs firsthand as they sought willing pioneers to learn how Lean could be used beyond the auto industry. For instance, Dan led teams of executives from the U.K. retailer Tesco and its suppliers to observe the vast amount of waste, delays, and checking along the supply chain from production to the point of sale in a supermarket. This triggered the first moves toward pull-based rapid replenishment in the grocery industry, inspired by Toyota's aftermarket parts distribution system. He also walked with groups of medical staff along the patient journey to begin to see the reasons for and implications of all the delays and queues in a hospital.

These approaches to "implementing" Lean undoubtedly delivered results, initially from getting rid of low-hanging fruit, but later from things like reconfiguring work from departments into U-shaped production cells, to introducing pulse lines for repairing and overhauling aeroengines and military aircraft, to creating flow through warehousing in retailing and visually managing the flow of patients through a hospital. Indeed, many pieces of Lean practice became well-known "tools" such as value stream maps and (later on) "A3 thinking." The more that Lean tools delivered "results," the greater a challenge it was to sustain these programs.

The shop floor pushed back against improvements that were done to them by experts. Occasional kaizen events did not give shop floor teams enough practice in solving day-to-day problems as buffers were removed from the flow of work. Experience told them that these improvement programs would come . . . and go again. Teams found it difficult—impossible—to create a flow of work across departmental boundaries. Top management was rarely actively involved and acted under the impression that Lean applied only to operations. As a result, support functions continued "business as usual," which created a great deal of tension within the organization. And so internal Lean experts and trainers ended up fighting fires constantly.

Meeting these challenges meant digging deeper into the Toyota management system. It became clear that maintaining any progress meant growing the capabilities of frontline teams by giving them daily practice in problem solving and kaizen, coached by line management and supported by experts. Experiments quickly showed how Lean could transform all the activities of the organization beyond operations. Yet management had to be actively involved and needed to learn some Lean tools if they were to deliver the business benefits. These included a Hoshin planning system that aligned shop floor improvements with the strategic objectives of the organization, using visual Obeya rooms in management and engineering and using A3 thinking as a common language for problem solving at every level in the organization. These could then be brought together in a Lean management system.*

But making all these changes was not enough. There is nothing wrong with any or even all of these elements of Lean practice. And yet they often function as barriers rather than aids in a complete Lean transformation. That's because they are often seen as "tactics" without understanding the strategic nature of Lean. Now we need to take one more step. What is missing is the different way of thinking and learning that underlies them and that delivers the true promise of Lean. It is time to learn from the pioneers like The Wiremold Company, that used Lean as a strategic initiative from the top to change the way of thinking across its organizations. As we noted earlier, it is no accident that Jim and Dan called their book *Lean Thinking*.

What Is Lean Thinking?

Lean Thinking was inspired by the fabled Toyota Production System (TPS). After 20 years of careful study of both Toyota's successes and setbacks as the pioneer in Lean thinking, and the many companies that have risen to Toyota's challenge, we are certain that Lean companies are more profitable than their competitors, thanks to their constant search for more sustainable solutions. Toyota, at the time this was written, was the largest automaker in the world, with twice the profitability of its main challenger of similar size, Volkswagen (VW). As we mentioned in the introduction, Toyota has led a revolution in cleaner cars with the first hybrid gas-electric engines and is now working on a long-term plan to introduce hydrogen-fueled cars. Operationally, its factories are smaller, lighter, more flexible, and greener than any other automotive manufacturer. It is the only original equipment manufacturer (OEM)

---

* Please note that throughout this book we often refer to terms that have become well known to the Lean community. If you need further definitions of terms beyond our explanations, we recommend *The Lean Lexicon*, Lean Enterprise Institute (LEI), Cambridge, MA, 2003. You can also get more background on the LEI site, www.Lean.org.

actively seeking zero landfill plants with a systematic Reduce, Reuse, Recycle, Recover Energy approach. And yet, in the United States, Toyota makes four times the profit per car than General Motors.

Since the publication 25 years ago of *The Machine That Changed the World,* also cowritten by Jim Womack and Dan, thousands of companies have taken up Toyota's challenge to build a Lean enterprise.[2] Two decades ago, *Lean Thinking* described the spectacular success of some such firms (including The Wiremold Company, where Orry served as CFO). Following the wide appeal of their two books, Jim and Dan dedicated themselves to spreading Lean knowledge across the world, creating the Lean Enterprise Institute (LEI) in the United States in 1996, and then setting up the Lean Global Network of affiliate institutes around the world.

Fifteen years ago, Dan, Michael, and Orry wondered whether Lean thinking could grow in France.* Today many other leaders, such as Jacques, have joined the movement, and we've been privileged to observe these companies up close, from workplace visits to discussions with their CEOs. In France, and in fact everywhere that we have observed companies seeking to adopt Lean, we have found many who enjoy short-term benefits— even in the most adverse economic or cultural conditions. And yet we encounter few who have truly captured the magic of Toyota's unique approach to building long-term success on the systematic elimination of waste.

A primary root cause for this problem is not that companies fail to commit to what they see as "lean production"; rather, they fail to understand the true nature of *Lean thinking.* There is no doubt in our minds that, first, Lean thinking is a way of thinking that is radically different from mainstream management's thinking and, second, that it leads to visibly superior performance and more sustainable profitability.

---

* France had a long experience with Lean because Toyota had installed one of its transplant factories in Northern France, and it taught its production system to its local suppliers (which Michael had studied for his doctoral research). As a result, the more productivity-oriented aspects of Lean were well known in the French automotive industry. On the downside, France has a history of negative labor relations and unions that are hostile to Lean. French executives are also very set on French exceptionalism, and they are reluctant to investigate anything out of the Cartesian, top-down tradition of French management. Dan, Orry, and Michael, with the help of Godefroy Beauvallet, created a university project to share and compare Lean practices in France, and Jacques was one of the first CEOs who joined with the firm ambition to learn Lean thinking so as to lead his own industrial group differently.

Why don't more organizations fully commit to Lean thinking? Beyond the usual resistance due to the "not invented here" syndrome, we've come to realize that most depictions of Lean thinking are "outside in." They are descriptions of how a Lean company should look: in order to eliminate waste and seek perfection, a Lean company has a clear definition of value, clear value streams run by a value stream manager, with better-flowing processes through a pull system, and a continuous improvement organization.* Executives therefore seek to Lean their organization by shaping it toward what we've defined as a Lean company. We've noticed that in doing so, they invariably achieve early visible results, but then Lean efforts tend to slow down and peter out, not achieving the hoped-for transformation and, often, unhappily sliding back.

Taking a fresh look at the few executives who achieved ongoing success with Lean, as did Orry's firm for the 10 years it followed the leadership of legendary Lean CEO Art Byrne (who has, throughout his career, conducted more than 30 Lean turnarounds first as a CEO and then as an owner-investor through his private equity work), we have realized that these companies adopted Lean *thinking* rather than Lean organization.[3] Successful executives, CEOs or COOs, did not reshape their businesses to make them Lean-er; rather, they changed their way of thinking about business, and then they taught this new way of thinking to their colleagues and teams.

And so we have come to the conclusion that in this book we should present Lean "inside out" and highlight how Lean is a strategy in the fullest sense of the term, both as a personal way of thinking and as a business strategy.

- *A new way of thinking:* Toyota did not invent a method to optimize traditional mechanistic organizations. Instead, it came up with a new way of thinking about work that is dynamic, people centric, and organic. Competitive advantage is sought by *learning* how to better satisfy customers by earnestly developing people, every day, everywhere. Market results are achieved by offering customers more value through encouraging employees to improve steadily the way they work and evolving organizations accordingly. The organization is no longer the main tool to access markets, but instead, it becomes the workplace conditions for

---

* These are the five principles Dan introduced with Jim Womack in *Lean Thinking*.

people development, seeking to earn customers' smiles by small, step-by-step improvements in products, services, and costs.

- *A new business strategy:* Lean thinking upends how one thinks about a business as a whole and what makes a business successful. Companies thrive by offering customers more value in the form of benefits they can't find with any competitors and that add up to benefits to society at large. Profitability is the result of a better use of capital through always seeking a higher level of just-in-time performance and better control of costs by constantly striving to be closer to right-first-time and higher first-pass yield. As we will see later, one of the key dynamics of Toyota is that it learned how to create a (near) seamless flow of work throughout its system (from order to delivery) supported by a (near) seamless flow of ideas from its people. Accelerating these flows supports greater service to customers and higher inventory turns, and, most importantly, it creates an attention to detail in operational processes that opens the way for smart improvement ideas and initiatives. As a whole, this opens the way for faster product development and a richer range to satisfy a greater diversity of customers. Competitors trying to follow with a traditional mechanistic worldview find themselves burdened with additional costs and increasingly resisting organizations that can't cope with the required flexibility. Accelerating the flow of work accelerates the flow of ideas through the business, and it sustains initiative and innovation in creating less wasteful products and processes, which are both more profitable and more mindful of the environmental impact of the business.

What Is Lean Strategy?

Lean strategy is about *learning to compete*—adopting a fundamentally different way of thinking at the workplace, one that is all about developing the capacity to discover and learn. Daily practice of this approach, at every level, creates resilient organizations that are better able to adapt and grow with a greater mindfulness in all things large and small.

The aim of a Lean strategy is to learn to solve the right problems and avoid wasteful solutions. We create flow (better quality, higher flexibility) in order to *find* our real problems; we then challenge ourselves to *face* them.

Relying on the Lean learning system, we then *frame* these issues in ways everyone can relate to in their daily work, and we *form* new solutions that emerge from a culture of problem solving and continuous improvement at all levels. As teams develop a deeper understanding of their work and get better at collaborating across functional boundaries, we shape new, innovative, companywide capabilities based on individual competencies and teamwork. Together we deliver higher quality by involving every person in finding new ways of working that achieve our shared purpose.

We do not mean to suggest that strategy bubbles up just from solving operational problems or that operational excellence is a strategy in itself. We believe that Lean CEOs confront their strategic intent daily by experiencing facts firsthand. They do so by looking into the problems their teams solve daily, supporting the teams in doing so, and thinking deeply about why the teams encounter these problems in the first place: which customer demands require greater flexibility and which organizational rigidities require greater competencies? This back-and-forth "helicopter" process of thinking at the highest level possible, while exploring work in the greatest detail, produces a deeper understanding of strategy in terms of what are the right problems to solve, what are the least wasteful solutions to look for, and what are the key organizational capabilities to develop from patient nurturing of individual competencies.

This form of strategic thinking fuels the strategy planning process used by Toyota, called Hoshin Kanri.[4] We focus on how leaders think, act, and learn in making strategic decisions and how they work to carry them through with frontline teams at the gemba. All our experience tells us that this is the key to solving the right problems and avoids wasting huge amounts of time solving the wrong problems.

Strategy is not the same as operational excellence. Rather, strategy sets the direction for the firm: what distinctive value proposition to the customer will give us a competitive advantage? We believe that this big picture view needs to be constantly compared to the reality in operations. What is the current condition? Where are there gaps between the current reality, and what we are trying to deliver to our customers based on our strategy? These gaps inform what we should be working on next. *

* We would like to thank Jeff Liker for his contribution to our thinking, particularly this passage.

STRATEGY

IT CAN BE SAID THAT SOLVING THE RIGHT PROBLEMS BY UNDERSTAND WHAT THE RIGHT PROBLEMS ARE LEAN THINKING AND

Toyota veteran and Lean thought leader John Shook believes that Lean thinking is an approach to strategy that is fundamentally different from conventional thinking (as represented and promoted by, say, most business schools and MBA programs). Lean thinking is at its core a different way of thinking about the development of capabilities that both shape and are shaped by strategy, about the role of leaders and managers to deliver it, and about the relationship between thinking and acting. Traditional business thinkers claim that strategy is a separate and more important thing than operations or organization, which they view as the mundane matters of how managers execute the strategic plan. Strategy is what separates winning from losing (as measured by financial results)—everything else is a mechanical decision that serves it. Lean thinking, in radical opposition, says that each shapes the other.

In the traditional approach to strategy, the leader defines high-level changes, which are then driven through the organization through either projects or systems. The changes create disruptive problems for value-adding teams, problems they then resolve as best they can (or not), often at great operational cost and inconvenience to customers.

The radical change proposed by a Lean strategy is that, by confronting his or her strategic intuition to obtain real firsthand facts experienced at customers' locations, at workplaces, and at suppliers, the leader expresses as challenges the top-level problems the organization has to resolve in order to thrive, frames the improvement direction to solve these problems, and expects each team to contribute controlled changes in order to form new solutions, sustained by a Lean learning system embedded into day-to-day work. This approach creates both rapid and gradual change without disrupting operations or customer experience, and it also engages employees further in their relationship with their work, and the relationship of their work to customer satisfaction.

We should note that a Lean strategy is a superior business approach: it clearly delivers dramatic advantages tracked by conventional measures such as cycle times and defect rates, use of invested capital, and enterprise value. We have found that companies that fully commit to Lean dramatically outperform their competitors over time.

A Lean strategy improves the flow of higher quality products and services as a means of discovering what value really means to customers and where our value delivery is better than that of our competitors. A Lean strategy also involves all teams in shaping better ways to work and discover innovative solutions, by developing the talent and pas-sion of all employees. In our framework, it accomplishes the following (Figure 1.1):

TEST QUESTIONS T-F

T

- Addresses and adapts goals continuously to external conditions (*find* and *face*)

T

- Improves internal conditions by freeing and increasing resources and competencies (*frame* and *form*)

T

- Achieves this by supporting and/or coaching people and their relation to their work (leveraging internal resources) and focusing their work toward the customers (leveraging external conditions)

- Lean provides insight into continuous innovation by using the learning system to discover value analysis (improving value in products and services currently in production) and value engineering (improving value in products/services currently in development) opportunities to concurrently develop engineering, production, and supply chain capa-bilities to deliver breakthrough (and industry-changing) innovation from team-based kaizen.

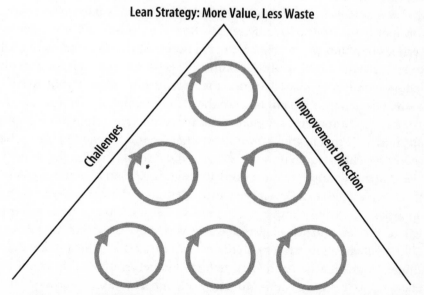

Lean Strategy: More Value, Less Waste

Challenges

Improvement Direction

Small-Step Controlled Changes by All Teams: Kaizen with Plan-Do-Check-Act (PDCA)

Figure 1.1 What the Lean Strategy Accomplishes

The goal is learning how to respond to changing customer demands by using a faster flow of value to strengthen the competencies of all employees in order to free up capacity and introduce new and improved products and services more quickly than the competition.

For all Lean's successes, we have also seen many companies fail at adopting Lean thinking because they try too hard to copy Toyota. They adapt those practices to their own organizations, failing to understand the underlying assumptions of these practices and thereby missing their deeper purpose. In the early 1950s, Toyota was a bankrupt automaker in postwar Japan. Its leaders were obsessed with the idea of making the first Japanese passenger car. They were equally obsessed with *self-reliance*: they would design and build their own automobile rather than buy designs from U.S. and European companies, and they would succeed through self-financing—that is, without relying on the banks that had forced massive layoffs on them to avert shutdown in 1951. They realized they would never compete on cost in a large-scale way as American automakers did.

They also realized they needed to introduce variety to satisfy steep competition in their home market, with a more frugal approach to investment because they wanted to remain financially independent. They had neither the volume nor the capital to build dedicated assembly lines fed on inventories of every single part, but they saw how massively inefficient industrial systems built on local efficiencies could become as variety and complexity were introduced. More importantly, Toyota leaders realized that the massive waste they saw all around them in operations wasn't the result of such and such practice but of wrongheaded *thinking*.

In this apparently upside-down perspective, right thinking is approached much the same as Michelangelo (allegedly) described sculpting: chip away extraneous matter, and find the form in the stone. By clearing away our misconceptions through hands-on experiments, Lean thinking teaches us to "clear the window" and see things as they really are, and then ask "why?" until a causal model emerges. Value is in there somewhere, hidden under the layers of waste caused by our wrongheaded ideas.

Toyota bases its strategy on the principle that the selling price is determined by the market, and after deducting a necessary level of profit, the challenge is to reduce actual costs to meet, or beat, the target cost (profit =

price − cost, not price = cost + profit). Every company making things has a core of fixed costs: wages, rents, and so forth. Crafting a strategy that was linked to its current challenges (limited resources and markets in Japan at the time), Toyota leaders considered ways to reduce the layer of costs generated by wrong thinking in operational methods, such as accepting defects in delivery or producing by big batches. Eliminating these costs contributed to creating competitive advantage, and it could be accomplished through continuous waste elimination by *changing the thinking that created them in the first place* (Figure 1.2).

Waste, Toyota leaders saw, is inherent in any process but not unavoidable. *Waste is the result of someone's misconception.* Consider the following two ways of thinking about inventory.

The first approach is to see inventory as a good thing to have. It feels instinctively better to have components in stock in order not to stop the assembly line for lack of parts.

It feels natural, for example, to stockpile tomato sauce in your cupboard to make spaghetti Bolognese when you feel like it. This mentality applies on the production line: the more parts that are built on one machine at a given time, the lower the production unit cost. Taken at face value, there is nothing wrong with these ideas, and indeed, most scheduling IT systems are built around them. But if we observe how things really work out, a different mindset can be applied. Excess inventory might in fact do more harm than good: having stockpiled tomato sauce in the cupboard doesn't stop us from coming up short if we have not replenished the stock of other

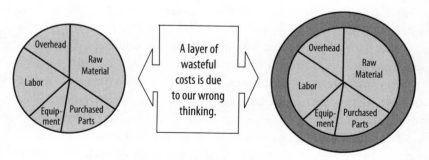

Figure 1.2 Eliminating Wasteful Costs

items needed on time. Furthermore, if we cook spaghetti irregularly, we might find that some of the sauce cans are past their use date.

Second, making more parts that we don't need right now easily leads to overinvesting in machine capacity that we don't need, as well as overinvesting in the carrying cost of inventory and all the logistic costs of moving, storing, and checking that these steps entail. The problem with the "economies of scale" thinking is that it focuses only on the task of making the parts and ignores the "indirect" costs (waste) that are created to support the production of parts that are not currently needed.

In other words, the ideas that can be "logically" right can also turn out to be completely wrong. Sure enough, as variety increases in industrial systems to satisfy customers' wishes for more varied products, the idea of holding stock for every component becomes ridiculous. At one time, prior to Wiremold's adopting a Lean strategy when operating in a Manufacturing Resource Planning (MRP) batch environment, Orry did a computer simulation as to the amount of inventory necessary to support varying levels of customer on-time delivery. He started with 95 percent and increased that level by 1 percentage point with each simulation. The increase in the level of inventory needed to support each additional percentage point of on-time delivery was exponential (mainly due to the "safety stock" levels needed to ensure that the changing levels of demand, due to forecast error, could be satisfied), to the point that at 99 percent the level of inventory required consumed more than the company's cash and required adding additional warehousing space. Similarly, producing mountains of parts in order to lower costs per part, and worse, moving the parts around the world to find the lowest-cost supplier, led to designing overcomplex, hugely inefficient supply chains.

And so while Lean and TPS are famous for touting a "just-in-time" approach with zero inventories, in actual practice, Lean thinking accepts keeping inventories in absolute terms. In fact, we have seen Toyota ask many of its suppliers to increase inventories in certain situations. The real problem is how one thinks about inventories. Knowledge is situational. No fixed ideology applies universally; and the difference between a wasteful outcome and a Lean one lies in how mindful or mindless the solution turns out to be.

What is known today as the Toyota Production System is not the Toyota production system: it is not the sum of Toyota's current production practices. Production practices evolve with time and circumstance. The name is confusing, but the Toyota Production System is in actual fact a *learning system* to teach you to think about production practices, not a fixed list of recipes or routines to apply this or that practice. Certainly, a management system needs to be put in place to support daily activities, but this, on its own, does not produce the kind of dynamic progress that will deliver superior performance (Figure 1.3).

The misunderstanding is often compounded by Toyota's belief that deep thinking can only occur through hands-on experience. Toyota insists on practice over theory, but it must be practice that is informed by the principle of *learn by doing*. As a result, there are practices, or "tools," in Lean thinking whose aim is not to design the perfect waste-free production system but rather to teach every employee to *think* about their job, to be *mindful* about the waste they inevitably generate, and to be *inventive* in coming up with new ways to do the job that will generate less waste and more value. (We shall, in fact, explore how many of the most popular Lean "tools" are in fact frames for learning, in Chapter 4.)

Michael first encountered Lean thinking when he studied how Toyota taught TPS to one of its early European suppliers as Toyota established its first transplant site in the United Kingdom. Freddy Ballé (Michael's father),

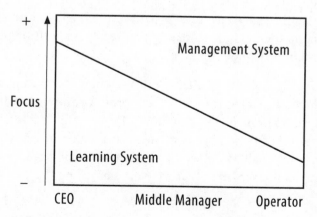

Figure 1.3   Balance Between Management and Learning Systems

then industrial VP of a large French automotive supplier, was already an old hand in automotive, and he had discovered Toyota as far back as 1975 and had regularly visited the company ever since. He convinced his CEO and Toyota's management to invest in teaching TPS to the supplier's engineers in order to improve quality and lower costs. In the traditional Toyota way, he was coached by an experienced TPS master (sensei) who had long worked with Taiichi Ohno—the legendary inventor of kanban and a key contributor to TPS.

The collaboration project centered on one cell building signal light casings, front and rear, left and right, with Toyota engineers visiting once a month and helping with the continuous improvement of the production cell. As they taught operators how to produce better quality with greater flexibility, they reduced inventory to almost nothing and improved productivity by about 30 percent in the course of two years.

It was the way they taught that defied conventional expectations. The supplier's manufacturing engineers had heard about "Japanese improvement techniques," and they expected an analysis of "waste" in the cell to distinguish value-added from non-value-added tasks and improve the ratio of value-added to non-value-added.

The Toyota engineers' recommendation completely blindsided them:

1. To start with, although the product was in a ramp-up phase and the Toyota truck would come to pick up parts once a week, the engineers asked the supplier to draw five lines on the floor in logistics, one for every day, and assign someone to pick up a container of products every two hours on the line, consolidating the weekly truck throughout the day and then throughout the week.

2. Previously, the supplier had large metal containers storing layers of parts, which accounted for the current production rate for an entire shift of production in one container. Toyota now asked the supplier to get rid of these large containers and replace them with dedicated five-part small containers, with built-in padding for each of the five products in each container to avoid damaging the parts during transport.

3. Furthermore, whereas previously the supplier would have made one long batch of right-hand indicators, then change the tooling and start

a long batch of left-hand indicators, Toyota now demanded batches of 25 parts maximum: five containers of five right-hands, then five containers of five left-hands, and so forth. Considering that any tool change took several hours, this seemed like pure madness in terms of production time loss. These guys were supposed to increase productivity, but instead they seemed to add cost at every opportunity.

4. Toyota engineers also requested an hourly production board held by the operators themselves who would write down every issue resulting from production loss, which the engineers would analyze with them issue by issue.

This first, early experiment proved to be a study in misunderstandings. First, the supplier's engineers failed to understand any of Toyota's logistical requirements and simply performed under duress, with rather bad grace, not seeing the point. The supplier was convinced that Toyota wanted to see the details of the line to use the information to negotiate the price of the parts down right away, although Toyota never asked for any money for all the help they were providing for two years. Then, the supplier engineers assumed Toyota would teach them "Toyota-like" advanced processes, while Toyota engineers were taking them through a list of technical difficulties on their own processes. Some issues became tricky internal political issues. For instance, at first, all tool changes were done by specialized setters, and there were few of them in the plant. The plant manager would never allow so much precious setter time dedicated to one small cell, accounting for less than 2 percent of his total turnover. It took the manufacturing engineers months before committing to simple tool changes so that the operators could do them autonomously, which they eventually did.

A deeper misunderstanding arose around the expected benefits for the supplier. As months went by, it became clear that Toyota was partly taking over the line to achieve the level of quality and productivity it expected. The supplier's early assumption was that it could codify what was learned on this "model" line and apply it across the company in cookie-cutter fashion. Certainly, some of this did happen (the so-called low-hanging fruit), but it turned out that this was not what Toyota had in mind.

During the entire experiment the sensei visited the line with the VP every two months. In retrospect, it appeared the line was an instrument to teach Lean thinking to the VP, and in particular the importance of visual management and employee involvement, as well as the logic of just-in-time. The supplier's engineers saw the line as a pilot for a "model line," which, once finally crafted, could be reproduced across the industrial group as a "best practice" to be followed (indeed, complied with). In fact, they were completely missing the point: *the sensei was teaching the VP how to think differently about production efficiency, and he was doing so through hands-on learning.*

Financially, what was Toyota after? The 30 percent productivity increase on the line remained the supplier's goal (it was not asked for by Toyota). Four years after the start of this experiment, when the new model came out, the new signal light casing was redesigned for 27 percent less of the total cost—a cost savings Toyota split with the supplier. The hard work of solving problems in order to achieve radically better delivery, quality, and productivity performance on the line (value analysis) was really the source of information (after a tough fight with the supplier's product engineers who didn't see the relevance of operator suggestions or even manufacturing engineering input in their own designs) to reduce the *total cost* of the part radically (value engineering). The supplier came to realize that local, continuous improvement leads to understanding the part better, which is the key to real waste elimination at the design stage (as the majority of the costs of any product are committed in the design of the product).

Earlier on, the supplier's engineers had created a "roadmap" to codify what they were working on with Toyota in the hope of spreading it across to the other sites. They then defined specific one-week workshops to get other cells started, largely ignoring Toyota's action plan of installing a logistics pull and communication with operators. Instead, they focused on calculating work content, balancing lines, and reducing operator movement within the line. Improving continuous flow across production lines across many sites did have a spectacular impact at first. Then it got stuck, as the sites as a whole failed to benefit from these improvements to the extent that they should. It wasn't until Freddy Ballé became CEO of another automotive supplier that, still coached by Toyota, he realized the improvement work started after the initial workshop when the team committed to continuous improvement—it was the very continuous nature of the effort that changed how people thought.

Freddy came away with several deep lessons from the experience. The first was that one had to improve *something* first in order to figure out what the real problem was; this was the only way to discover what really needed to be learned. In the lighting cell, for example, the first thing to learn turned out to be how to fix plastics issues and better control plastic injection presses. The second issue to learn was how to modify assembly equipment so that the operators—mostly women—could change production from left to right or rear to front on their own, autonomously, without needing setters' help. The third—unexpected—lesson, obvious in retrospect, was understanding the unnecessary costs built into the part at the design phase, mostly from lack of understanding of the practicalities of the production process. This understanding was a lesson Ballé later put into extensive use as CEO by constantly urging better cooperation between product design, manufacturing engineering, and production. This type of cooperation is one of the hallmarks of Toyota's own way of working. Upon reflection, Ballé realized that you don't know beforehand what the lesson is going to be unless you make progress with the improvements firsthand. Static optimization of what is there largely misses the point. True efficiency lies in the learning from *dynamic progress*.

The second hard lesson was to stop seeking "people-free solutions" and best practices. Engineers are typically taught to design and implement people-free solutions that can then be applied in any conditions in the same way: one ought to be able to assemble a McDonald's Big Mac the same way in any country in the world, from Downey, California, to Ho Chi Minh City, Vietnam. First comes the *solution,* and then people are staffed into it. The Toyota engineers' approach was noticeably different in its *people-centric* approach—by working with the people in the cell at solving issues, they came up with new ways to solve previously intractable problems. They did so by using the TPS system of tools to construct the proper scaffolding for people's learning, which consisted of a set of exercises to visualize the problems and properly analyze the situation in order to come up with smart ideas. The scaffolding was only just that, something to support learning, not to be confused with learning itself. TPS, it turned out, was the finger that pointed *at the moon*, not the moon itself.*

---

* At the time, Michael was just as convinced as the supplier's engineers that Toyota engineers were working from a secret book of Toyota "best practices," and he was never quite convinced by their perplexed answer that they actually solved one problem after the other as the problems appeared. One day, exasperated by Michael's badgering, the Toyota lead engineer exclaimed: "We do have a golden rule: we make people before we make parts."

The Toyota engineers didn't come up with the Toyota secret way to make signaling casings—why would they know better than their supplier? What they did know better was *how to learn faster* about making signaling casings. They established a pickup every two hours to visualize whether they were early or late. They packaged parts in small containers of five, carefully protected to inspect the quality. They reduced batches to five containers of five parts each to focus on the parts in small quantities. Then they made things even better by working with every issue the operators encountered. Doggedly. Sure, this delivered productivity—but that was only the visible side of the iceberg. An increase of 30 percent productivity on labor costs, which are about 10 to 15 percent of the total cost of the part, is not that much (and it is about the 3 percent improvement classical Taylorism can deliver).

What they were really after was the *knowledge* from value analysis in production to significantly reduce the total cost of the part by value engineering both the part and the process. Cutting the total cost of the part by a third is significant competitive advantage—figures that were thoroughly unbelievable at the time. But they did not do so by the traditional manner of studying the problem first, coming up with a better mousetrap, and then executing with discipline. They got these results by making things better locally until they made things better globally. And they knew how to do that because they had been taught to *think differently*.

It is easy to misinterpret requirements such as "produce in smaller batches" as organizational changes. To some extent, we all did. When first confronted with Toyota's approach, we all thought they had a new set of organizational processes, such as these:

1. Organize the company by value streams to better satisfy customers.

2. Organize better flows of work by reducing batches and steps to reduce lead times.

3. Organize a pull system to create the tension necessary for waste elimination.

4. Organize the constant search for perfection to involve people in continuous improvement.

And yet, as we visited more and more Toyota sites (while experimenting with Lean initiatives outside of Toyota as well), we came to realize that no two Toyota sites ever had the same organizational design and that although very high-level principles could be recognized everywhere, the specifics of each solution were quite different from one another. Right from the start, when Dan cowrote *Lean Thinking* with Jim Womack, the feeling was that Toyota engineers did not reason the same way as their competitors. Indeed, another early book on TPS by Benjamin Coriat was called *Thinking Upside-Down*. It finally dawned on us that the true revolution of Lean was cognitive, not organizational. Toyota engineers had evolved a different way to look at business issues, a different way to come up with solutions, and a different way to work with people. The organizational changes we were witnessing were no more than the outcome of this different way of thinking.

What Toyota pioneered was a different way of facing challenges, an adaptive strategy to thrive in turbulent, harsh markets by systematically developing competitive advantage from developing people. It recognized that all of the physical assets it had did nothing by themselves and that people were the only resources that could in fact recognize abnormal conditions and create countermeasures to address them. It also realized that the more it invested in teaching its people to recognize and solve problems, the better the company could serve its customers' needs at lower costs. In effect, it realized that sustained competitive advantage truly is all about the people . . . not some of the people, but all of them.

In the following chapters, we will show how Lean thinking is a personal strategy to change your way of thinking and become more effective at facing challenges. Next we will share how to teach Lean strategy toothers as a way to turn individual competency into a business capability. And finally, in the third section, we will discuss how to act on this: to improve the business's performance at all levels by achieving better sales, greater cash flow, lower costs, smarter investments, and sustained innovation.

CHAPTER 2

Think Differently

Lean is a completely different set of assumptions about moving from reflection to action.

Jacques vividly remembers the day that he realized that becoming Lean would mean that he would have to *think differently*. While working with his sensei to improve the horrendous ergonomics of an assembly workstation, his coach told Jacques that he was "nice—but cruel." While Jacques was furious to hear this, he reflected more on his sensei's explanation: "You mean well at a policy level with many progressive policies in the company," said his coach. "But at the work level you have not solved *any* of the difficult problems workers face with every day, every hour, every minute. This is cruel because you, unwittingly, keep them struggling with no hope of improvement."

Up to that point the sensei had been pointing out practical shop floor issues that neither Jacques nor Frédéric Fiancette, the chief operations officer, could relate to their wider problems. The company was faced with pressing issues ranging from failure to deliver products when promised, safety issues in assembly and logistics, MRP-triggered chaos caused by last-minute changes, and endless rework and unacceptable reject rates (up to 30 percent) of produced parts. They struggled to see how their global challenges related to the seemingly trivial problems emphasized by their sensei.

And yet when challenged to help make things better right here, right now, as a means of tackling the greater problems, Jacques was able to accept a different mindset regarding his role. Previously he saw his role as CEO as being smarter and more imaginative, taking the longer view, and above all coming up with better strategic thinking so that he could align his teams to tactically execute the strategy. He felt, not unreasonably, that his ability to achieve this alignment, mostly through a focus on communication and sharing of intent, was the key to his previous successes. Up until then, he had externalized all the problems as gaps between his innate knowledge and the failure of others to keep up. To paraphrase Orwell, he realized that when the CEO "turns tyrant, it is his own freedom that he destroys."*

Jacques's "mental model" that his strategic vision for the company should serve as its compass had blinded him to the reality of the situation. He could not see how the shop floor itself could be a source of transformation—or, indeed, how, as the old-time Lean senseis used to say, "the gemba [the Lean term for "real place, real products, real people"] is the greatest teacher." His deeply held beliefs were being attacked by the very concreteness of shop floor evidence ("Fact is fact," another old-time saying).

He realized that he had reached his own level of incompetence, particularly on the one point he really cared about: respect for people. Every day his management system created dangerous or meaningless work, which, on top of everything else, belied his own promises to customers. This was not the fault of other people not doing their job well, he realized. Rather, as a leader, he had to change his own outlook.

Jacques realized that *to transform your organization, first transform yourself.* Any revolution (Lean or otherwise) starts from within. Lean transformation requires a personal transformation at the leadership level about how to think about solving problems before there can be an enterprise transformation. So bear with us as we backtrack to where Toyota's way of thinking deviates from the mainstream thought habits. Many readers will be familiar with the Plan-Do-Check-Act (PDCA) problem-solving methodology that lies at the heart of Lean. However, this concept does not adequately capture the thought process leaders go through in deciding what problems need to be solved. After much observation and reflection, we have come up with the following framework to deepen our understanding of this significant change in thinking.

On the whole, humans are largely self-directed (at least at a supervisory or higher level), particularly at work: they establish goals and then go about achieving them. The full process looks something like this (Figure 2.1):

- *Define: Thinking about a situation*—pondering, mulling over it, and so on

- *Decide: Deciding on an intent*—meaning to do something about the situation and thinking about how

---

* From George Orwell's famous and oft-reprinted essay "Shooting an Elephant," 1936.

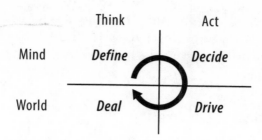

Figure 2.1 The Define → Decide → Drive → Deal Cycle

- *Drive: Doing something about it*—getting on with it, either by following a deliberate action plan or shooting from the hip, and driving the action until there is some resolution

- *Deal: Experiencing consequences and dealing with them.* Most situations are complex and fluid, and effects don't necessarily follow from action, so consequences are often hard to parse, particularly since humans are very vulnerable to a confirmation bias, which means we feel that positive consequences are the result of our actions, while negative consequences are the result of unforeseen conditions, someone else's screw-up, or plain bad luck.

This cycle is one of thinking in the privacy of our own heads, acting on the world, and then trying to figure out what is what. Learning occurs as we draw the right conclusions from such cycles and progressively decide and act more accurately to reach our goals. In business, managers are expected to carry out an investigation phase, outlining alternatives as well as the costs and benefits for each available option. Then an executive chooses one of the options and draws an action plan to "make it so." Middle management is then charged with implementing this action plan through the rank and file, and at some point, success or failure will be evaluated, conclusions reached, and a new set of options looked for—and so on.

Both everyday experience and modern cognitive psychology show how this define → decide → drive → deal representation is profoundly flawed.*

It is often nothing more than an exercise to support what Google's Eric Schmidt calls the "highest-paid person's opinion" (HIPPO). The boss might not be always right, but he or she is always the boss, and so elaborate

---

* Explained in depth by cognitive psychologists—notably in the influential book by Daniel Kahneman, *Thinking Fast and Slow*, Penguin, New York, 2012.

corporate rain dances are performed to ensure that the boss is always seen to be right. Then, not surprisingly, reality fights back, as real people confront real problems in applying the instructions they get from above and still serve customers.

Lean Thinking Is Different

Lean thinking starts with acting: solving immediate problems to better understand the deeper issues. It differs radically from the mainstream approach. In fact, the traditional mindset of seeking quick solutions and trusting cognitive power over learning and adaptability is a key reason why most people interpret Lean instrumentally—as a simple way to get tangible results.

Of all the Lean efforts we have observed, most, sadly, are attempts to adapt Lean tools to traditional financial management thinking. Improvement tools often "work" by producing early results from picking low-hanging fruit in the first couple of years, typically convincing management they should invest more in the program. Experience shows, however, that these local benefits do not increase the bottom line, fail to visibly improve the business, and are usually achieved by yet more pressure on employees who feel let down when the promise of greater involvement turns into the usual increase in management control of irrelevant costs, forcing people into open spaces, and head count reduction. This is not Lean.

To truly grasp Lean thinking, you must do the hard work to acquire the discipline of another way of thinking, as shown in Table 2.1.

Traditional financial management is about optimizing the current situation and, when it is felt that this is no longer enough, restructuring in order to find a new (more!) optimized situation. The underlying metaphor is the organization as a vast machine that can be fixed by replacing the broken parts. Not surprisingly, this approach suffers from endless change management and change resistance setbacks as people naturally resist things they don't understand, where they don't see the benefit either for the company or themselves. Profitability is achieved through violence done to the organization and its people, whether by strong cost control or brutal reorganizations.

The Lean alternative looks for results in a completely different way. Lean thinking looks to dynamic progress. The traditional mainstream

	Financial Management	Lean Thinking
Define	Look at the numbers, find the profitability problem, and think of alternative options.	
Decide	Decide and commit to a course of action (a "strategy"), and draw up an action plan.	
Drive	Execute the action plan and monitor the realization of line-by-line actions.	Support local kaizen efforts in every process to make things better and see firsthand the strengths and weaknesses of products, people, and processes.
Deal	Evaluate the impact of the strategy by looking at the numbers and finding after-the-fact explanations.	Build ad hoc physical measures to quantify business outcomes beyond what appears in the financial reporting.
Define		Mull over the big questions of how you want to make the world a better place, and figure out what the improvement dimensions should be at the company level, as well as understand the pushback mechanisms in place.
Decide		Commit to capability development through managing learning curves by supporting kaizen in standard processes and looking for innovation breakthrough where it is needed.

Table 2.1 Traditional Thinking Compared to Lean Thinking

	Think	Act
Mind	1. *Define* the situation in static terms of where we are, where we ought to be … the "gap."	2. *Decide* the best course of action that will take us from where we are to the vision of where we'd like to be.
World	4. *Deal* with the fact that things rarely go as planned, and we rarely end up where we thought we'd be (and we'd promised) so that we can live to fight another day.	3. *Drive* the action plan to implement the decision in the face of resistance and obstacles to achieve the stated goal.

Table 2.2 Traditional Mainstream Thinking Framework

thinking framework, still taught at business schools today, can be described as shown in Table 2.2.

By contrast, Lean thinking starts with *find*, in the real world, by identifying immediate problems right now, moves to *face* as we grasp which problems are easy to solve and which aren't, what our deeper challenges are, then to *frame* these challenges in a way others will understand intuitively both (a) the problem we're trying to solve and (b) the generic form of the solution we're looking for, and then *form* the specific solutions through repeated try-and-see efforts with the people themselves until we, all together, build a new (often unforeseen) way of doing things (Table 2.3).

These four phases don't happen at once but are worked on in a continuous loop. Finding, facing, and framing (what Toyota calls "problem awareness") lead to forming solutions sustainably by step-by-step problem solving, progressively building the capability to sustain the new solutions in the very process of developing them. Lean thinking leads to *sustainable profitability* because profitability is built into growth, through the virtue of constant improvement. In that sense, "Lean" is not a noun. It is a verb. Lean thinking is about sustaining the continuous "Leaning" of operations, from product design to manufacturing to supply chain to administrative support, by working with the value-adding teams themselves in order to create more value while generating less waste. It's a dynamic, not a *state*.

Lean thinking is really, really different. On one hand, we have the traditional thinking of the leader defining the situation, deciding what to do, doing it or driving the changes through to get it done, and finally dealing with the consequences, particularly the unexpected ones. On the other hand, we have Lean thinking, which starts with working with people to improve things right away, building mutual trust and finding out the real problems, then facing these problems and sharing this across the group by measuring outcomes, and then thinking deeply and framing the issues in

	Think	Act
Mind	3. *Frame* the situation in dynamic terms of improvement dimensions and pushback mechanisms.	4. *Form* the solution by developing capabilities and shaping it as you go with key stakeholders.
World	2. *Face* the real problems by committing to measuring our experience beyond existing numbers to grasp what is really going on.	1. *Find* what the issues really are at the customers, the workplace, and the suppliers.

Table 2.3 Lean Thinking

terms of improvement dimensions and finally forming the solution with the people involved by building capabilities through progressively developing existing skills and new competencies (Table 2.4).

The building block of learning by doing is the *plan-do-check-act* (PDCA) cycle that Dr. W. Edwards Deming popularized in Japanese industrial companies in the 1960s, and then in the rest of the world. Deming's own teacher changed this linear thinking into a circle, the *Shewhart circle*, to describe how learning occurs on any product. Effectively, the idea is that to learn anything, we first have to change something and then carefully check the results to evaluate the impact.

Deming described this cycle as consisting of four fundamental steps:

1. *Plan:* Plan a change or a test aimed at improvement.

2. *Do:* Carry it out, preferably on a small scale.

3. *Check:* Study the results. What did we learn?

4. *Act:* Either adopt the change, abandon it, or run through the cycle again, possibly under different environmental conditions.[1]

Traditional Thinking	Lean Thinking
Define: The leader defines the situation by explaining how things are, how things ought to be, and how she intends to remedy the situation using a visionary strategy.	*Find:* The leader encourages improving things as they are to build relationships and find out what the real problems are according to what is easy or hard to improve.
Decide: The leader commits his organization to one path out of several in order to achieve the goals he has set.	*Face:* By creating ad hoc measures and indicators, the leader shares the problems with everyone so that all can see where they stand and face the situation.
Drive: The leader either does herself or drives the changes through by getting them done through action plans executed by the hierarchy, demanding loyalty to her "vision," rewarding followers, and overcoming resistance.	*Frame:* By thinking deeply about what improvement has revealed about the situation and how people see it, the leader frames the situation in terms of improvement dimensions, not a destination, and he involves everyone in making their own steps forward.
Deal: The leader deals with the consequences, often unexpected, of his action and the pushback from real-life conditions that will affect the cleverest strategies.	*Form:* By building capabilities progressively with the very people involved along the improvement dimensions, the leader shapes the new situation and better outcomes from improved performance.

Table 2.4   Lean Thinking: Starts with Working with People

PLAN
DO
CHECK → ACT

This PDCA cycle is considered, to this day, as the core improvement tool by Toyota, which sees itself as an organic sum of PDCA activities. The main change Toyota has made to this cycle is to consider concrete facts rather than data as the ultimate source of knowledge. Data remains important, for sure, but the emphasis in Lean thinking is on facts—firsthand grasp of the situation.

PDCA is how we conduct every activity of the four *find*, *face*, *frame*, and *form* (4F) *phases*. PDCA is used to solve problems in the find phase and to see which problems yield easily and which unveil trickier issues, which problems are mundane and which reveal competitive challenges. PDCA is used in the face phase to plan the right measures and to see whether they correctly represent the challenges revealed by facts at the gemba, and to adopt them or modify them until they do. PDCA is the basis for correctly framing challenges in a way that every employee can relate to—a new frame is planned, tested, checked, and either adopted or adapted. And, of course, PDCA is the main driver of the form phase where different solutions are tried by all teams on all levels.

PDCA is also fractal as it can be used at the higher level of the 4Fs in the form of, in Lean parlance, *hansei*, which is the self-reflection to recognize mistakes in order to avoid reoccurrence. Even when something worked well, it can be fitted within a PDCA cycle to reflect on issues that remain unclear and opportunities missed. As the formed solution emerges from framing and facing the challenges revealed by the problem finding, we can check whether that solution gets us closer to our original goals and either adopt it or plan to try again.

The 4F reasoning is built with the bricks of PDCA thinking at all levels. The point that Deming saw early on is that in order to learn, you first have to make a change. Conversely, changing without checking the impact will not produce any new learning, nor any new knowledge. PDCA is the engine of Lean thinking because it captures the dynamic thinking of continuous improvement in day-to-day work.

Traditional thinking is essentially mechanistic—one unsatisfactory situation has to be replaced by a better one—and the language is one of visionary strategy, disciplined execution, and overcoming resistance to change (creating a full industry of "change management" consultants). Lean thinking is about crafting solutions with the people doing the work by continuously sharing the understanding of the improvement dimensions and experimenting locally in real life.

Indeed, Lean thinkers usually avoid talking about "solutions," preferring the awkward term of "countermeasures," because no solution is ever final and every action is an attempted countermeasure to an existing problem. Lean thinking is organic inasmuch as the specific shape of the solution will emerge from working with the people in the process (although the improvement directions are firmly set and shared) and formed by everyone's efforts, inventiveness, and will to contribute to move the organization forward. People's buy-in is built into the Lean thinking method as the systemwide improvement dimensions are derived from each local effort and initiative. Lean thinking is a dynamic process, not a static one. One is never Lean. One is always practicing Lean.

"It's easier to act your way into a new way of thinking," wrote John Shook, "than to think your way to a new way of acting."[2] One of the original, powerful—and disconcerting—aspects of this new form of reasoning is refusing the separation between thought and action, between strategy and execution. A deep, personal grasp on reality is developed by trying ideas immediately, in small ways, and watching what works and what doesn't. Deep thinking comes out of pondering "why?" and then "why?" repeatedly. Solutions emerge out of doing with others while somehow balancing a common direction of inquiry with the leeway to be creative for each single person. In this sense, although it sounds awkward, Lean thinking is a practice. Nampachi Hayashi, Freddy Ballé's teacher, used to quote his own teacher, Lean legend Taiichi Ohno, as saying, "Don't look with your eyes. Look with your feet. Don't think with you head. Think with your hands."

Lean thinking is the practice of dynamically moving *from finding problems* to *facing challenges*, from *facing challenges* to *framing directions* for progress, from *framing directions* to *forming solutions*, and then continuing by finding the next order of problems and so on. Lean thinking is based in the most concrete way on learning by doing, or, in John Shook's terms, on acting yourself into a new way of thinking.

Improve to Grasp the Situation

Lean thinking proceeds from a completely different set of assumptions about the process that leads us from reflection to action. The Lean thinking process starts with the "act" phase: we conduct many quick, short experiments to *make things better* in local conditions, mainly by improving the flow of operations:

- Flow of motion in employees' work (getting rid of obstacles to fluid, safe, and value-adding work)

- Flow of work between workstations so that value is added more consistently without breaks for transport, storage, sorting, and other non-value-added work

- Flow of information to avoid batching and to change more seamlessly from one work to the next to better flow with real-time customer demand

These early, quick actions are not meant to solve any large issues but, rather, to grasp the hands-on reality of the workplace, to better understand what customers really prefer, what people can and can't do, and what technologies are heritage (good) and which are legacy (bad). The aim of these repeated experiments is to figure out the strength and weaknesses of products, people, and processes firsthand. By improving things as they are right now, we discover what is easy to fix and what problems resist any efforts. In effect, we are discovering our real problems directly.

The root idea of all Lean thinking is *kaizen*: continuous, small step-by-step improvements done by the people who do the work themselves. The emphasis in kaizen is on self-reflection about how one does one job, seeing waste in terms of either customer annoyance, work difficulty, or unnecessary cost, and coming up with ideas that don't require investment to improve things. As one improves by taking fast small steps, one will discover the *root* cause of waste, and then address it directly.

Kaizen can be done either singly, in the form of suggestions or problem solving, or as a team, to improve the team's work methods. Lean thinking starts with looking for opportunities to kaizen one's own work to improve flow and, as a manager, to encourage and support kaizen in one's teams. For instance, any frontline team can be asked to do the following:

1. Find some performance improvement potential (safety for team members, better quality, faster delivery, less inventory from smaller batches, increased productivity from waste elimination, or simply work made easier).

2. Study their own work methods (list the steps they go through as well as the manpower, machine, material, and method issues they typically encounter at each step).

3. Come up with new ideas to make the work easier, less wasteful, and flow better.

4. Propose an adoption-and-approval plan to try out their new ideas (which often requires some management interest, support, and handling of other departments involved).

5. Try their ideas and measure the impact.

6. Evaluate their new method, correct it if necessary, and then adopt it.

Small-scale, focused kaizen efforts serve in effect as prisms through which management can gain insight and clarity about broader strategic challenges. While CEO of an industrial group, Jacques and his team were struggling with strategic problems such as their overall supply chain strategy and their investment decisions in warehouses and facilities. He asked each of the department managers of his main sites to improve their operations. Logistics started with improving on-time delivery by visualizing the day's hour-by-hour service status and improving the final picking to package customer orders. Assembly worked on a few products with very high reject rates from automated processes. Machining looked into reducing setup times to reduce batch sizes and making sure the right products were available at the right time. Production planning focused on leveling the production schedule and organizing regular pickup loops in the factory. The CEO dedicated a weekly slot to visit these improvement efforts, encourage the teams, and take away organizational hurdles.

These improvement efforts challenged many of management's beliefs: the quality of their products was not as good as they thought. The supply chain might benefit from switching from looking for the cheapest supplier in low-cost countries to looking for the most reliable supplier closest to supply routes. Investing in costly, oversophisticated machines that couldn't cope with parts sourced from China was not worth it. Over a couple of years, by patiently looking into the improvement efforts of all local teams and actively supporting them when they were stuck, the firm's management team completely redesigned its supply chain strategy and led a complete turnaround of the firm's cash position, tripling the inventory turns from 5 in 2007 to more than 15 in 2014. By learning from his frontline team's improvement effort, Jacques completely changed the story of his company from sourcing everything in China and reducing the offer to customers, to keeping a wide catalog for customers and sourcing as locally as possible for quality and responsiveness (short lead times). This story enabled Jacques's company to regain the competitive edge that had been progressively eroding as competing on costs alone turned every product into a commodity.

The real benefit of a kaizen effort goes way beyond the performance improvement you (almost) always get. The value lies in the learning for the team (they learn how to do their job better) and for yourself (you better understand the issues of the process).

In a completely different context, another question kicked off the find phase at another company. "Why is this machine so large?" was the first question the Lean sensei asked Christophe Riboulet and his engineering team at their first meeting, looking at the flagship product of this high-tech company. Riboulet is the CEO of Proditec, a firm that makes specialist equipment for tablet inspection for the worldwide pharmaceutical industry. Each machine is roughly the size of a gasoline dispenser, and the sensei insisted, "Considering the size of the tablets, and the size of the value-adding elements—vision and ejection—why is this machine not the size of an expresso maker?" The engineers were incensed. They knew exactly why the size was needed—it required a certain length of conveyor to maintain the stability of the tablet's trajectory at high speeds, a sufficient size of the frame for rigidity, and other features such as being able to hold the various mechanical elements to see both sides of the tablet and having places to put in the various computers. This is a high-tech product, and competing machines are just as large.

Notwithstanding the engineers' outrage, Riboulet was intrigued. He actually agreed with the sensei. He knew the demand for Proditec machines should continue to grow as regulators kept increasing the pressure on pharmaceutical companies to increase their quality; and although the company was doing well, he had a nagging sensation that they were not growing as fast as they could be. He also knew that, to respond to regulators' pressure, manufacturers were resorting to manual inspection of suspect batches of tablets, which amounted to both millions in value of the drugs and huge inspection costs. Furthermore, Riboulet found that asking human beings to inspect tablet after tablet visually for surface defects was terrible and his aim was (and is) to replace manual inspection with automated systems—machines that don't tire or get bored, and don't have anything more value adding to do with their lives.

Riboulet invited the sensei in because he had a further vision of some-how inspecting tablets in line with production to bring inspection closer to the source (as opposed to inspecting full batches once they had been produced). This was technically impossible because the speed of pro-duction machines could not yet be matched by inspection machines and the inspection machines were so large that it was difficult to integrate in a production line. Curious about the idea of better flow, Riboulet listened carefully to the sensei's questions on the shop floor, and against the general opinion of his team, he suggested that they explore the Lean approach.

Although the company's sales were healthy, Riboulet was worried. The company was not handling the influx of sales well, managers were con-stantly putting out fires all over the place, and when he looked at this 2012 plan, he realized that he had absolutely no sense of where the next sales would come from. He mentioned these concerns to the sensei who, typ-ically, asked about the main sources of customer complaints. On the top of Riboulet's mind were long lead times (it took too long to get a machine delivered from Proditec) and stability issues once a machine was installed. The sensei suggested two practical experiments, to better make the deeper problems visible:

1. *A boutique:* Although each machine is customized to each individual client according to which type of tablet or capsule they want to inspect, the bulk of the machine is generic. The sensei suggested that rather than wait to have a firm order from a customer in order to launch supply of parts for assembly, the company could create its own "bou-tique" or front shop window and have one of each machine type pre-customized and ready at all times for customers to see and purchase on the spot for further customization.

2. *After-sales complaints board:* Rather than let after-sales deal with cus-tomer complaints separately from the rest of the company, the sensei suggested that each customer complaint be visualized on a large board, analyzed in terms of cause and countermeasure, and shared with all engineers to create a common thinking space about how customers really used the machines and what they struggled with in practice. This simple action turned out to be nothing short of revolutionary in a company where each department was accustomed to solving its tech-nical problems on its own and where rework because of misunder-standings was considered normal as well as passing the blame and the

buck around until Riboulet himself had to weigh in and decide. Facing customer complaints directly and collectively as they came in was a shock to all.

To Riboulet's surprise, these two simple activities revealed many more, and far deeper, issues than he'd anticipated. The "boutique" action challenged his entire approach to manufacturing. His strategy up to that point had been to focus on the engineering and delegate all manufacturing to suppliers—he was in the process of developing an Indian supplier to reduce assembly costs from his local suppliers. In establishing the discipline of always having a precustomized machine ready for purchase on each model of his range, he discovered how his lead time was mostly dependent on his suppliers' scheduling practices, who would use the high-content low-volume work from Proditec as an adjustment variable to their own planning. He also started seeing the communications difficulties between his own engineering teams and supplier assembly operations. Information from Proditec was often vague or incomplete; suppliers tended to interpret assembly instructions as they chose, causing serious issues during customization or beyond.

Worse, working on the complaints activity, it suddenly hit Riboulet that although company sales were doing well in 2011 and 2012, his traditional customers had stopped reordering. The financial crisis had certainly dampened internal investment processes in large pharmaceutical operations, but Riboulet asked himself a more painful question: "What if the company's reputation for quality was deteriorating to the point that the company was living off new customers who needed to mechanize inspection but was losing the trust of its established customer base?" Furthermore, new entrants were appearing in South Korea and Eastern Europe with interesting products free of legacy issues. These machines had their own problems, so they posed no immediate existential threats, but they did start to win some competitive bids on price or flexibility of the machine.

Working on these early Lean shop floor exercises delivered rapid results. Before Lean, production was entirely outsourced. The supplier delivery time was four months from order to Proditec delivery for final testing, with a resulting lead time of six months for the final customer. In addition to the long lead time, the existing process was not capable of absorbing any increase in production volume. As a result, to maintain a capacity to deliver to its customers, Proditec had to order machines for its inventory, ordering batches of several units several times a year.

With the boutique idea, the company aimed to have a machine ready for the next customer in the boutique and to be able to restock a new finished machine in the boutique after five weeks. Because of the increase in customer demand, the boutique never stayed filled as orders came in too fast. However, by the end of the year 2011, Proditec had managed to deliver a record number of machines, matched the expected customer delivery times (two to three months lead time), and as a side effect, found itself with twice the amount of cash in hand. Although pleased to have successfully passed this peak in sales, from all the hard work resolving the exercises set by the sensei, Riboulet now saw more clearly the challenges that had been nagging at him—although he had no clear idea how to solve them:

1. *Resale ambition:* Build a trust relationship with major customers, and rebuild that relationship with existing customers, to equip their inspection machine department and collaborate technically to better respond to their needs.

2. *Concurrent engineering:* Rethink the supply chain to tighten the links between engineering decisions and assembly operations in order to learn how to both reduce lead times and improve quality.

3. *Technical performance:* Take a hard look at the technologies used by Proditec, distinguish legacy from heritage technologies, and recapture a technical competitive edge to fight off new entrants.

Riboulet was discovering the first step of Lean thinking: *find*. Previously he defined his strategy by thinking in terms of markets (where to push, which markets to withdraw from) and technologies (which technologies to bet on, which to avoid) and take decisions that were then more or less accepted by his engineers, who did what they felt comfortable (or interested in) doing, and he ignored the rest. Now, working on the shop floor at solving the concrete problems set out by his Lean sensei, he was slowly radically changing his mental picture of his business. He was also finding out that, having changed his mind, he now needed to convince his management team and his frontline engineers.

Measure Outcomes to Understand the Real Issues

Choosing what to measure and what not to is one of the most important decisions in running a business, and it is a proxy for a company's priorities. A clear, succinct list of indicators is a loud statement of the outcomes sought, beyond simply counting output. Measuring accidents and customer complaints first, for example, sends a clear message that the first issues faced by leaders are customer and personnel safety and customer satisfaction. In traditional business thinking, key measures are generally financial ones, and they are supposed to flow from the management accounting system to run the business "by the numbers."

As we will describe in Chapter 6, these financial measures fail to reveal problems on the ground, and they tend instead to hide areas where improvement can happen. Lean focuses on physical measures, while constantly questioning which indicators we look at. Measurement is not taken for granted, and it is the occasion for ongoing discussion and kaizen; your dashboard largely frames how you perceive the environment. The measurements you choose reflect the problems you choose to face.

Lean thinking constantly focuses people on what actually happens when we do experiments. In order to fully understand the import of the many short quick experiments carried out through kaizen, we need to evaluate the impact on operational performance. This calls for measurements that will enable us to quantify what is really happening in the business and on the markets, beyond the numbers reported by financial management—using numbers that enable us to gauge how well the experiment worked, so we can adopt what worked and avoid what did not.

There is no set list, obviously, but in a business, we can start with figures such as these:

- Sales

- Margins

- Accidents and near accidents

- Quality returns and complaints

- Market shares

- Response times to customers

- Inventory turns

- Productivity

- Sales per person

- Sales per square foot

These operational metrics reveal whether or not there is a smooth flow of good products with the least waste of resources possible. Other such measures can and should be created as countermeasures to specific problems as they occur at the departmental or technical level. The point is that running experiments and experiencing consequences is an ongoing process. It is more to accelerate the learning cycle—to learn and respond, then grasp with the current situation, then adjust again—than it is to establish large-scale goals and compare our progress to them on an occasional basis rather than as a constant state. Companies must use meaningful metrics to understand meaningful actions.

As CFO at Wiremold, where CEO Art Byrne joined and led a complete Lean turnaround, Orry realized that the traditional management accounting system gave a skewed vision of the company, one that did not reflect either the real problems or the real progress happening on the shop floor accurately. Although Orry had begun experimenting with alternative presentations of financial information, it wasn't until after Art joined the company that wholesale change in the accounting processes took place. Orry realized that any financial measure (for example, dollars or euros) was merely the result of a quantity of something (for example, units sold, pounds of steel consumed, number of hours worked, or kilowatt-hours consumed) multiplied by its price (or a cost), and that to understand the financial performance of the business, he needed to go beyond standard costs and measure actual physical quantities. The company's traditional financial accounts didn't reflect such essential features of the physical health of the company such as development lead time, production lead time, productivity, and supplier networks or inventory turns.

After participating in several kaizen events, Orry and the rest of the management team continued to create a system of nonfinancial metrics that focused attention on the physical improvements that would eventually translate into financial improvements. On the shop floor, employees developed charts that tracked physical activities (such as hourly takt time performance), but these metrics were used where the work was being done, and they were never aggregated for reporting. The goal was that when the financial statements were prepared, they would contain no surprises, either bad or good. If they did, then that meant that they did not have the right operational metrics.

In addition, he realized that traditional standard cost accounting obscured both problems and progress, so he created an alternate system of reporting financial results that gave more transparency to what was really happening in the business—including what he called a "Plain English P&L" that would be understandable to anyone in the company, not just the accountants. These efforts are more fully described in Chapter 6. Orry's work in focusing on the "real numbers" of the work, rather than some mythical Taylorism-driven numbers, together with the work of several other CFOs dealing with the same issues, went on to found the discipline now known as "Lean accounting," which is based on this insight.[3]

The metrics in Table 2.5 summarize some of the financial and nonfinancial results over a 10-year period.

By measuring specific aspects of the situation with these types of metrics, we are in effect committing to understand what is really going on. Numbers on a chart don't mean much unless you can relate every instance to a real-life case you have experienced, firsthand. This approach is, in fact, much closer to the scientific mindset of conducted repeated experiments

	1990	2000
Sales	$100 million	$450 million
Assessed Value	$30 million	$770 million
West Hartford:		
Sales per employee	$90K	$240K
Gross profit	37.8%	50.8%
Throughput time	4–6 weeks	1 hour–2 days
Product development time	2–3 years	3–12 months
Number of suppliers	320	43
Inventory turns	3.4	18.0
Working cap % sales	21.8%	6.7%

Table 2.5 The Wiremold Company Before and After Lean

to test hypotheses and look for closer fit-to-fact explanations. This is not a static exercise but, rather, a dynamic one that leaders are supposed to carry out all the time, much the way a scientist never ignores newer data sets and is always looking for better, more precise ways to measure what is observed.

Christophe Riboulet accidentally followed Orry's lead. Having decided to fully master Lean thinking, Riboulet joined a study trip of kaizen-driven companies in Japan where he met another CEO who had been impressed with Orry's notion of a Plain English P&L. Riboulet decided to establish the key measures that could be shared by his management team to face the problems he currently saw but that they did not want to consider. He set up a monthly tracking for the following:

- Sales (planned and actual)

- Cost of goods sold (planned and actual)

- Cash

- Inventory turns

- Employees

- Customer lead time

- Customer complaints

Although sales were high for 2012, existing customers were trying out new entrant products from Asia and Eastern Europe. The focus on customer complaints on the service side of the company showed that customers found Proditec's machines difficult to operate because of their inherent system complexity and the uneven stability of settings issues.

The CEO added "churn" to his list of indicators—that is, the percentage of customers lost over total number of customers; and the management team started focusing on returning customers versus one-offs and on solving the former's issues. Throughout 2012 to 2014, the rate of customers that stopped ordering jumped alarmingly from 10 to 40 percent. This revealed to the management team that they were busy chasing new customers (often with price rebates) rather than solving problems for their existing customers. By the simple act of looking regularly at churn, Riboulet had now started to change the story of the company—he made his management team face a problem they had previously missed.

In response, Proditec refocused its resources on quality and performance. All existing issues at customer sites were taken as opportunities to improve products one change at a time, such as replacing neon tubes with LED lighting for more stable lighting. At the same time, Proditec identified the next generation of technology that made machines simpler to use, more stable in the customer production environment, and better at detecting smaller defects at a higher speed. In 2015 and 2016, the company efforts started to pay off: customer churn decreased from 40 to 10 percent, and the number of recurring customers was multiplied by 3 compared to the lowest level of 2013. Proditec rebounded to its 2012 sales level, only now with a much stabler customer base. They could harvest the sustainable growth of farming, rather than hunting and gathering for every new opportunity.

Think Deeply About Which Improvement Dimensions to Pursue (and Where the Pushback Will Come From)

The TPS and Lean thinking framework hinges on *purpose*. Why are we doing these activities in the first place? The thinking phase is where we think bold thoughts. How can we make the world a better place? What is the change we want to effect? Bill Gates wanted to put a PC on every desk. Steve Jobs wanted to liberate individual creativity by taking away the barrier in the human-computer interface. We want to progress toward a waste-free society by introducing Lean thinking to executives. Thinking bold thoughts is hard because our thinking is easily constrained by what we know already.

To think big thoughts, Lean thinking expresses *improvement directions* rather than specific solutions. To start with, let's imagine an ideal *without* waste, which we'll take as a North Star: always far on the horizon, never reachable. In Lean thinking, a starting point to sketch out this North Star would be the ideal flow of value:

- Customers' problems solved completely, in ways they like

- 100 percent defect free

- Large variety of choices

- Delivered immediately on demand

- Built without any accidents

- One by one in sequence (with no inventories)

- 100 percent value added (without moving, checking, or stocking)

- 100 percent energy efficient

- 100 percent employee satisfaction and engagement

- Cheaper than the competition (yet profitable)

Fully achieving these ideal targets is but a dream. However, by standing firmly in the current state we've explored through experimenting with local improvements and clarifying the experience of consequences, we can now come up with improvement dimensions.

In Lean thinking, we look for critical improvement dimensions by carefully scrutinizing every "problem," or instance where actual performance falls short of what we believe should be the standard. Then we examine the numbers that frame this in a way we can learn from, and we use that to think deeply about how to move forward—even if we don't know exactly what the ultimate solution we reach will be. Starting from where we are:

1. What would be the ideal waste-free situation?

2. What is the key improvement dimension?

In thinking this way, we can now focus on three different kinds of gaps:

1. *The gap between the current situation here and now and the best we can do:* What is the specific waste getting in the way that stops us from being the best we know how to be?

2. *The gap between the best we can do and the next significant step:* This is a gap we don't yet know how to close because we need to learn the techniques that will enable us to move forward.

3. *Issues no one has ever looked into:* These are new problems that weren't even considered as problems, which left people without an idea of exactly how to get started. File this under the "we don't know what we don't know" category.

Unlike mainstream approaches, Lean thinking accepts that we do not know the shape and form of the solution beforehand. Thinking is about defining what the outcome should look like. Although this kind of thinking is rarely easy, it helps in avoiding the typical frame blindness of solving the wrong problem because you're fixated on a specific result and/or method.

To return to Proditec, Riboulet had discovered some deep problems that were hidden by the accidental success of a good year of sales (and the subsequent order book drop), and he had made the company face some of its deep issues by including customer lead time and churn in the monthly indicators—that is, Orry's Plain English P&L. Out of the many kaizen activities at the company over the years, some struck the CEO as particularly instructive:

- First, the sensei had suggested the engineers open up the black box elements of the system such as purchased cameras or custom-made electronics cards to see how they competed with state-of-the-art vision products in other industries. In doing so, they realized that in many cases they were building work-arounds to get the maximum out of obsolete equipment without challenging the elements themselves and looking for open source, catalog products that could now do the job just as well.

- Second, in trying to catch up with the deliveries at the peak of demand, the CEO started the experiment of hiring a skilled assembler and asking him to put together a full machine from the chassis onward— as well as write down the planned work content and write down all the problems he encountered. This opened a Pandora's box of issues from unfinished drawings from engineering to poor quality parts received from suppliers as well as systems complexity from difficulty in assembling elements drawn from different departments in the company.

- Third, this exercise led to an arduous, painstaking effort to draw the entire value stream of a product, with a detailed understanding of every aspect of lead times, including rework and supplier rescheduling.

- Fourth, focusing on solving stability problems with installed products led to the realization that the company as a whole treated quality problems (not delivering the promised performance consistently) as performance problems (increasing the promise) and that Proditec engineers knew how to solve the issue at the customer by changing the system to deliver more performance but did not know how to reduce variability and deliver greater consistency—which was fine with clients but extremely costly and ultimately unsustainable.

Out of all this experimenting and thinking, the CEO framed the need to improve the company in four clear directions, which could be shared across the company:

1. Better partnering with existing customers to slow down the number of innovations per machine (while continuing to be innovative as a company) and deliver to customers exactly what they needed for their quality assurance

2. Better teamwork between engineering and assembly in order to avoid rework, and finding smarter, more stable engineering solutions, which involved reintegrating a large part of the assembly and supply chain

3. Better distinguishing quality problem solving from performance improvement through a better understanding of the product's modular architecture and interfaces between software, vision, and mechanical engineering

4. Better management of the young engineers the company was recruiting who were looking for greater involvement and teamwork and felt stymied by the "you do your work and let me do mine" attitude of the old timers

This framing of the company's direction for improvement also radically changed the CEO's vision of how to lead his company. He realized that his marketing plans on "which machine to develop for which market" were wishful thinking because, ultimately, all customers responded to capabilities—what the machines did and what they did not do. Framing his strategy around four core challenges enabled him to give a dynamic impulse to the company as well as work these dimensions in very concrete ways, every day with engineering and the budding production and supply chain. To his mind, this was much less "neat" than the previous vision of a grand strategy driven by high-level processes, but it was far more practical and effective for a high-tech company, and it created the kind of dynamic spirit needed to turn the company around and get back in the competitive race.

Lean framing of critical must-win problems will change from company to company, and indeed, from industry to industry. As a self-described Lean pioneer, Dan started Lean initiatives in a number of industries, from fast-moving consumer goods to healthcare to even government. In doing so, he discovered that, as shown in Table 2.6, each industry had

Industry	Improvement Dimension to Make Each Industry a Better Place
Automotive	Improve standard work, flow, and parts delivery
Process	Improve the separation of stock replenishment for high volume and made to order for the tail
Retail	Improve basket fulfillment and rapid replenishment
Service	Improve the predictability of unpredictable work
Software and IT	Improve rapid experimentation with automated testing and feedback
Construction	Improve the specification of design up front
Healthcare	Improve discharge and the visibility of the work plan
Government	Improve synchronization of services delivery
Finance and administration	Reduce unnecessary demand created by the system

Table 2.6   Improvement Directions for Lean Initiatives

specific conditions and the improvement directions were not necessarily all the same.

The aim of Lean thinking is to grapple with the situation until one can scope out how to make the world a better place by moving forward in an improvement direction. The basic assumption is that the world will never be fully known or understood, and we respect that it retains some of its mystery even as some improvement dimensions become clearer.

A further aspect of the situation that experienced Lean thinkers focus on is understanding the forces *against* the improvement. Much of this resistance can be seen not as ill intentioned but as a clash of ideas—what Lean terms might see as misconceptions. Waste is generated in processes by focusing too narrowly on one result and ignoring the overall outcome. In Proditec's case, for instance, a force of pushback is the difficulty in motivating older engineers to take the time to discuss problems with teams and "waste" time in what they think are useless discussions—time they could spend working down their long to-do list. Getting veteran engineers to see that many of the things appearing on their to-do list are precisely the result of misunderstandings and poor communication of intent, and that some of those things are specialist solutions that are too narrow (and that create problems in all the other technical functions) is definitely a challenge in itself. The simple misconception that "if everyone did his or her job well and independently, then the whole company would go well" often turns out to be costly indeed, and it can bring the company to the very edge of losing contact with its customers, which in turn can cause the company to be blindsided by competitors.

Waste at the industry level typically occurs when the side effects of selling a product or consuming resources are ignored. Waste at work mostly has to do with unnecessary work, such as dealing with defective products for customers, performing non-value-added work for employees, or poorly utilizing capital at the enterprise level. Waste doesn't happen by accident: it's created by the methods used to organize operations.

Waste typically occurs when a decision leads to batching, which over-burdens the weakest point of the system and creates breakdowns or poor quality, which generates further costs—all of which are compounded by the flawed decisions in response (Figure 2.2).

An unfortunate side effect of our industrial history is the deeply held belief that volume drives down cost. "Common knowledge" says that volume brings down cost: you get sales discount volumes, machines that always go faster to handle greater volume, IT systems to batch together orders in order to produce enough volume in one go, and so on. Each of these decisions, which are based on the assumption that "economies of scale" always produce lower costs, are hardwired into the financial accounting systems.

Such misconceptions produce massive waste. Batching encourages you to produce more than is needed at any one time, creating excess inventory, which needs to be handled, stored, and so forth. The financial accounting system reinforces this belief with rules that require that a specifically iden-tified set of costs be included in the product costs, and other "secondary" costs be excluded and treated as period expenses. Moreover, batching is likely to place unreasonable demands on operations in an irregular manner. On Black Friday, for instance, retailers are driven to open as early as 4 a.m. in order to sell goods at massively discounted prices, which encourages shoppers to purchase things they don't really need, or won't buy later

---

Mura (Batching) → Muri (Overburden) → Muda (Waste)

Figure 2.2 How Waste Typically Occurs

on when they would have needed them. Preparing for Black Friday sales requires massive inventory buildups for manufacturers, inducing further waste. Overall, beyond the debatable fun of such collective frenzy shopping days, one can see the overall waste created by volume-for-discount decisions through, first, batching and, second, overburden.

The decision → batching → overburden → waste → worse decision cycle is common in most business decisions, particularly those driven by financial management, and it explains how firms can make the "best" decision every time and still end up bankrupt. Suboptimal decision-making is the norm because systems thinking (which is needed for Lean thinking to thrive) is discouraged by function- and silo-based organizational structures. Point optimization prevails as each piece of the system seeks the "most" (something that is invariably rewarded by the financial system). Understanding how these forces line up against future improvement is an essential part of Lean thinking and a constant reflection topic for Lean thinkers. We often create our own misery, although we're hardly aware of it. The question Lean thinkers ask themselves is this: "How am I behaving right now contrarily to my goals without realizing it?"

To sum up, Lean thinking asks the following questions:

1. What is our purpose? How are we going to make the world a better place?

2. What is the North Star, the waste-free ideal?

3. What are the key improvement dimensions?

4. How do we define a "win"?

5. What waste-generating mechanisms are in place and are likely to push back?

As you practice, you'll soon realize that none of these questions have obvious answers, and that's the whole point. "Common sense" tells us otherwise. Our minds are designed to jump in, frame the problem in familiar ways, come up with the obvious solution, and then build the case for it. We fight hard for our "best" solution and view it as a success when a team of managers approves this plan. Lean thinking approaches this differently. The Toyota Production System was explicitly designed to make people think beyond their usual patterns, in the specific context of car making. Lean thinking has the same aim: to usher a different way of thinking. We realize that it's hard, but the fact is that if you miss that, you'll miss the entire point of Lean—and end up surprised when the results from Lean efforts are not what you expected.

Commit to Capability Development

The more that we learn through kaizen at the workplace, the more we see that we don't know how to do what we need to do. That's why we need to *commit to a learning curve rather than an action plan.* This is another radical departure from mainstream thinking in that it's less about fixing the immediate problem. The question is: how do we create the conditions for learning?

Here again, Lean thinking differs fundamentally from the mainstream "get it done" action plan. You can make people execute an order, but you can't force them to learn. Therefore, a few key questions can help shift focus from engineering results to targeting meaningful learning:

1. *Who is going to learn and whom with?* The first question to answer is how the learning situation is going to be engineered. Whom will we learn with? Whom will they learn with? Learning means teaching as well as firsthand experimenting, and a key issue is having access to knowledge (which, in practice, means access to knowledgeable people), which typically will be outside of the organization's fences.

2. *How is the experimental space set up?* Learning requires repeated experiments with clear trial-and-error signposts. How do we structure the self-reflexiveness that is most likely to produce real learning? In other words, how is the learning curve managed?

3. *What are the incentives to really learn?* Most organizational environments are biased against learning because they assume that scarce resources should be spent on reinforcing proven strategies rather than exploring unproven ones. Learning is difficult inasmuch as one cannot predict when or where breakthroughs or intractable obstacles will show up, and one needs to keep the learning teams motivated through long periods of uncertainty. The incentive structure for learning must be considered early on to make sure real learning happens as opposed to quick copying of existing solutions or, conversely, tackling too early tasks that are too difficult and setting yourself up for failure.

Performance improvement is the result of fast learning, itself the outcome of structured problem solving and repeated experiments on difficult topics. In Lean thinking, the real "decision" is to commit explicitly to learning and to creating the conditions for learning by developing people individually through teaching them rigorous problem-solving skills, and collectively through teaching them kaizen team skills. This is learning in the sense of learning to do what needs to be done (and we don't know yet), not just learning to comprehend the generalities of the topic. Which brings us back to kaizen, or repeated continuous improvement experiments. We started our Lean thinking cycle by asking frontline teams to think of ways to improve processes across the board. In fact, there are three main uses for small-step improvement efforts:

1. *Daily performance problem solving* to train employees to better understand their job and engage them in their own self-development, which provides a good idea of the level of personal competency of your staff

2. *Team kaizen efforts* for teams to study their own work methods and for team members to learn to work better as a team and with the rest of the organization, which will let you assess the real capabilities of your organization

3. *Targeted experiments* to learn something new in which you can follow a team's learning curve as they struggle to master new skills, and out of these new skills build new capabilities

As both Jacques and Christophe Riboulet experienced, Lean thinking is a profound transformation of our very modes of reasoning, which leads to an equally profound change in how we act and how we pursue goals. Rather than defining the situation on paper and deciding in the boardroom, then driving the execution through the ranks and dealing with the consequences as they arise, Lean thinking is about engaging with real-life problems by improving the flow of good products for real-life customers, facing the hard question most people in the organization would prefer to ignore, framing the space and pace of dynamic progress through improvement directions, and forming the new ways of working with the people themselves as they solve one problem after the other and discover innovations from repeated experiments. We will present four key practices to transform the strategy of your organization by transforming your own way of thinking:

1. *Lead from the ground up* to first find what the real problems are and then face the underlying challenges.

2. *Master the Lean learning system* to frame the challenges you face in terms of improvement directions that all can understand and organize for learning.

3. *Change ways of working one change at a time* to form new organizational patterns from repeated continuous improvement activities by the people themselves.

4. *Craft strategy* from both building capabilities step by step and looking further, and keep focused on what really matters to win both in the short and long terms.

CHAPTER 3

Lead from the Ground Up

Learn by doing, and by developing people-centric solutions.

Jacques bit the bullet. He decided that he would stop trying to look for a global solution and, instead, work with his guys pragmatically to solve the safety, quality, and flow problems the sensei was pointing out. Locally. This first meant facing the problems. On the shop floor, chief operations officer Frédéric Fiancette set up a flat screen to show the level of truck readiness throughout the day. Logistics calculated, according to incoming orders, whether the outgoing truck would be complete or not at cutoff time. Throughout the day, in logistics, every person could see if the truck preparation was "normal" ("If we continue like this, we will keep our promise") or "abnormal" ("If we continue like this, we will not keep our promise, so let's look up from the work and figure it out"). As logistics employees started working with this system, they came up with a few ideas and many, many concrete new problems to solve, and Jacques began to see how, indeed, the gemba could be a great teacher.

In assembly, Eric Prévot, the continuous improvement officer (who had previously been in charge of supervising the productivity projects with the outside consultants), came up with a simple scoring scheme for physical actions—red, dangerous; orange, so-so; green, OK. He taught their system to each area production manager, who came up with his own local improvement program to eliminate all the reds. Things started moving and Jacques and Fiancette kept to the discipline of coming personally to see the final results of activities and recognize and encourage efforts. Jacques still didn't see how any of this would solve his much larger problems, which continued to pile up, but he also appreciated the engagement dynamic growing in the company.

On the quality front, each of the production managers set up red bins at every workstation, chose one glaring issue, and addressed it with technical teams. Here again, previously intractable issues got solved one after the other, never in a spectacular way but steadily and continuously. Review after review, Jacques realized that people were not only solving technical problems that had previously been felt to be part of the normal cost of doing business, but they also saw that some of the doors opened had much wider implications for the business, such as supply chain policies. In the terms of the philosopher Montaigne, Jacques was learning to "think against himself," and he realized that he was indeed learning from the shop floor—not only was he discovering some deeply held misconceptions about operations but he was also discovering new, hitherto unknown, technical solutions.

It came to Jacques as a shock to realize he was now asked to present choices rather than make decisions. Progressively, he saw his strategic "wide offer/better service" approach in a different light, and he realized that all the decisions that he, and his management teams, made every day were inconsistent with this approach. They would react on a case-by-case basis to events, such as the choice to cancel all temporary workers in logistics in response to the fall of the order book in the aftermath of the meltdown. Yes, Jacques realized now, he needed a more flexible workforce, but arbitrarily taking people out of logistics would simply stop the trucks from filling and renege on the next-day promise. Jacques was discovering the meaning of "leading from the ground up."

 "From the ground up" is a strategic concept that Emile Simpson coined in his pleading for a radical rethink of modern military strategy.[1]

Simpson argued that many of the strategic blunders of recent Mideast wars were caused by the innocent-looking practice of drawing allies in blue (our guys) and enemies in red (theirs) on PowerPoint maps. This assumed a stability of relationship that was nowhere near the case in a region where alliances shift by the minute according to circumstances, temperament, and opportunity. Commanders on the ground who realized that fact had real successes in focusing on developing the stability of alliances rather than simply hitting the "bad guys," but it took years before the top brass took notice and started changing their stance about the nature of the conflict. Generals can't help fighting the previous war, and they need to learn the current war all over again, from the ground up.

Leading from the ground up means leading the exploration of the strategy from the "shop floor" (a generic term that also includes all support activities, be they factory or office) by looking deeply into factual data points and connecting the dots to form a new strategic picture, rather than imposing one's preconceptions on the reality of operations. Leading from the ground up is not a random walk. It's a determined approach to improve flow (of work, of products, of information), reveal obstacles to flow, and ask "why?" repeatedly with ground teams to figure out what the deeper issues are. It's a leadership act because this exploration is rarely easy or intuitive. Each improvement effort is like a scientific inquiry into what works and what doesn't, what matters and what doesn't. It requires clarity of purpose and a show of confidence of local teams for them to open up and say what they think without fear that the executives will shoot the messenger. It also requires confidence in the leader's genuine curiosity about the situation and interest in improving customers' experience, through better products, services, and processes.

Leading from the ground up means that (1) we show we care by looking into local issues and supporting their resolution and (2) solutions will be built *with* people, not against them. Gemba-based solutions integrate learning-by-doing and people-centric answers. The ultimate aim of leading from the ground up and solving concrete problems is to figure out what the real challenges are, as opposed to what we'd like to do. Making things better locally teaches us to see where the real problems are. And it develops capability by having the people involved in kaizen hone their skills and acquire new ones. The various Lean tools are self-study methods to leverage learning by doing.

Making things better locally requires a rewiring of our ways of *thinking* as well as our models for how to organize ourselves to get things done on a large scale. Modern companies are a legacy of nineteenth-century bureaucracies, influenced by the military successes and reforms of Frederick II the Great. Frederick's fascination with the automation of his time led him to organize his armies as automotons, or mechanical men.[2]

People were turned into mechanical components by techniques we now consider standard: rules, roles, top-down decision-making, and bottom-up reporting (to inform the top-down decision-making). This kind of reasoning leads to solutions with distinctive features. (1) One feature is the separation of strategy and execution—the strategy is devised by reports and in-room analyses, and only once it's been refined, debated, and "sold" does it roll out to the troops to be executed. (2) A second feature is that "people-free" organizational designs are made to work regardless of who is staffed in the role: regardless of personality, individual expertise, motivation or morale, and personal ethics.

Frederick Taylor is remembered for articulating these two principles for the business world, calling them Scientific Management. He was one of the first of a long line of management consultants with advice on how the detailed study of work could lead to new best practice performance. The work of management was essentially to ensure compliance with these new standards designed by experts. These ideas had widespread appeal in an era when the industrial workforce in the United States was swelling with waves of immigrants who spoke many different languages. The Taylorist method of modern management has retained many of these characteristics. The unfortunate consequence of this way of thinking is that even though the average education level of today's workers is higher than it was a century ago, we still send the message to people that they are not expected to "think," just "do," which leads to workers going home at the end of the workday bored and sometimes angry at their diminished feelings of self-worth.

The next challenge during World War II was to train an army of largely women workers to manufacture munitions for the soldiers who went off to fight. The remarkable Training Within Industry (TWI) program was the first large-scale industrial training program teaching factory skills through learning by doing.[3] It used scientific methods to train workers and supervisors in how to carry out tasks (job methods), how to train others to do so (job instruction), and how to work together (job relations). It also was based on three important criteria—namely, simplicity, usability, and standardization. Although it was highly successful, TWI was largely forgotten when the original workforce returned from the battlefield.

When TWI reached postwar Japan, Taiichi Ohno used it as the basis for his own training of TPS. But he took these ideas one step further, using them as the basis for building a system for teaching employees not only how to do their work but how to learn to improve it. As we will see later, the interrelated elements of TPS provided the frame for a deeper understanding of work and how it could be improved to create additional value for customers.

So Lean thinking solutions are (1) crafted through learning by doing and (2) designed to be people centric: they are evolved with the people themselves. Lean leaders figure out with the people themselves what "better" means and draw the overall conclusions, rather than stepping in with a readymade story and imposing it on the people on the ground. Lean leaders do things *with* people, not *to* people. TEST

Learn by Doing

The first skill of a Lean leader, whether the leader of a team of five people or of a multi-billion-dollar company, is to lead kaizen firsthand. This involves enlisting and engaging others to follow you in the change you all learn is necessary and getting them to work for it.

Such an approach contrasts starkly with traditional models of leadership, in which a few gifted individuals with grand strategic visions and a steely will get every last person in line with the plan. This type of change leadership hinges on strategy and execution. The leader and a close guard come up with a strategic plan and then tap into a cadre of richly rewarded enforcers to impose the changes on everyone else.

The costs of this traditional approach go beyond bottom-line losses; they tend to waste human capital. In this approach, the rank and file are rarely involved. Forced to change without understanding the benefits to the organization or to themselves, many people will keep their heads down hoping this will pass them by. In the end, most comply but in the least cooperative way, and not surprisingly, the resulting changes are far from effective. Change initiative failures are far more likely to be attributed to operational resistance than strategic mistakes, whereas the whole approach to change is in question.

Lean thinking's view of change rests on individual commitment to self-development. If people understand the "why" of the changes and have the autonomy to contribute in a way that makes sense to them, change—adaptiveness, in fact—can happen continuously at a much smaller cost and without as much pushback. Change is seen as an individual skill, developed daily within routine, run-of-the-mill work situations by kaizen. Experience shows that when people develop the habit of frequent small-scale changes, they become far more capable of dealing positively with larger ones when necessary.

Above all these leadership approaches represent a challenge to the rise of bureaucracy. There is no known way to scale up any organization

WRITE PARAGRAPH OF
bureaucracy ✓

without setting up some bureaucracy because people need some clarity of roles, chain of command, procedures, departments, and stable task scope. But at some point any bureaucracy becomes obsessed unavoidably by the permanence of its own structures and systems at the expense of focusing on real-life customers with concrete, present problems and focusing on clear and present business conditions. Turning inward, bureaucracy devolves into red tape, where the letter of the procedure matters more than outcomes, departmental borders are the occasion for power struggles, and meaningless work becomes habitual. The traditional approach to fight such bureaucratization is to change policy at the top and watch these changes somehow trickle down through the organization, where they rarely, in fact, reach value-adding work level.

Lean leadership fights these bureaucratic challenges daily by sustaining local kaizen and learning within day-to-day activities. The goal of a Lean thinking leader is to engage all individuals in their organization in making their job better. How? By knowing what to ask for, and knowing how to ask. This means always practicing Lean in a visible manner every day and keeping people focused on a clear improvement strategy based on these principles:

1. Improve customer satisfaction.

2. Improve the flow of work.

3. Make it easier to get tasks done right the first time.

4. Improve relationships.

These improvement directions are navigated by Lean leaders with the following attitudes:

1. *Go and see for yourself.* Rather than listen to what people tell you in the meeting room, go to the source, and see the facts firsthand with customers using the product or service and the people doing the work. In doing so, you can make sure that people agree on the problem before jumping to solutions. Better observation and better discussion lead to better outcomes.

2. *Put problems first.* Leaders who are adamant about putting problems first and do not blame people for them are living proof of respect for

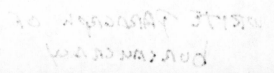

people and their opinions and experience. Listening without blaming people, making an effort to hear their point of view (no matter how weird or biased), is a foundational attitude in building mutual trust.

3. *Try, see, think, try, see, think, to learn faster.* Actively seek out new ideas, and whenever someone does come up with one, encourage her to try small, somewhere, with materials at hand or scrounged resources and see what the impact is like, and then think about it. After she has tried, you commit to help her convince her colleagues and get the financing if necessary to go bigger when appropriate. By encouraging small steps and supporting people through the struggle of learning by doing, you can engage staff in doing something without succumbing to the temptation to invest in untested ideas. Making it easy for workplace employees to try out ideas is more than an attitude. It's a skill—and a stepping stone to your own discovery of the reality of the workplace.

4. *Intensify collaboration.* The quality of problem solving, initiatives, and indeed, the ability to reach real breakthroughs is largely linked to the quality of the collaboration. Collaboration is the ability to bounce off of each other's ideas, to take different perspectives in and take them one step further, and to do quick back-and-forth until something difficult finally works. To better collaborate, teams need both greater clarity in the purpose of what they're asked to do and in the confidence that the team is a safe environment to speak out in one's own voice, propose new ideas, and challenge existing problems.

By personally supporting workplace teams in improving their own work methods, leaders learn to grasp firsthand the larger challenges their organization needs to face and how to go about it. GOOD

When John Bouthillon took over as president and CEO of the family construction business, PO Construction (POC), the previous CEO had grown it to 100 million euros in sales and . . . zero profit. As a result of the 2009 financial meltdown, in the first year of his tenure the company experienced a drop in sales of 40 percent. Bouthillon's interest in Lean had been awakened by reading articles about Toyota's resilience and Jeff Liker's seminal *The Toyota Way.*[4] Knowing the business inside out, he could see all the waste involved in constructing apartment blocks, and he became persuaded that Lean was the way forward to turn the company around. At a

Lean conference, he persuaded a sensei to help him prove that construction could be both less dangerous and less wasteful. The problem was that he had no idea of how to do so (and to be fair, neither did the sensei who had reluctantly agreed to help, knowing nothing of construction either).

John established a routine of visiting four construction sites every week, seeing all his sites every two months on average. By visiting work site after work site, it soon became apparent that one of the biggest differences between construction and traditional manufacturing was the evolutionary nature of any site—the site itself changed from one day to the next as the building grew from digging foundations, to building the structural work, to plastering, painting, flooring, and fitting all final appliances. Traditional Lean techniques didn't seem to apply intuitively.

The second big difference from manufacturing was the large reliance on subcontractors to do specialist work. At most work sites, Bouthillon discovered that his engineers spent most of their time in the site offices looking at spreadsheets to satisfy head office demands for reporting and having legal contractual fights with their subcontractors. Indeed, it became clear that the story of construction was one of negotiation and execution. It was assumed that all was known about how to make a building, so what really mattered was (1) negotiating the lowest price and then (2) controlling the execution. Not surprisingly, this created a toxic work environment, ripe with conflict and distrust, which made it very hard to look into technical problems and find smarter solutions.

To explore these issues more fully, Bouthillon chose to tackle safety and order in the work sites first by requiring his engineers to spend more time on the ground and develop a culture of 5S, a Lean tool focusing on *sorting* and eliminating what is not useful, *straightening* the work area before starting the work itself, *sweeping* before and after, *standardizing* the three previous S practices in normal work, and then *sustaining* by disciplined involvement of site management. This approach revealed how much time workers spent looking for materials and tools in the course of their day and how much rework was considered natural due to unclear communication or lack of detailed planning of the day's work.*

---

* 5S is a Lean tool to help operators improve the flow of their work by better arranging their work environment. The 5Ss are, in fact, five steps. (1) *Sorting* and eliminating: going through every object in the work area and asking oneself whether it's useful or not, and then eliminating

Example of waste 'WASTE

Leading from the ground up led him to formulate two initial strategies he asked all his site managers to get involved with:

1. Work safely by controlling the work space.

2. Get it right the first time, or fix it right away (as opposed to waiting until the opportune time to fix the problem).

Interestingly, because of the varied and evolving nature of building sites, there was no one set way to achieve both principles. Bouthillon asked his site managers what these two strategies meant according to the specificity of every site and the phase of the project they were in.

On the supplier front, Bouthillon started arguing with each of his site managers for a more collaborative approach to working with the subcontractors, looking for astute technical solutions where both the contractor and the company could win in terms of time spent or effort needed. This involved asking site engineers to look in detail at the very first work done by the contractor so as to establish safety ground rules, quality expectations, and a specific improvement point to collaborate on. Bouthillon also took a more strategic approach to this issue, investing in subcontractors of each different trade to learn their issues from the inside and seek win-win opportunities.

He figured out that two major issues confronting subcontractors were that (1) the previous guy had not completely finished his work and would have to come back, which caused technical problems to the next contractor in the work flow, and (2) because contractors worked at different speeds through the building, the faster ones coming behind did not want to be blocked by the slower ones ahead of them, and as a result they took safety margins by delaying when to send their teams to the site, which added considerably to the project's overall lead time.

Step by step, Bouthillon formulated his next two general strategies:

---

anything that isn't useful. (2) *Straightening:* figuring out the best place to locate all useful objects and defining that space. (3) *Sweeping:* making sure everything in use is well maintained and cleaned after use. (4) *Standardizing:* developing the routines that will keep the workplace spick-and-span while doing the job. (5) *Sustaining:* maintaining management support and interest in making sure the workplace is kept spick-and-span according to the 5Ss at all times. 5S is not a "neat workplace" exercise but, rather, a thinking discipline of daily creating a fit for purpose where the environment supports easy, quality work. 5S is a key Lean discipline with the deeper purpose of developing mutual trust between management and employees as workers take responsibility for their own workplace (and organize it as they see fit) and management takes responsibility for giving people the means they need to work effectively.

3. Finish the job completely before leaving the area.

4. Tighten the handover between one trade and the next.

The impact of changing his site managers' approach to running the projects was astounding. In the first years, the company reduced its project lead time on average by 20 percent (not all site managers participated in the effort with equal vigor), which meant that although the company had seriously lost ground on turnover, it now found itself to be profitable, and it was able to recapture lost sales.

At the site level, these "strategic" initiatives rarely looked so grand. Beyond requiring site management teams to develop and sustain their 5S work space approach, the main tool of Bouthillon's transformation was a humble daily problem analysis sheet where the site manager explored with his team one problem a day on the basis of the following:

Date	Problem	Cause	Countermeasure	Impact

Junior engineers were asked to spell out a problem, analyze the cause (and find out what the gap to industry standard was), figure out a counter-measure, and check the impact of this corrective action. Nothing grander. But on the sites where the manager understood the exploratory nature of the exercises and used it to discover the technical strengths and weaknesses of his team and coach them to better understand their job, this delivered spectacular results.

One unlooked-for aspect that particularly interested Bouthillon was the emergence of smarter solutions for the energy performance of the building as a whole. Looking for simpler ways to do the work, engineers also found more energy-efficient ways to both make the building and do the work—two of which led to patents, something that had never happened in the company. This enabled the CEO to formulate the fifth item of his overall strategy:

5. Improve energy performance.

As the cumulative results of many kaizens became apparent, POC designed a new building that performed at 20 percent less energy con-sumption, using traditional construction methods more mindfully. In this instance, we can see that improving all existing processes and techniques and combining them smartly can lead to radically better results and unexpected new thinking. Here again, this achievement did not come from deciding it up front and investing in "making it so." It occurred as Bouthillon progressively devised his strategy to improve how regular buildings were constructed, and how all sorts of improvement ideas accumulated and could finally be brought together in a breakthrough result.

As Bouthillon continued to visit sites every week, he noted that when faced with questionable approaches on the site, the project managers would be asked to explain how their choices helped to work more safely, succeed right the first time, better prepare for the next contractor to come in, improve the hand-off, and improve the energy performance of building or construction. As they themselves worked their way through the questions, they would often see what they hadn't grasped in their first approach. Leading from the ground up is a way to craft strategy while developing competencies with the people who do the work themselves.

The question remains: how do we make sure these various improvement efforts don't go all over the place but, rather, as in Bouthillon's case, converge in improvement that can be seen in bottom-line figures? As we've seen, improvement direction is not random, and there are 60 years of Lean tradition to help us steer, which is where making the effort to learn the Lean tools in depth comes into play.

Look for People-Centric Solutions

"Greatness in people," explained Akio Toyoda, Toyota's current CEO, "comes out only when they are led by great leaders. We say at Toyota that every leader is a teacher developing the next generation of leaders. This is their most important job."[5]

The modern corporation, regardless of happy talk about empowered employees and "people are our most important asset," is essentially based on *people-free* solutions familiar to us all: Rules are inflexible corporate laws, not guidelines that can be adapted situationally. Roles are functional positions that have no personal relevance. Hierarchy exists to ensure compliance. Managers make the decisions that "hands" execute. Information systems that gather and compile the right financial "numbers" lead naturally to the best decision-making. And formal contracts are the key to managing relationships.

Such ideas, which we're brought up to consider as perfectly normal common sense, lead to people-free problem solving. A company's issues (or beyond that, a society's) are solved independently of the people composing the firm. Once a people-free solution is determined, the next question is how to make people comply with this solution—hence the insistence on proper "change management" and buy-in. The equation is resolved by top management irrespective of people, and then it has to be applied through a mix of incentives, persuasion, and pressure.

Lean thinking markedly breaks away from such reasoning. No solution is people-free. Indeed, since solutions appear by the cumulative impact of local improvement and are dependent on the skill building needed for capability development, solutions are *fundamentally and inalienably people centric*. Each person's very personality, engagement in their own self-development, initiative, and creativity make up the seed from which new capabilities will grow and from which, by combining new capabilities, new solutions will appear. People are not the problem. They are the solution.

People centric means turning toward people often and accepting that their personality, experience, expertise, morale and ethics, and more importantly creativity are elements that will deeply form the end solution of the problem we're trying to solve. Because Lean solutions rest on developing capabilities, and capabilities are institutionalized skills, people matter as people, not just as cogs in the machine. People centric involves turning toward people to see how they understand the challenge, what problems they experience, what ideas they have, and ultimately, what direction they'd like to see the full organization going. In practice, this involves the following:

- Showing frequent interest for what people have to say, not just what you want to hear them say. Going to the workplace to see firsthand is the foundational technique of all Lean thinking because there can't be interest without proof of interest. Walking to the workplace to see for yourself proves that you *care*.

- Understanding that some of the things you'll say will touch on deep insecurities in the people in front of you—insecurities from their perception of their environment, what they feel is open to them or not, what they feel comfortable with or not, and so on—and that these insecurities, rational or not, will not be disclosed. Creating a physically and psychologically safe environment is a prerequisite to collaborative discussions.

- Realizing that each person has her own opinion about how things are and how they should be, where the company is as a whole and where it should go, regardless of how much you agree with these opinions. You can force people to do something against their better judgment, but if you really want them to contribute, you'll have to first reframe their thinking—which takes building a relationship and mutual trust from frequent expressions of interest and repeated explanations of what you're trying to do and, in particular, leaving them space to think and to experiment with their own ideas as well. They will surprise you. There is no stronger way to marry someone to a cause then to recognize his personal contribution to it.

- Finding the people with the greatest learning-by-doing abilities and connecting them to others across silos in order to develop teamwork. And then promoting them as a means of strengthening the learning capability of management teams in order to enhance the capacity of the entire organization to grow and learn.

People centric doesn't mean bottom up: leaders lead, and they have a disproportionate impact on the direction and the way work is performed. But leaders explain and listen, support as well as teach, and accept that every specific situation is felt differently by the people on the ground, where things actually happen. People centric involves thinking differently about our traditional organizational reflexes, which is reflected by Lean thinking's specific vocabulary—different because the underlying thinking is different from the command-and-control habits instilled in managers in both their education and their previous work experience. In short, the core idea of Lean practice comes down to this: *Making things better starts with making better people.* Mainstream thinking leads us to decide the solution in abstract terms, plan for its implementation, organize accordingly, and finally staff the organization with people who will then be directed and controlled. Lean thinking does not seek this type of static optimization but, rather, dynamic progress. First we choose our allies, the people we'll face our challenge with. Then they tell us how they wish to organize themselves and how we'll coordinate to face the challenge together. This states clearly that the quality of the solution directly depends on the knowledge, judgment, and leadership of the people involved in the problem (it is in any case, but people-free thinking tends to mask this).

Unfortunately, we're not taught to look for people-centric solutions, and even when we should know better, our reflex is to solve the problem in our minds and then rely on the bureaucratic mechanisms to implement it. For instance, when Jacques acquired a smaller company to complete his range with electrical drivers, he immediately thought he needed to "Lean" the newly acquired company. Having succeeded at turning around his traditional business with his COO (Frédéric Fiancette) and his Lean director (Eric Prévot), he asked the latter to spend some time in the new company and establish the same standards. The CEO of the acquired company, still reeling from changing management, simply did not see the point. They were a small firm of just about 40 people, half in assembly and half in product design and administration, much too small for Lean. The company had revenue of 6 million euros, 1.1 million held in inventory, and an on-time delivery performance of 86 percent.

Focused on releasing a new product, the CEO let the Lean director conduct kaizen workshops without paying it much mind. Still, as they applied Lean techniques to flow work, and as sales increased by 20 percent with the new product, the inventory remained at 1.1 million, jumping turns from 2.8 to 3.6. Unfortunately, not only did on-time delivery fail to improve but the operators started complaining, softly at first and then increasingly bitterly, about the deteriorating ergonomic conditions of the line. The throughput was far faster, but the work was much harder. Typically, assembly had used Lean techniques to improve flow, but the CEO, being vaguely supportive but not personally engaging, had done nothing on either quality or pull.

Management then decided to stop all further progress, take a step back, and work with the CEO and his production team (or not at all). For starters, they went back to flow principles by pacifying the lines with a regular pull, and then they worked with each operator team in turn to solve all ergonomics issues. They invited in an ergonomics specialist to create a measuring system the operators could use themselves. They studied different work scenarios, alternated workstations, multiskilled the workforce, and gained 20 percent productivity. Three years after the start of Lean, sales had grown a further 16 percent to 9.3 million, and inventory had reduced by 40 percent to 680,000 euros. Turns had jumped to 8.5, and, more astonishing, service had climbed to 96 percent—something no one thought could ever be achieved considering the high-mix low-volume nature of the business.

More importantly, by refocusing on a people-centric approach to improvement, collaboration between product design and production improved, and solutions now kept pouring in from the engagement of all employees. Progressively, production learned to abandon batches altogether and work only on demand, while enduring quality issues were resolved with engineering. Operators coordinated themselves to work with management with a more flexible labor hours system to be able to respond faster to spot demands. Improvement work then moved on to the supply chain and working more closely with suppliers—again with many unforeseen improvement ideas resulting from more intense collaboration. In the end, the company did achieve similar results to the acquiring company (Table 3.1).

Temptation is always strong to apply to others what one has learned and revert to a "I say, you do" strategy-and-execute style. As we'll discuss later, both Prévot and Fiancette (Jacques had retired by then) had a long experience of transforming sites. If Prévot hadn't done a superb job of being resilient in the face of the acquired CEO's passive resistance as well as listening to the operators' complaints on the line, management could easily have done what many other companies do—be encouraged by early results on turns and continue to force progress mindlessly. In this case, Fiancette and Prévot reverted to *find* and understand that their early improvement results did not show the same things that they'd seen in their own sites (the products were functionally very different, as were the people and the company history). They went to *face* the issue and work on creating

	2009	2015	Gains
Sales	6 million	11 million	+80%
Inventory	1.1	0.44	2X
Turns	2.9	15.5	+500%
On-time delivery	86%	99%	+15%
Sales per person	150,000	290,000	+90%
Backlog	3 weeks	3 days	7X

Table 3.1   Lean Improvement Results in Acquired Company

a measurement system for ergonomics (something they imported back to the other sites later), and from then on to *frame* the situation by using the size of the firm for it rather than against it. Its small size meant that the main improvement dimension should be intense collaboration between production and engineering (again, something that proved difficult in the larger, older acquiring sites) in order to *form*, spectacularly, new solutions invented with the CEO and around the production and engineering guys, not by forcing them, through carefully developing manufacturing, engineering, and logistics capabilities, with many an impact on the very design of new products.

Studies of mergers and acquisitions put the failure rate somewhere between 70 and 90 percent, and, unfortunately Jacques had some experience of that with a previous so-so acquisition.[6] When acquiring this new company, he'd been specially careful not to overwhelm it with his own procedures, systems, and culture. Unfortunately, in most acquisitions situations, the strength of our bureaucratic conditioning is such that we implicitly believe the acquired company should adjust to our people-free strategies (after all, they're acquired to fill a gap in the strategic portfolio), roles (they need to join corporate management schemes), and procedures (some of them required by law, such as Sarbanes-Oxley) and, they should, well, bloody do as they're told. As a result, in many such acquisitions of technical companies, the smartest engineers leave, and you're left with a bureaucratic shell deprived of its smart core.

Orry's former company, Wiremold, acquired 21 companies from 1991 to 2001, and it developed standards for both pre- and postacquisition. One of those standards was that on the first day that the company became part of the Wiremold family, the employees of that company received a few hours of introduction to Wiremold and its Lean strategy—with a focus on the improvement dimensions. This was followed by the formation of a couple of kaizen teams that began working that day on the improvement of two significant problems. In every case it was the first time that the people doing the work were asked to be involved in identifying their problems and given a say in putting countermeasures in place. After a couple of days there was no doubt in their minds that life would be different from then on and that their input and engagement would be central to both their success in the new environment and the success of the company as a whole.

Lead from the Ground Up to Face Your Real Challenges

VERY GOOD (handwritten)

A key part of having sustainable, consistent results with Lean thinking lies in avoiding huge, wasteful mistakes. We learn to fail early, in small, quick ways in order to sidestep catastrophic failure in large ways. Small mistakes are part of learning by doing. Large errors are costly. Succeeding in the mid to long term has much to do with the ability of leaders to face the real issues their organizations are dealing with. Facing one's real, deep problems is the point of firsthand kaizen. Learning about the people around us by working through issues with them, learning their strengths and weaknesses, their preferences and red buttons, are all aspects of forging better dynamic outcomes.

Lean thinking's people-centric approach doesn't mean "soft" (as in "soft skills") or a free-for-all. It means following the compass of better flow to support learning curves and avoid readymade solutions, which can take quite a bit of management grit. It's a completely different way to grow the business. Make no mistake—doing so certainly imposes pressure on employees to perform at a high caliber. That's because team leaders keep an eye on high-level goals while at the same time holding people accountable for better results: forming the future company one kaizen at a time, one team at a time, every day, everywhere, and keeping the dynamic of small, continuous, people-led improvement.

As Lionel Repellin, the CEO of the company Jacques acquired, shared, "I really didn't believe in any of this Lean stuff because I did not see how it could apply to a company like ours, a small technical company. I must now admit I never would have believed any of the results we've had would have been possible at all. I've learned a lot, and, most surprisingly and encouraging, after a rough start, relationships within the company are better than they ever were." Processes can be managed; people must be *led* if real challenges are to be faced, together, from the ground up.

TALK ABOUT
MAKING SMALL
MISTAKES & AVOID
Huge MISTAKES

CHAPTER 4

Framing for Learning

Use Lean tools and methods for increasing understanding, teamwork, and improvement.

Having seen how the shop floor itself could show the way how to make daily decisions consistent with the larger strategic choices, Jacques as CEO, Fiancette as COO, and Prévot as CIO were quick to adopt the Lean learning system as a framework to structure their exploration:

1. They established a list of key indicators to reflect the safety, quality, lead time, productivity, energy performance, and morale challenges in each plant.

2. They built pull systems to handle variety through better planning at takt time, created continuous flow cells, and implemented logistics internal pull with a small train and *kanban cards*.

3. They worked with each production manager to stop at every quality problem and to make equipment and materials progressively more reliable to assemble more seamlessly.

4. They worked on the basic stability of each of the production halls, through 5S, team stability, and daily problem solving.

As this work progressed and the cash curve improved, Jacques realized that his intuitive strategic choices were being framed with greater consistency, and in a way he could communicate with the entire company, from boardroom to shop floor. First, he had to deliver a wide catalog of products the next day while maintaining low inventories through an extended supply chain. For instance, having realized that China shipped one container of components a month, the logistics team set up a cross-dock operation in China to mix the content of the container according to demand, and thus reducing in one go the total inventory by about 20 percent.

Second, Jacques had to deliver quality parts, not only through final inspection and rejection at testing of the faulty products but first through self-inspection at each workstation (and solving the machine problems), and further on with source inspection at the suppliers. This led to a deeper engineering problem of designing products more tolerant of poorer dimensional quality casting parts without affecting the performance of the assembled product.

Third, he had to continue to machine and assemble parts and find a way to mechanize assembly to take away ergonomics problems without investing in large oversized robots with overcapacity (and costing cash)— which led to the thornier problem of scheduling more production through local machining to lower the overall product cost, without being penalized by western high labor costs.

Jacques was seeing his industrial problem with a depth of under-standing he had not grasped before. He began to see the problems with greater clarity and granularity. He realized that each of these problems could be narrowed down to specific activities on the shop floor so that the people themselves could pragmatically address local problems revealed by the Lean system. In other words, as people at the gemba learned to solve their daily problems, they were showing Jacques how to solve his larger, strategic issues. As they learned, so did the CEO. This revelation completely revolutionized Jacques's understanding of what a learning organization could be. For the past several decades of experimenting with learning orga-nizations, Jacques had always separated actual "work" from the "learning" that would take place elsewhere in classrooms, or "learning labs." Jacques now saw how the Lean system framed issues in a way that brought learning *within* daily work—operational learning, as it were. Jacques discovered that shop floor Lean "tools" were in fact learning labs brought into day-to-day operations, helping every person form solutions every day, everywhere through repeated experiments on the larger challenges.

As a manager, Jacques found himself progressively tougher on problems and softer on people. He would no longer accept "can't do" answers—the problem had to be solved—but he would be patient about trying different things until they found a workable solution, actually curious about what would come out of the process in the end and hoping for a surprise (both good or bad surprises are *learning*). By accelerating the speed of practical change on the shop floor, Jacques grew more confident about having a hands-on way to shape the company with more input from everyone and far less soft resistance. The Lean tools revealed specific shop floor progress where he could help by showing interest, encouraging, and removing bureaucratic obstacles when these came up.

"Give me a fulcrum and a lever long enough and I shall move the world," Archimedes once quipped. The world does change, and it changes from combinations of tools and ideas. What is a telescope without the theory of gravity? What is a printing press without the idea of personal theology? Or the Internet without the idea of a World Wide Web connecting every page? Ideas are the fulcrums, and tools are the levers on which the world moves. Lean thinking can change the world if we understand the idea of making things better and using the various Lean kaizen tools to do so.

These large ideas are called *frames*. Frames structure how we understand a complex situation and scaffold our learning to point us to the next step (as in, literally, the picture frame through which you see the world). The frame, however, doesn't tell you what you'll find: you need to look through it and see. To understand the essence of Lean thinking, it's critical to see many of what are popularly interpreted as powerful tools as *frames*. Not as instruments for quick results, but as methods of engagement, understanding, and, yes, framing. Just-in-time, for example, is a frame stating that we should make only what is needed, when it is needed, and in the amount needed. Taiichi Ohno tinkered for many years with the idea of *kanban* (cards for each container) to make the frame work. Once kanban was perfected, the just-in-time frame could then be explored in much greater detail.

The Toyota Production System (TPS) is in fact a system of a few powerful frames: customer satisfaction, built-in quality, just-in-time, standardized work and kaizen, and basic stability. Within Toyota, the TPS is sometimes called the "Thinking People System." In remembering his training with Taiichi Ohno, Toyota executive Teruyuki Minoura recalled, "I don't think he was interested in my answer at all. He was just putting me through some kind of training to get me to learn how to think."[1] The system emerged through trial and error in solving practical problems and meeting the needs of the company.[2]

It was only by developing a loose collection of techniques into a full-fledged system that they were able to spread its influence throughout the company, says Minoura. Still, veterans of the early days of teaching TPS repeatedly warn that, in the words of another sensei, the risk with a system of tools is "creating a Buddha image and forgetting to inject the soul into it."[3] Without the tool, the idea remains a fantasy; without the idea, the tool leads to the wrong understanding.

The trick to framing hard issues productively is avoiding global solutions and tackling them in ways that are not overwhelming. One learns to be disciplined and to rely on a *scaffolding*—that is, a framework to express challenges in concrete, chunk-able bites, in line with a long tradition of others who have done this before. Mastering the Lean learning system is the key to framing the issues we face in a way that others can understand.

The TPS is, in essence, a vast mental scaffolding structure to teach people to think differently, working on the assumption that you don't think yourself into a new way of acting, but you act yourself into a new way of thinking. The TPS defines challenges and exercises to help you understand your own business differently. It's a learning method, not an organizational blueprint. Furthermore, it's a learning method designed to teach every employee how to participate in Toyota's overall strategy. Consequently, to fully grasp the importance of the TPS one has to see the following:

- Toyota's overall approach to competitive advantage in the automotive market

- How the TPS tools teach each employee to participate in creating this competitive advantage in his or her daily job: not just to make value, but to *add* value

When visiting Toyota operations, most people are impressed by how incredibly flexible the production lines are (handling one model after another without batching); how productive the people are (most people you see follow a standard cycle fluidly—without strain, but without stops); how responsive the lines are to operator concerns (the andon call signal lights up every minute or so); and how many suggestions employees come up with (99 percent of which are accepted and implemented). There is no doubt that Toyota has created a superior industrial system with greater discipline on safety and with greater attention to quality, a system that is also visibly both more flexible and productive. The temptation is to interpret this industrial system in our own traditional Taylorist terms and jump to the conclusion that Toyota has better manufacturing engineers who design better processes and a more disciplined management line (Japanese culture, here we go) that executes those designs more rigorously and interprets TPS as a vast standard-policing machine.

Again, we are in no way arguing that Toyota is a perfect company: it is emphatically not an embodiment of best practices to follow blindly. Thinking that way would be falling back into the Taylorist notion that something designed elsewhere can be applied in cookie-cutter fashion. We are saying that 25 years after the original study, Toyota remains the strongest competitor in its field and that, in the process, it has become the world's leading automaker, pushing General Motors into bankruptcy along the way. Astonishingly, Toyota has succeeded in being profitable every year since 1951, barring 2009 when the bottom fell out of the auto industry (fewer new cars were sold than cars were scrapped).

Interestingly, for one of their top executives, the conclusion of the 2009 period was that Toyota was able to make money from its factories even while they were operating at 80 percent capacity . . . and yet the aftermath of the global financial crisis drove volumes below 70 percent. And therefore the company needed to learn to make such flexible factories that they could operate profitably at 70 percent of full capacity: another gutsy challenge. The aim is not to be perfect and rigid but to be never satisfied and always be striving to find a better way. As a result, as Professor Hirotaka Takeuchi explained, Toyota appears full of paradoxes and contradictions, as a way of life, compared to our notions of "perfect" systems.[4] The company's system supports human creativity, as opposed to restricting it, which allows Toyota to both make cars rigorously every day and absorb breakthrough innovations regularly without risk to customers.

Right from the start, Toyota has described TPS as a training system to engage workers in detailed problem solving to deepen their understanding of quality for customers and involve them in kaizen with their teammates, and with the company at large, to find ways to produce greater variety without generating so much waste. Lean thinking leads to *sustainable profitability* because profitability is built into growth, through the virtue of constant kaizen. In that sense, *Lean* is not a noun. It is a verb. Lean thinking is about sustaining the continuous "Leaning" of operations, from product design to manufacturing to supply chain to administrative support, by working with the value-adding teams themselves in order to create more value while generating less waste. It's a dynamic, not a state—and TPS is the learning framework Toyota has created to support this learning with challenges from clear ambitions, respect from jidoka conditions, teamwork from just-in-time conditions, and continuous improvement at the work-place from kaizen and standard work.

How Did Toyota Choose to Compete?

As Dan and his colleagues have explained in their study of Toyota, the company came up with its business system as a response to three deep (and largely self-imposed) constraints in the 1950s and 1960s:

- *Intense competition:* The world's automotive market of the 1960s was dominated by the United States' big three players. National auto-makers were struggling to survive, and they lobbied government to protect internal markets. Contrary to the wishes of the Ministry of International Trade and Industry (MITI), Japanese automakers of the postwar period chose to compete on a full range of cars rather than split up the market between them. The MITI believed that because of the small size of the auto market in 1950s Japan, there would be room for only one manufacturer per segment, but instead Toyota, Nissan, Mazda, and Mitsubishi went for all-out competition, and as a result they faced great pressure to release new products frequently to seduce the growing population of Japanese motorists.

- *Self-funding:* In 1950 Toyota went nearly bankrupt and was bailed out by banks, who forced it to lay off workers and restructure (sepa-rating sales from production). Toyota leaders swore they would never be reliant on banks again. As the company churned out new model after new model to keep up with its competition, this meant that new models had to be assembled on existing production lines because the company did not have the means to afford dedicated single-product lines like the Ford system in use at the time.

- *Value analysis/value engineering (VA/VE) with suppliers:* In contrast to the traditional approach of squeezing suppliers for price cuts, Toyota realized that a huge part of the value of their cars rests with the suppliers. Consequently, rather than view suppliers as outsiders to be gamed, Toyota asked for innovation from their suppliers. They progressively incorporated key suppliers into their just-in-time supply chain, pushed them to engage in VA/VE projects, and shared the gains that resulted.

- *No strikes:* As a result of the brutal strikes leading up to the company breakup and revival in 1951, which triggered the resignation of the company's founder Kiichiro Toyoda, Toyota's leadership committed to a policy of collaborative labor relations based on the front line's management relationships with unions, with the firm intent of not experiencing strikes again. In their global expansion, the no-strike policy is less rigorously observed because the company has encountered different union setups, but strikes are still regarded as something to avoid at almost all costs.

Toyota therefore worked hard to find an engineering and manufacturing way of (1) proposing attractive new products at a regular cadence for each market segment while (2) assembling new models on existing production lines in order to manage sales variation by (3) involving all employees in developing the proper way to engineer, supply, and manufacture a wide range of products productively. Out of the mad scramble for survival in the automotive Japanese market of the 1960s, Toyota devised a sensible approach to customer satisfaction through quality, variety, and price—which economists now recognize as customers' preference order in hypercompetitive markets.

Toyota's approach to sustained sales is that (1) if you buy a Toyota, you should never regret it so that (2) your next car will be a Toyota as well and you will find the model for your evolving needs in the Toyota product range (3) at a reasonable price. The company leaders set out to solve three basic problems: First, how do you guarantee the quality of every car both in design and production? Second, how do you offer variety (with quality) without burdening yourself with impossible investment costs? Third, how do you deliver quality and variety productively? Most manufacturers consider that both high quality and high variety generate additional costs and are in fact necessary trade-offs. Toyota believed that the highest quality and greatest variety should be compatible with lowest costs.

Quality was defined as attractiveness with peace of mind. A Toyota car should be OK to look at, pleasing to drive, and carry all the expected features—with greater robustness. A Toyota car should run longer, without needing repairs (thus ensuring a high resale value). In purchasing a Toyota, you're not acquiring the sexiest style or the fastest ride, but you're buying "no trouble"—the one feature Toyota delivers more consistently than any other automaker.

To achieve this, Toyota leaders came to the conclusion that quality could not be inspected out (inspect every product and set aside the poor quality ones) but *built in* (whenever you have a quality doubt at any operation, stop and investigate rather than continue to assemble and assume that any defect will be sorted out at inspection). The argument was that if you allow faulty products to go all the way to final inspection and then try to select them out, you'll miss some of the flaws and you won't learn because you won't see the defect as it's *put into* the product.*

They figured that the only way to learn how to solve quality issues was to see when the problem happened in real life to be able to fix it. This meant stopping nonquality at the step of the process where it happened, when it happened.

Built-in quality has two essential dimensions: *GOOD.*

- *Design robustness:* Features need to prove their robustness before being included in the final product, which means largely relying on known engineering standards and a cautious approach to innovation. Toyota is known as a "fast follower" because it follows the market in terms of innovation, and it is very cautious in adding innovative features until they have been fully tested and mastered. The built-in quality frame applies at all levels of the system from the largest—don't put on the market a feature you're not 100 percent sure of—to the most detailed— don't pass on to the next worker a job you're not 100 percent sure of.

- *Stop-at-every-defect:* In assembly, every operation is inspected through a "finishing touch," and whenever the operator has a doubt or the machine's auto test shows a slight problem, the line is stopped, and the problem studied so that every product comes out confidently within standards. This, in turn, creates a huge database of what kind of problems to expect at every stage of the process, which both feeds back into engineering and into training and inspection checklists for further assembly.

Building quality in rather than inspecting defects out puts *outcome ahead of output*: there is no point in producing anything quickly if a large percentage is at risk of creating customer issues and will be thrown away (or reworked) because it is considered defective. Whatever productivity is gained from speed is lost through the efforts to inspect defects out after

---

* "Jidoka captures the principle of building quality into the production process—of designing work so that the people making the product have the means and mindset to be constantly vigilant for what is okay and what is not," wrote Tom Ehrenfeld in his article "Lean Roundup: Jidoka," *The Lean Post*, Lean Enterprise Institute (LEI) blog, October 27, 2016. See also the *Lean Lexicon*, Lean Enterprise Institute, Cambridge, MA, 2014.

the fact. Better to slow things down on the first pass and fix problems than suffer the cost of inspection and elimination of defects later. For Toyota, however, such a system required day-to-day, minute-to-minute attention to mindful work. To be able to stop at every defect, employees need to *care* and look for inconsistencies in order to flag them, which in turn involves a relationship with management where problems are welcomed and speaking up daily is encouraged.

The second aspect of Toyota's sales approach is variety. Today— as half a century ago—Toyota strives to offer customers a more complete range (with lowest cannibalization between models) so that when lifestyles evolve, consumers can find what they need within the Toyota family. This core thinking led the company to come up with a luxury brand from scratch (Lexus) to offer cars to their most successful customers (and compete with the German high-end brands in the United States) and a youth brand (Scion) targeted at younger, first-car owners (which it decided to discontinue in 2016 as a "failed" experiment).

The obvious problem of producing a wide range is investment cost. Back in the 1960s, manufacturers believed that the only way to keep costs down was Henry Ford's approach: specialize production lines and facilities, produce large batches, and lower unit costs through economies of repetition. Toyota, however, could not afford to invest in new lines and equipment with every new model. The hypercompetition in Japan drove the company to come up with new models too often, they were committed to self-financing their development, and they would not go to banks to fund new facilities. As a result, they resolved that any new model would be assembled on an existing production line.

As Toyota transplants opened around the world, a "young" plant would learn to achieve top quality at a required output on one model first, then cope with variants of that model, and finally add an additional model, and so on, striving to reach the flexibility of lines in Japan that can handle several platforms in sequence. The impact on capital efficiency has been considerable. New plants are designed to cover the basic market with a single model, and extra volume is taken care of in the Japanese flexible plants, so that Toyota has never found itself (except for the exceptional year following the financial collapse) in the structural overcapacity situation that plagues all its competitors. Indeed, they have been profitable every year of their history, apart from the one disastrous year of 2009.

The third element of Toyota's sales strategy is reasonable price. Toyota manages to keep costs down through its commitment to quality. Simply choosing not to produce defective products turns out to be a very cost-effective strategy (indeed, non-quality-related costs can easily amount to 2 to 4 percent of sales in most companies we know, directly affecting profitability). The company also has higher capital productivity, through producing high variety on the same equipment, which makes a Lean company far more cash and capital efficient.

Driving all this is kaizen. Built-in quality and variety with flexibility *with* labor productivity come down to solving millions of detailed technical issues. Toyota's approach to doing so is through the engagement of all its employees in kaizen—making things better every day. As a result, a thousand-foot view of what Toyota achieved can be summed up in organizing:

- A *flow of value* by offering not just one model but a flow of models at a regular rhythm to try to reach customers better with each new generation

- A *flow of ideas* by encouraging and supporting suggestions from all employees throughout the company

- A *flow of work* by creating a work organization getting closer and closer to full right-first-time and one-piece flow to support both variety and productivity and thus solving the industrial conundrum of finding a cost-effective way of offering a wide range of products

Since the 1990s, Toyota has added a further dimension to its sales approach: emissions and energy performance. Deeply involved in energy efficiency both in their products and processes since the 1980s, Toyota introduced a radical innovation to the automotive markets with the gas-electric hybrid Prius in 1997, and it has since bet its entire brand image on energy-performing cars since, recently introducing the first hydrogen fuel cell car, the Mirai. In typical Toyota fashion, energy performance is sought in both product design and process improvement, and every plant has stringent zero landfill and zero carbon emissions targets.

How Does TPS Develop Competitive Advantage?

Toyota's Lean system provides thinking frames to develop people-centric solutions: employees are expected to think of ways to make their work better in a manner that supports quality, flexibility, lower costs, and greater energy performance. Furthermore, the overall sum of their contributions, both at the management and frontline levels, will shape the system as a whole. Still, this approach poses four serious challenges that contrast with all previous management styles:

1. You cannot force people to have ideas. You can only encourage them to do so and support them when they do.

2. You cannot tell people what kind of ideas they should have. You can only show them the sort of suggestions that fit within the wider scope of what you're trying to do.

3. You cannot focus on error avoidance alone. It is useful, in order to delve into technical issues, but people also need some thinking space for initiative and creativity.

4. You can't expect people to experiment and learn during their normal daily work if you don't create specific space for them to think and try new things.

Taylorism was born on the belief that no one could be expected to do the work and think about the work at the same time. Taylor's insight was to separate those who work from the experts who study work and write down the "one best way," to be enforced on those who work. People behave as human robots following the engineer's work program.

This framing of the organization as a machine with interchangeable parts (people) was perfected at the executive level at General Motors by the Alfred Sloan followers pursuing what Peter Drucker described as "management by objectives." A manager's work was not specified as line work, but the idea was to force middle managers to make the "right" decisions according to the executive function. By defining financial objectives and linking pay for performance to achieving these objectives, corporations found a way to force managers to make certain types of decisions—even when they felt the outcomes of those decisions were questionable.

A slew of financial and personal measurements drives organizations and their people to pursue short-term and often counterproductive and/or contradictory goals. Middle managers will repeatedly say, "I'm sorry, I realize this might not be optimal, but I need to reach this target in order to get my bonus." Or the sales managers may want to give customers more generous payment terms to earn a bonus for increased sales while the financial manager may need to reduce the number of accounts receivable days outstanding to earn her bonus, creating an organizational (and personal) conflict.

Note that neither Taylorism nor management by the numbers engenders real initiative from either workers or managers. The real difficulty lies in "orienting" people's minds so that they understand what is sought from them, as well as making improvement opportunities in their jobs visible. To do so, Toyota leaders developed a framework over time to structure work environments that support creative tension between where we want to go, where we are now, and how we're supposed to get there. This enables people doing the work to orient themselves to improvement goals at any moment, create the conditions for improving within daily work, and understand how to do this specific work with their teammates.

Ambitions

To achieve competitive advantage, first, you've got to *want it*. This sounds like a truism, but many executive teams have worked themselves into such a reactive posture that they've let go of the ambition of being better than their competitors. The first step of the learning system is putting daily new energy into challenging ourselves to be better, like athletes on the track. The second step is to describe this ambition in terms of concrete goals for all to understand and aspire to.

"Better" in Lean thinking starts with seeking to earn customers' smiles—more complete customer satisfaction (more exactly, aligning customer satisfaction, employee involvement, and benefit to society), or value. In this perspective, the customer is not a "consumer" to be milked but a client to be helped: (1) helped to achieve what they want to get done, in their terms; (2) helped through uptimes and downtimes and helped when they need you; (3) helped in a way they find more valuable (and overall more cost-effective) than your competitors' offers (4) so that they generously let you prosper by rewarding you financially. A 5 percent increase in customer loyalty is estimated to be worth 25 percent in greater profitability. Customers are not prey to feed on. They are long-term friends to be supported in their lifestyle choices.

The TPS framework defines customer satisfaction challenges in terms of *safety, quality, cost, lead time, morale,* and *energy efficiency.* In any situation, one can ask oneself the following questions:

- *Safety:* How can I reduce accidents by half?

- *Quality:* How can I reduce customer returns or complaints by half?

- *Cost:* How can I double labor productivity and halve component costs?

- *Lead time:* How can I cut lead time from order to delivery by half (or double inventory turns)?

- *Morale:* How can I improve employee morale, reduce absenteeism by half, and double creative ideas?

- *Energy efficiency:* How can I cut carbon emissions and energy use by half?

If we have already faced the problems and measured the problems, each of these questions yields a mathematical answer. The result might seem impossible but will orient the creative thinking. If we make the effort to take the numbers seriously, we will naturally start listing the obstacles that stop us from achieving these goals—mostly issues with our current level of technology or practices. This will lead us to find promising topics in terms of value analysis (improving value in products or services currently in production) and value engineering (improving value in products or services being designed for future offers), with value determined as the formula of function over cost.

These challenges form a system inasmuch as they can't be looked at independently of each other. There is not much point in increasing quality if it also increases costs or conversely in reducing costs if it affects quality the wrong way. The fundamental idea is that by improving all indicators simultaneously, one is certain to improve one's competitive position—even if we don't quite achieve all our demanding targets.

In any case, by measuring these values for your activity, and doing the simple math of dividing current bad numbers by half or doubling the good ones, you can easily create your own range of goals in any situation and any position, to get the creative juices going: "What do I need to solve in order to reach these goals?"

Conditions

The two next main frames of TPS are *built-in quality* (also known as *jidoka*) and *just-in-time*. The built-in-quality frame holds that it's better to stop work than to pass on a defect down the chain (stop, solve the problem, and start again) in order to catch the problem just as it happens and see the facts in real-time context. Just-in-time is about making only what is needed, when it is needed, and in the amount needed. Obviously these two frames overlap since making only exactly the products needed assumes that all products are good (no inventory to cover throwing out bad apples after inspection) and being able to check every product so as to not pass on defectives requires making products one by one in sequence, that is, just in time.

These Lean frames are not simply about ideas. They also function as learning scaffolding. As we previously discussed, Lean thinking seeks to learn by doing and find people-centric solutions. As a result, a unique aspect of Lean technique is creating the right workplace conditions for day-to-day learning by doing. This is probably the aspect of Lean that is the most arduous to learn, and it requires one to be steeped in the TPS tradition, which has developed these various techniques over decades.

The two basic pillars of workplace organization are:

1. *Jidoka conditions:* Creating a visual environment where it is possible to get work right on the first pass, every time. In jidoka conditions, any person doing any work can recognize that something is doubtful, call for an immediate second opinion, and if the problem is confirmed, stop to fix the issue and return to standard conditions before continuing rather than working around the problem.

2. *Just-in-time conditions:* Coordinating all departmental, machine, and human processes to work continuously without accumulating inventories or requiring overcapacity. In just-in-time conditions, anyone can know what she is immediately working on and what the next job is going to be, with only the needed materials and equipment on hand to complete the job to avoid any stagnation of work or accumulation of parts.

The aim of the Lean learning system is to teach individuals and teams to achieve (1) quality (safely) (2) within the target time (3) with increasing variety and (4) at lower cost and the best energy efficiency. Jidoka and just-in-time conditions are visualization techniques to make the ideal appear visibly and intuitively at the workplace so that all can see at a glance whether work is occurring in normal or abnormal conditions and all can have ideas to improve the situation and overcome obstacles. Each of these "pillars" have specific component parts.

The deeper point, and most difficult to grasp, about jidoka and just-in-time conditions is that none of these tools are improvements per se. Rather, they are the techniques to create a workplace environment where everyone can orient themselves to (1) do their job right and (2) take initiatives to improve in the following ways:

- *Jidoka conditions are geared toward individual training at standards.* By "stop-at-every-defect," operators and technicians have daily opportunities to better learn standards (is this OK or not OK?) and hone their problem-solving skills to return to standard when a problem arises. Training actually works both ways: by calling out issues, operators also have the chance to teach management (and engineers) where to find opportunities for value improvement.

- *Just-in-time conditions are geared toward encouraging teamwork and opening up opportunities for kaizen.* By level pulling as close to takt time as can be and creating continuous flow, many problems will appear as many opportunities to challenge the way we currently work and coordinate between various departments: scheduling, engineering, production specialties, supply chain, and so on.

Jidoka and just-in-time conditions can always be improved, of course—whatever one's given level on both conditions, one can always move forward. You can better detect problems, and you can deliver faster from order to delivery. In actual fact, every work environment works at a certain level of jidoka (when does a mishap become acknowledged as a problem?) and just-in-time (how long does it take to respond to a demand?). The trick is to constantly tighten these conditions to make smaller and smaller problems appear. Tightening of jidoka and just-in-time conditions creates the dynamic that will improve performance *if* people are engaged in honing their standards and improving their own work methods.

Let's examine the tools in more detail to see how they act as learning frames.

Jidoka Conditions

Toyota's secret to both quality and productivity is to seek built-in quality: every job is done right the first time on the first pass. At any step of the process, we can look for the following:

- The ability to do the job right, which is the probability the work will come out defect-free on the first pass

- The ability to detect issues on the work before problems occur, which is the probability that any defect will be spotted during the work, or even better, before (Table 4.1)

No process is ever in perfect jidoka conditions, and rather than try to improve capability up front, we start by improving detectability. This creates space for employees to think and then suggest how to improve capability without investing randomly.

Jidoka is often assumed to be a form of quality assurance: if a problem appears, operators pull a cord or push a button, which lights up an *andon board* (a signal board) and stops the line. The team leader rushes to see what the problem is, and then, if the line remains stopped, the team leader is joined by the supervisor and others further up the food chain. The aim is to get the line working again as fast as possible by bringing the situation back into standard. Every line stop is examined and analyzed (by asking

		Detectability		
		Poor: No Way to Detect Whether Work Is OK or Not OK	*Average:* Some Detection, but Not-OK Work Still Gets Through	*Good:* All Bad Work Detected at the Process
Capability	*Good:* All work is done right the first time without any rework.	Poor	Average	Good
	Average: Most work is done well, but there are some defects, or some reworking is needed.	Poor	Average	Average
	Poor: It's hard to get good work, and many jobs are rejected or reworked.	Poor	Poor	Poor

Table 4.1 Ability to Detect Problems

"why?" repeatedly) until the root cause is identified and a countermeasure found. The first dimension of jidoka is never allowing a known defect to be passed on down the line. *LECTURE* ✱

Jidoka is the dynamic system teaching us how to produce effectively by (1) teaching the employee how to perform the job and (2) teaching management to remove all issues that get in the way of easily getting it right the first time. Jidoka creates the space for both a sequence of experiments with each single product or job and for learning to occur with the individual operators of the process. Jidoka has four basic elements:

1. A clear definition of the work

2. A way to stop work and call for help whenever a doubt arises

3. Mechanical tricks to check whether the work or the equipment is OK or not OK

4. A systematic analysis of stoppages and the further separation of human work and machine work

The primary responsibility of the line managers is to guarantee their staff's success, as well as the company's success, by personally training the employees to do productive work, which means teaching them the work standards and how to think about improving work. The managers' primary focus is on helping the employees work productively, asking: "What do these people need to work confidently and get it right the first time every time?" Managers are therefore expected to work daily with their direct reports to build up confidence, first in the employees themselves and then in each other. Managers are also expected to learn from the various difficulties people flag. Jidoka's various tools, from the simple hourly production analysis board and the humble red bin to highlight defective parts, to the more sophisticated andon button or cord and andon board, are there to support observations and discussions with value-adding employees at every opportunity.

The first issue employees will face is this: how do they know whether they're making good work or bad work? Without being able to judge at each step whether one is doing a good or bad job, it becomes difficult to move on to the next step with confidence. Employees then live in the casual dread of working as best they can and still being told off apparently randomly by their management whenever a problem does occur—not the best way to grow mutual trust.

And so standards are created as mechanisms for understanding (not controlling). Distant and irrelevant metrics are not designed to control, reward, and punish; instead, real-time measures are developed to track quality, support coaching, and frame problems productively. Quality issues start by asking the following:

1. Is there a standard at all?

2. Is the standard clear and well understood?

3. Are some aspects of the standard difficult to achieve (for instance, a standard for right-handers might be awkward for lefties)?

4. Is the standard just plain wrong in some situations?

5. Are there ideas to improve the standard?

Managers are expected to check and develop each person's understanding of the following:

1. *Right and wrong from the customers' point of view:* What makes work meaningful is helping customers achieve what they want with our product or service. Therefore, the first step in knowing the job well is to clearly understand what the final customer considers to be a good or bad job and how this translates for one's own immediate customer, the next person in the value chain.

2. *Seamless progression through a sequence of tasks:* If you want to cook pasta with confidence, you have to know to first boil the water before putting the spaghetti in rather than dumping the pasta in water and then heating it—and you need to know this without having to ask the chef. Autonomy also means knowing what to do next once the pasta is cooked: should we add tomato sauce or basil and oil? Should Parmesan be added on the dish or brought separately to the table? Mastering work means understanding the breakdown of any task into separate work elements and knowing the right sequence.

3. *Knowing OK from not OK for each job element:* The next part of being autonomous in any job is knowing the OK/not-OK judgment criteria for every task. This applies not only to making products but also to any creative work. For instance, with writing, one can ask: How compelling is the argument line? How clear is each paragraph? How simple is each

sentence? Criteria should be shared without having to go and refer to a manager or inspector at every step. How long should you let the pasta cook? Cooking time won't be the same for linguine and spaghetti. And does the customer prefer al dente or softer?

4. *Understanding good or poor conditions of their work environment:* Does everyone have all the information they need to do a good job? Are the tools working properly? Is the work environment uncluttered and functional? Is the work method clear? What are the good and bad safety habits at this station? And so on. Close work with employees in the work environment feeds into discussions on how to improve manufacturing engineering or software design to make work easier, and then on how to put together the product or service so that it is easier to get right the first time. Teaching employees to take control and ownership of their environment is also a mainstay of motivation and job satisfaction—as long as management helps them to do so.

5. *Being confident in addressing problems:* Problems will always arise. That's a fact of life. Being autonomous means being able to face problems serenely and attack them with confidence where others would freeze, put the problem aside, or try to work around it rather than face it. The first step in addressing a problem is to correct its impact immediately if at all possible—which often requires skill. Then, the next step is to check the necessary conditions for each work element to spot where the problem originated. This, again, requires knowledge as the person needs to know what the proper conditions should be in terms of information, training, quality of the materials, and so on. The basics of problem solving are observing, assessing which conditions are out of joint and how to bring them back to where they should be, . . . and then ask oneself why they went awry. And then why? And why?

The second key dimension of the jidoka concept highlighted by Toyota engineers is the *separation of human work from machine work.* This cumbersome phrase means designing machines that can work autonomously, without needing human babysitting. For instance, if you cook a meal the old-fashioned way using a kitchen stove, you'll have several pans going on the fire, and you will need to keep a constant eye on each to make sure your dish is cooking the way you want it. There is no separation of human work and machine work as the cooker does not work autonomously. On the other hand, a microwave oven works autonomously: you place the dish inside it, press the button, and move on to do something else. The oven cooks the dish and pings when it's ready, but you can come and pick up the ready meal at your own pace—you are not tied to the machine.

Autonomous equipment is the key to freeing people to be able to focus on their job. Every time the machines we use require attention, such as when your computer suddenly needs upgrades or it has compatibility problems, you are interrupted in your flow of work, and there's a risk that you'll make mistakes and lose time. Making equipment more autonomous is a true revolution in equipment design and engineering because presently, so many machines or systems need constant human supervision to do their job. Autonomous machines also enable you to place the machine in a flow of work so that the person leads the work and not the machine.

In the end, it's about *confidence*. Creating jidoka conditions means setting up a workplace where people can confidently focus on their flow of work, knowing the environment will help them learn and maintain their work standards and that the equipment will support them, rather than their needing to support the equipment. Confidence in the workplace is the bedrock of engagement and suggestions, and jidoka gives us a clear blueprint on how to improve physical conditions for greater personal assurance.

Seeking to reach a higher level of jidoka conditions is a gold mine of improvement opportunities that help both managers and employees to see what needs to be concretely improved in the workplace to contribute to overall quality and productivity.

Just-in-Time Conditions

Jidoka conditions create an environment where every person can learn the minutest details of their job while they work. The *andon* mechanism of stop, and then call and get someone else to look at any problem you encounter in your work, is first and foremost a training device: one that allows all employees to check their knowledge and understanding of standards as they go. Jidoka conditions are revolutionary inasmuch as they don't separate work from learning but, rather, build learning into work, creating a stimulating environment for ideas and suggestions.

Jidoka conditions mainly focus on individual learning. The second "pillar" of TPS, just-in-time conditions, emphasizes teamwork and better learning to work together across boundaries. *Teamwork*, in the Toyota sense, means using individual skills to solve problems across organizational boundaries. Just-in-time conditions are about creating a collaborative work space where better coordination allows for less wasteful production.

Yet most businesspeople (and possibly the entire business press) understand just-in-time as a logistics system to supply goods as close as possible to when they are actually needed—which is possible only if demand is stable or forecasts are accurate (as if anyone has ever encountered either!). By contrast, Kiichiro Toyoda, the founder of Toyota Motors and the man who coined the term (in English in the Japanese text), has said, "The ideal conditions for making things are created when machines, facilities, and people work together to add value without generating any waste."[5] Just-in-time conditions aim to improve cooperation across functional departments. True, logistics are an important feature of just-in-time as they provide the tools to enhance this cooperation, but here again we must make sure we don't confuse the tool and the idea. The idea is seamless cooperation; the tool, as we'll try to show, is a specific form of logistics.

The broad problem just-in-time aims to answer is how to increase variety to better fit customer preferences without increasing the response time to customer demands or adding capital to cope with variety—that is, working capital in the form of inventory and late invoicing, fixed assets in the form of more square meters (for dedicated lines and warehouses), and more dedicated equipment.

In Jacques's old business, for instance, one production hall was filled with one or two operator-isolated cells that made only one product each. Because demand varied and was rarely as high as sales forecast, no cell was fully busy all shift long. As a result, at any one time, a few operators would work in busy cells, building up an inventory of these parts, and would then be moved to another cell to replenish the inventory of another type of part. These inventories were then forklifted to a warehouse, from which they were picked up when needed to fulfill customer orders. In order to improve productivity, manufacturing engineering was considering robotic cells that could build some of the parts without manual assembly (but would still need someone there for packing the parts). At a glance one could see that less than 20 percent of the surface and equipment was used at any one time, and when asked, the supervisor estimated that 20 percent of overall working time was easily lost in moving operators from one cell to the next.

Jacques and his Operations Director Frédéric Fiancette brought in the just-in-time pull system of keeping all inventory at the cell and having a small train pick up only what was required by customers every hour. Immediately the total unproductiveness of the system became obvious: achieving more parts per hour per operator (the argument was that some products were always missing, so more production was needed) was revealed as precisely the wrong solution. Doing so by investing even more with automated processes seemed bizarre.

As the problem jumped in their face, the supervisor and the plant manager grappled with it, and they began by combining two workstations to make two products in one cell and clear some space for all the parts inventories now encumbering the alleys. Step by step, they worked at it until operator teams stayed at their cells and all components were brought to them to make a variety of products as needed (which involved very hard work with component logistics).

Two years down the line, half the space was freed, most of the inventory was gone (freeing some further space in the warehouse), and on-time delivery had increased—shifting the problem further down the value stream at inbound logistics. Not surprisingly, just-in-time also improved productivity as operators now worked in a steady rhythm without the hassle of having to set up in a new cell every couple of hours. This was prompted by the jidoka work the supervisor did with the employees—training them about the products, fixing all issues in the cells, and going much deeper into assembly support with manufacturing engineering.

Just-in-time conditions frame production in terms of making products one at a time. Well, of course products are made one at a time, one might think. In actual fact, executives tend to think of products as generic— that there is a generic process that produces generic products, and so they treat the process as a black box. Making products one at a time revolutionizes this thinking because it creates a challenge to do just that: focus on one single product, and then the next. By steadying the rhythm of production to match with real customer demand (*takt time*), creating a more continuous flow of work sequence (*continuous flow*), and reducing batches (*pull system*), just-in-time conditions bring managers, engineers, and employees to focus on each single product, one at a time, and build a mental picture of generic issues from looking into each specific problem one after the other (not, the opposite, from preconceived ideas about production or delivery processes).

Takt Time

Takt time is one of the most powerful—and least understood—tools in the toolbox. You can always decide, more or less arbitrarily, on a *takt*—that is, a rhythm for any activity—and thus visualize a steady stream of output in ideal conditions. *TEST QUESTION*

We're all familiar with the idea of production rate: in order to secure a certain output, we need to make a number of jobs per hour. For instance, if we want to write a weekly column, we need to write four columns per month. This can mean, of course, that we don't write anything for the first three weeks of the month and then hurry to produce four columns in the last week. The monthly production rate is achieved—at the expense of dedicating a huge chunk of time in the fourth week to column writing. By calculating a time *rhythm* rather than a rate, we can think differently about delivery processes. For instance, organizing to write a column every seven days is very different from organizing to write four a month: the scheduling of time will be very different.

In the early 1960s, Toyota engineers realized that for the chassis they were making, many parts did not arrive on time, and they could not assemble much in the first half of the month, and they were struggling to fulfill the production plan the rest of the month, once they had gathered the parts that arrived intermittently and irregularly. In Taiichi Ohno's words, they realized, "If a part is needed at the rate of 1,000 per month, we should make 40 parts a day for 25 days. Furthermore, we should spread production evenly throughout the workday. If the workday is 480 minutes, we should average 1 piece every 12 minutes."

At the highest level, we can establish for ourselves a rhythm of new product introduction. Consider automobile models. Classical thinking is, "We need a new car that will take the entire segment." Lean thinking, by contrast, maintains, "We need to learn from the previous model and adapt it to its times to retain our customers." These are two very different engineering strategies. The classical, mainstream one is an all-or-nothing strategy; the Lean one is a learning strategy.

In fact, the radical idea behind a takt of model releases is a flow of new models, of versions of the same car, to respond to the same market segment but to evolve continuously in sync with the segment itself by reinventing the car for changing generations. Leading-edge tech products, such as the iPhone, now routinely adopt the same strategy. The iPhone releases a new generation at roughly an annual pace, with a new iOS release each time. Any iPhone is not just here and now but also part of a cadence of new products, roughly one a year, where faulty features are either fixed or deselected, while the boundaries or technology are tested with new features.

Calculating Takt Time

In production, takt time is calculated by assuming that the law of large numbers will even out spot variations and that we can start with average demand to calculate the rhythm of customer demand against the production time available:

$$\text{Takt time} = \frac{\text{daily available production time}}{\text{daily averaged customer demand}}$$

The heart of Toyota's Lean strategy is to (1) achieve quality (2) at takt time (3) with increasing variety on the same production line. So, to take a classic Toyota example, if the overall demand for all models on one line is 9,200 units per month, and we assume 460 working minutes per 20 days, we get a takt time of 1 minute: we need to see 1 car roll out of the line every minute.

The line, however, makes three car models: a sedan, a hardtop, and a van. The monthly requirements of each of these models will differ, and so will the product takt time. For instance, if the monthly requirements are 4,600 units for the sedan, 2,300 units for the hardtop, and 2,300 units for the van, the takt time will break down as shown in Table 4.2.

This simple calculation allows us to make an ideal consumption calculation. In our leveled simulated world, customers would walk out with the following pattern of cars:

Product	Monthly Averaged Demand	Shift Requirement	Takt Time
Sedan	4,600 units	230 units	2 minutes
Hardtop	2,300 units	115 units	4 minutes
Van	2,300 units	115 units	4 minutes
Total	9,200 units	460 units	1 minute

Table 4.2 Takt Times for Sedans, Hardtops, and Vans

Sedan, hardtop, sedan, van, sedan, hardtop, sedan, van, sedan, hardtop, sedan, van, etc.

So we should strive to make cars in the same pattern in order to adjust the production pace as much as we can to the sales pace. Obviously, programming work in such a fluid manner is not easily achieved because most processes have been designed to work in batches. The traditional pattern would have been:

Sedan, sedan, sedan, sedan, sedan, sedan, hardtop, hardtop, hardtop, van, van, van, etc.

By visualizing takt time, we create a clear target for the most leveled, most flexible way to work and now know which way we need to improve our production scheduling and flexibility of our line. Takt time calculation gives a powerful image of how sensibly we are working to avoid the waste created by bunching work and working faster or slower than real customer demand. A given cadence changes everything because processes are now dimensioned to deliver regularly. Cadence creates a capacity plan around the recurring jobs, and lets one-offs fill in the rest of the available time.

Continuous Flow

Producing at takt time means being mindful of making things one at a time, focusing on each and every one. The best way to do this is *one-piece flow*: any assembled part or product is passed from hand to hand like a baton in a relay race. *Continuous flow* means that all activities to make a product or to deliver a service are organized so as to never break the flow of work. We should not have to put the job down and go and do something else in order to finish the full job.

Continuous flow in any operation allows every individual to see all the places where work is inefficient and where people would either wait or stumble if they had to pass the part hand to hand immediately. Management usually allows inventory to hide this: even a few parts between stations will hide most of the problems employees encounter in every cycle.

Toyota has identified four main causes for poor delivery and high inventories:

1. *Large batch sizes:* Large batches are handy from the producer's point of view because they let the machine or the people run without the inconvenience of changing production, which is always a struggle as we first saw with the Toyota line at the automotive supplier. The trouble is that large batches will guarantee inventory because you have to store all parts made somewhere, but they will not guarantee delivery because you're unlikely to be building the exact parts needed to complete an order.

2. *Complicated flows:* Meeting the simple goal of producing today what was ordered yesterday, whether in manufacturing or services, is often thwarted because of batch size (people are busy building a long batch of what was planned) and complex flows. This problem occurs because each part has its own route through the plant from one machine to one waiting queue, to another queue and another machine and, so on, much the way patients in a hospital walk around from test to waiting lines without ever following the same journey. The more complex the flow, the harder it is to finish on time and the more likely it is that parts accumulate in all the various holding areas.

3. *Misalignments between work and sales pace:* Producing today what was ordered yesterday should sound like common sense, but it contradicts the Taylorist obsession that everyone and everything should always be working as hard as possible. It is intended that operations are set up to maximize productivity: the number of parts, files, or patients seen within the available time. Now, sometimes this might mean that we're producing one part of the product much faster than clients are consuming it, and so the extra goes into inventory, and at some other times we're lagging behind demand. This second situation should be OK because parts are held in inventory, but too often, because of the complexity, there are too many parts not needed right now and not enough of what is needed at that instant. As a result, the intended level of on-time delivery and productivity is never achieved.

4. *Poor conveyance and logistics:* Reducing batch size by more frequent changeovers won't help much unless you also pick up parts more frequently, which was Toyota's first lesson to its supplier as discussed in Chapter 1. Experienced Lean practitioners learn early on that productivity is in fact directly linked to the frequency and rigor of part

conveyance and logistics. This comes as a bit of a shock to most operations that tend to consider logistics as a means to move stuff from one place to the other and not as the main tool to actually run the plant.

And indeed the learning process depends on the rigor of logistics: leveled plan for every part, kanban, and trainlike regular pickup logistics.

Leveled Plan

A *leveled plan* means committing to produce the same quantity every day for a week or two, and then projecting what is expected in the weeks to come. Real customer daily demand will vary, of course, but the assumption is that what customers don't buy today they'll buy tomorrow, and if they buy an extra one today, they won't buy one tomorrow. The point is to take away volume variations from production worries for at least a week or two if we can, and see what changes we can anticipate in coming weeks.

Again, the aim of this tool is to *visualize* the most stable plan, so as to see that volume variations are not necessarily the main causes of output variation. The leveled plan doesn't just teach you to "level" the plan. It teaches you all other internal reasons for production rescheduling. In fact, you'll be drawn to track these schedule changes and ask "why?" Most of them are the result of mindless decisions from another part of the business. Creating (and holding to) a level plan teaches the assembled frontline managers to stabilize operations so that value-adding teams can work at their best and think of ways to make things better in a more stable environment. This is a critical capability to create a learning environment.

Pull with Kanban

A *kanban* is a card. A *kanban system* is a card system that materializes information so that we can "think with our hands, look with our feet" on information as well as material flow. Typically, information flows are much harder to grasp intuitively, and they are thought of as "the system." By materializing information as physical cards (digital kanban doesn't make much sense as it loses the material aspect), we can intuit more easily how information flows through the system and what information triggers what action. There are two sorts of kanban cards:

- *Withdrawal cards:* These are like checks with which to buy containers of products or parts. One card is exchanged by one box. Materializing the demand across the whole delivery flow means that no box can be "purchased" without the corresponding card. In practice, this means that if the production cell chooses to build stuff to stock, without a specific customer demand for it, it will have to keep the containers around because they can't be pushed ahead onto the next process without the proper withdrawal kanban card—that is, the purchase instruction.

- *Production instruction cards:* Whenever a box is being purchased (with a withdrawal kanban card), the production instruction card that accompanied the box is sent back to a production queue. This materializes production scheduling as if there were a physical line of customers waiting to be served at the counter. By materializing the production queue in this very concrete way, we can see both the problems production encounters to deliver on time and also all the various issues caused by batching or reversing orders (imagine that the clerk at the counter decided to ask the person behind you to pass you in the queue because she looks like a more convenient customer).

Both purchase instructions and production instructions are handled through a material kanban system that helps logistics visualize the flow of information and the flow of material throughout the entire operation at all times, and so to see where blockages occur and analyze why. In this sense, kanban is closer to acupuncture (releasing the blockages in the energy flows through the body) than surgery (reengineering one part of the process that is broken). Kanban is the tool that made just-in-time possible, and it is the root tool of other Lean tools, so it's important to understand its historical background.

The Toyota Production System didn't emerge fully formed from some staff department, like most corporations' current XPS, that is, the "X [fill in the company] Production System." Toyota's founder, Kiichiro Toyoda, had a vision of creating just-in-time, but his efforts to do so were thwarted by the company's takeover by the military during World War II and postwar hardships. In the 1950s, Taiichi Ohno, a machine shop engineer, was inspired by the way that customers picked only the items they wanted from shelves at American supermarkets, and he figured out how to make some of this work by tinkering with cardboard cards called *kanban*.[6] A brilliant engineer and demanding boss, he made many enemies, but the value of his work was recognized early on by Toyota's real leader, Eiji Toyoda, who had returned from a study trip at Ford with two key insights: first, he had not understood a word of Ford's statistical jargon of quality control, and second, he had been very impressed by Ford's suggestion scheme (which Ford was about to stop, ironically). Kanban imposed a drastic discipline of changing dies often with cumbersome processes such as presses in order to produce no more than was needed. Getting it right meant that hard engineering work had to be mixed with operator involvement in suggestions to make the cumbersome equipment more flexible. Progressively, "Ohno's system" began to spread throughout Toyota as the "kanban system" under Eiji's impulse. Taichii Ohno got promoted and went on to sell his kanban system across the company.

As just-in-time spread within Toyota, it soon hit the barrier of suppliers' delivering large erratic quantities of parts. Toyota's senior executives took it upon themselves to teach supplier CEOs how to reduce inventory and increase quality through applying Toyota principles of just-in-time production and built-in quality. As Toyota grew and internationalized, the need was felt to write this "system" down to diffuse it more rapidly. Taiichi Ohno resisted this at first, arguing that his teaching system was organic and ever growing, but he eventually relented. The first *Toyota Production System* leaflets appeared in the late 1970s and early 1980s, and they spread within Toyota's supplier group. Taiichi Ohno wrote the foreword for the first leaflets and explicitly stated that the TPS was about "practice over theory," that it comprised interrelated activities to teach people how to see and eliminate waste in order to reduce cost, improve quality, and improve productivity. He saw it as the application of the scientific mindset to production, stating, "On the shop floor it is important to start with the actual phenomenon and search for the root cause to solve the problem." The explicit aim of the TPS was to train people to think for themselves.

Taiichi Ohno reasoned that the ideal way to work would be one part at a time in the correct sequence according to customer demand. Work should not be scheduled according to forecasts, but instead, it should be scheduled the way a supermarket manages its stock, where customers come and pick what they need from the shelves, and then the shelves get resupplied accordingly in small quantities. Toyota engineers had three aims in mind concerning the *mission* of every value-adding team member:

1. *Line of sight:* How can the team member working a machine know whether he is busy making the part needed now or busy making a part no one needs immediately while some parts are missing just because the forecast got the instant-demand figure wrong (which it will always do even if the forecast is roughly correct in the midrange)?*

2. *Autonomy:* How can team members be confident about what needs to be done now and what needs to be done next? And how can they have a practical way of ordering the materials needed to carry out present and next jobs without holding lots of inventory and without having to break their pace of work?

3. *Improvement:* Cards are used to get closer and closer to the ideal of one-piece flow, treating jobs one by one in sequence. The cards make this possible because the cards are pulled out of the loop as problems are solved. Improvement is not just seen as a win for the company but also as a way for employees to find satisfaction in their jobs and for management to sustain motivation by recognizing real efforts.

What they came up with were *kanban cards* (that is, cardboard cards). Each card corresponds to a fixed amount of work, and the cards are placed in front of the team member in order that they know what to work on now and what to work on next, much the way orders taken in a restaurant are placed in order in front of the cook who then prepares the dishes in the *same order*. The purpose of kanban cards is to have the least possible amount, to correspond to the reality of customer demand as closely as possible. For instance, if team members have to deal with an entire stack of cards ahead of them, this defeats the purpose of using cards.

Kanban doesn't apply only to production. For instance, the CEO of AIO, a company Jacques knows well, Cyril Dané, makes ergonomic support devices for Toyota and other leading manufacturers in the aeronautics and automotive industries. Karakuri, as these devices are known, are zero energy smart devices developed to improve operation time and working conditions for operators.[7] Using only simple principles of physics, such as gravity or elasticity, designing these devices is a constant challenge

---

* We are grateful to Tracey and Ernie Richardson for enlightening us on this topic in their excellent book, *The Toyota Engagement Equation* (McGraw-Hill, New York, 2017).

for the teams, requiring them to think with their hands and engage in substantial teamwork.

As every one of his projects requires some engineering, Dané realized he had a flow problem in his design department. But how did it apply to the engineering team's workload? Ideally, in order to work in the best conditions, we should tackle only full jobs at one time and get them done in full before starting a new project. Putting down an unfinished job on your desk to move on to another one and so on is not only unproductive (there is as much as 20 percent loss of time every time you do that) but also risky in terms of overall quality as you break continuity and concentration. The brilliant part of kanban is that it forces you to limit the jobs taken on in parallel.

Reality seldom cooperates, and management always comes up with one more *urgent* task. That *is* the point. Kanban is about separating a backlog of projects and jobs to be done (a backlog is pretty much an inventory of jobs to do rather than of parts done in advance) and what is open on the desk. The problem, of course, is that few tasks can be done in one go. Kanban acknowledges that most jobs require inputs and responses from other people and simply can't be done in one go. By limiting how many jobs you can open at the same time, you'll find ways to improve the flow of work by making it as continuous as it can be—and solve many quality issues in the process.

In practice, a kanban consists of two whiteboards: One whiteboard holds all the jobs to be done—without prioritization—and the other holds the jobs in process with a limit of how many jobs one can tackle in parallel (one per line) (Figure 4.1). Kanban rules say that you can put a job in

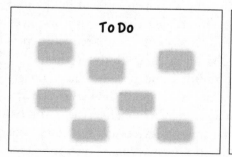
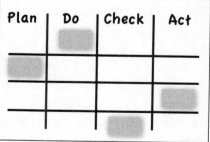

Figure 4.1 Kanban Whiteboards

production (move it from the left board to the right board) only if a lane has been freed. At any one time there are only a set number of jobs in production in parallel—in our example, four.

The learning frame of kanban works by visualizing the information flow to make it intuitive and replace scheduling decisions based on forward-looking forecasts with making the most timely decision every time the information passes through our hands, as a card. Kanban is a simple device to control the flow of work from intake into production that enables you to look at every job singly and to start the learning process. It will improve the flow of work, and it will improve team members' accountability through visualization of shared work expectations.

Kanban *never* comes naturally because it forces us to look at every job separately and think, whereas our instinct is always to regroup and batch and do it as quickly as possible. Kanban is the key to quality and learning, and it never comes easy. Kanban will have an impact on capacity as jobs get processed faster and so the intake or backlog will be eaten quicker, but that's not the main function of kanban—kanban is not there to solve your problems as a middle manager. It's there to help you discuss jobs on a one-by-one basis with your team members.

The simple kanban at Dané's company immediately reduced the workload on engineers' desks and accelerated the flow of projects. But more importantly, it revealed where engineers were struggling. To complete the kanban, Dané asked the engineering team leader to stop everyone whenever someone received a customer complaint so that the team could gather round and discuss the problem, which led them to the next step. Engineers instituted a daily meeting to explore how to do karakuri. Every morning for about 20 minutes, a member of the engineering team presented to his colleagues how he was going about his current design and how this fit with both customer expectations and what AIO was trying to do in terms of delivering value: improving ergonomics and reducing costs for clients.

This daily meeting was a revelation for Dané: because the engineers now tackled projects one at a time, problems could be looked at one at a time and discussed, and standards could then be written in earnest. This led to an in-depth exploration of value in karakuri devices and hard questions about what distinguishes a "good" karakuri from a "poor" one. It became apparent that both company and client engineers tended to overengineer their design in a clear-cut case of overprocessing (harking back to Taiichi Ohno's seven wastes) and that *elegance* in karakuri design was indeed hard to pinpoint.

Dané's self-described mission is to reduce ergonomic burden in every industrial operation: people should never hurt themselves or develop professional illnesses in the course of their work. Karakuri is a large part of the answer, but only if it's an accepted response: customers need to find this relevant and like working that way. In order to achieve his larger goal of changing how industry thinks about workstations, Dané had first to change the internal story of his own company and not see products as generic devices, but focus on each design one by one, to get engineers to both (1) better understand the fit to customers and (2) progressively learn to narrow down and master what, exactly, makes a karakuri smart and fun for the user. Using engineering kanban to focus on projects one at a time opened up a completely different qualitative vision of what the product really was: it changed the frame from needlessly complex designs to simpler, smarter, more robust supports for operators.

Regular Pickup Trains

Toyota converts the leveled plan into regular pickups, which can range from hourly to 20 minutes, simulating for the line a real customer needing the parts to assemble them on his line. This involves three core practices:

1. The production cell owns all its finished products and keeps them in the cell, not in a distant warehouse.

2. Logistics employees come and pick up what is needed to levelly fulfill the plan every 20 minutes (a normal concentration window for any person), with withdrawal kanban (each card acts as a check to "buy" the containers from the cell).

3. Although some processes require batching, the cell's operators replenish their finished products stock in the very order of the parts pickup, through the use of kanban (withdrawal kanbans translate into production kanban in a queue at the production process).

The regular pull from logistics creates an hourly schedule of work for each cell, which, in turn, asks a specific question of management: does the team have everything they need to achieve 100 percent of the scheduled plan? The discipline of regular trains teaches us to look at every cell and wonder whether it is ahead or late, and again, to learn to see the working conditions of the cell:

- Are all the components there that are needed to make the variety of products required in the quantity required (by the way, is the train also supplying components?)?

- Is the standard method to produce good parts well known by all operators in the cell?

- Are operators all there and all trained?

- Are all machines working as well as they should?

- Is the team working on an improvement idea?

The tension and discipline of regularly scheduled pickups are the mainstay of just-in-time conditions, and they transform the workplace by creating a visible "pull" for jobs that threads itself throughout the entire site, from customer delivery to supply of parts (or information). Trains correspond to newspapers' famous deadlines, but every 20 minutes. They create a rhythm to work that reveals every accumulation, every late work, every stagnant station. They teach you how to work regularly and efficiently, and more importantly, they teach all departments to work together to deliver to each other on time in full.

However, look beyond the logistics. Just-in-time ultimately reveals how well distinct departments are helping each other succeed. They are now connected, and to maintain the flow, they must help each other, not by compensating for each other's mistakes and hiding problems but, on the contrary, by creating an orchestrated ballet in which each department shows up on time and department heads discuss among themselves how to make it easy on each other to deliver in a coordinated way.

And so this mechanism that many perceive as a logistical procedure has in fact a broader systemic goal. The elimination of waste at the company level is the result of cooperation in which each player helps to make each segment succeed at its part and do so in rhythm with all the others. Making only what is needed, when it is needed, and in the amount it is needed, contrary to what it seems, is not a simple logistical target but a mutual help and collaboration target.

Action: How to Manage to Learn on a Daily Basis to Support Employees' Work Satisfaction

A core lesson, oft repeated and ever hard to learn, of TPS is that you can't have customer satisfaction without employee satisfaction. Now, as we all know, in real life, employee satisfaction is hard to grasp because, first, it depends on each person and, second, conditions and collective moods can change rapidly. Being practical, Lean focuses essentially on two components of satisfaction: *engagement* in one's work and *involvement* with one's team:

- *Engagement* mostly comes from one's own confidence in doing the job well and dealing with daily issues that crop up (conversely, stress is born of the feeling of not having the inner resources to cope with the challenges of the job). By daily working on formulating standards and solving problems, Lean thinking helps people hone their skills, develop their autonomy in solving unexpected problems, and, overall, feel more self-confident about doing their job and more interested in solving problems.

- *Involvement* is born of the feeling that one can work in a team without having to "wear the corporate face." One can be oneself, express how one feels and face difficulties, and take initiative and be supported by colleagues as opposed to being put down or ridiculed. To support this environment, the practice of team kaizen is all about letting teams own their own working practices. In finding performance improvement potential, reviewing current process, and trying new ideas, teams progressively develop ownership of their own ways of working together, which deepens the involvement of each person in the team through the very process of improving.

Both engagement and involvement, however, require a radical reframing of the managers' role. Managers must become teachers, which means shifting from *deciding* (who does what) and *controlling* (checking to see that it's done) to *instructing* (do we understand how this should be done?) and *improving* (how could we do it better?). This change is possible only in just-in-time conditions because the pull system removes the need to make scheduling decisions about who works on what because the kanban cards make each continuous flow production cell autonomous in knowing what they have to do (basically, follow the production orders from the kanban cards). Frontline management is therefore focused on eliminating the obstacles that stop work and stop people from flowing smoothly by working with the people themselves.

The basic idea is that in order to satisfy both external and internal customers, people have to work mindfully rather than mindlessly. One part of this is creating the right working conditions, through jidoka and just-in-time. The other is developing their autonomy in better understanding their work and solving their problems daily—so senior management can do its part in helping them solve the greater issues thrown at the people by the business environment or the organization itself. The role of frontline management is to develop each person's autonomy in doing her job well, taking responsibility for issues (no one would walk past a child looking into a well without pulling him back, and the same applies to work concerns), and knowing how to help resolve them. As in medicine, the teaching method is "problem-based learning." Developing people means teaching them to be autonomous when solving typical problems: taking responsibility for acting when the problem appears and knowing how to solve it correctly in a variety of different contexts.

The Lean approach is a type of *action learning*.[8] The basic premise is that learning is the result of (1) instruction in existing knowledge and (2) questioning to trigger personal insights. Both instruction and inquiry occur through problem solving with three broad types of problems:

1. We know what we should do, but something happens to stop that, so problem solving is correcting the situation by getting back to how we already know it should work.

2. We don't know what we should do, or we have found out that what we know is not appropriate, so we have to figure out what we should do and then bring the situation in line.

3. We know what we should do, and actually, we are doing it, but we can think of a way to do it better (add more value, generate less waste), and we'll try different ways to make it so.

In other terms, in Lean thinking, a job is redefined this way:

$$job = work \text{ (with standards)} + kaizen$$

Frontline managers have four basic frames to help people with their own development, both as individuals and in teams: *standards, visual management, daily problem solving,* and *kaizen*.

Standards

How do we feel confident about how to tackle a task? How do we know what we know? Does anyone ever actually read a manual? At work as in life, we tend to muddle through with work habits we've mostly acquired from watching others do things or by repetition of very basic instructions—the way anyone learns to use a new gadget. No one in his right mind ever seeks to take advantage of the full capability of a new software program—we naturally latch on to the few features that get the job done satisfactorily and move on to something else.

In Lean, standards are not procedures. Nor are they rules. They're an expression of knowing what we know. Standards are knowledge of work, in terms of 4Ms:

- *Manpower:* Basic skills to handle the job confidently

- *Machines:* Understanding of how the equipment works best

- *Materials:* What we need to know about components and elements

- *Methods:* How the product or the service is put together and how elements combine to create quality (or fail to do so)

The manager's job is to clarify and teach these basic components of knowledge of work, so that every employee can grade herself on the 0 to 10 scale and learn to master each element. In rapidly changing environments, the main part of a manager's job is to keep this knowledge up to date and to train people—and then train them again. In practical terms, standards can be thought of as the training material any one needs to work with to handle her job with confidence.

Visual Management

A key management skill in Lean thinking is *visualization*—that is, learning to make standards come to life at the workplace so that anyone can tell at a glance, intuitively, whether the situation is within standard or not, and take the responsibility to solve the problem and therefore learn.

To make it easier for people to stop and look up and deal with problems as they occur, Lean tradition has developed tricks to visualize problems concretely as gaps between standard and not standard conditions. This starts as simply as bright lines drawn on the floor to show that boxes are not stacked at the right place, but these cues can be as sophisticated as measurement tables on complex measuring equipment. Your computer's spellchecker is a visual management device: it underscores a word dubiously spelled so that you can stop and think about it.

Visual management helps reveal problems as they occur (as opposed to posting historical management reports like PowerPoint charts on the wall!). Standards must be expressed in a visual, intuitive way so that anyone can see whether they are within standard or not—much like white lines on the road separate one side of the road from the other and tell you where you can pass and where you can't. Visualization is a technique unique to Lean to bring the workplace alive and make it easy for people to take responsibility for problems because they jump out visually. For instance, the kanban card queue at every workstation (whether production or engineering) visualizes whether we are behind in work (kanban cards have accumulated) or ahead (no more kanban cards).

Daily Problem Solving

Visual management and standardized work are frames that highlight problems to make it easier to learn through daily problem solving. *Daily problem solving* is the basic mechanism that allows our minds to fight habituation and keep our knowledge fresh by investigating every day how things really happen as opposed to how they should have happened. As a thinking exercise, once a day, we can ask people to look at how a problem was solved in terms of the problem, its cause, the countermeasure, and the check (Table 4.3).

Making the effort to visualize a problem as "a gap between the actual situation and an ideal standard" creates the mental tension between

Problem	Cause	Countermeasure	Check
What gap to the standard outcome occurred due to what issue in the process?	What deviation from a specific standard caused the problem? How is our theory wrong?	How did we get the situation back into standard conditions?	Did it work? To what extent? Is the customer satisfied by our response? What do we need to investigate further?

Table 4.3 Thinking Exercise: How a Problem Was Solved

the person's experience and what he knows, which establishes a circuit between working memory and long-term memory, which is key to learning in adults.

Furthermore, by asking the person to look up not just the problem but also the standard (original documentation by the machine, existing procedure, or something else), we engage the mind in investigation. Learning standards is not so much about learning in a classroom situation as it is about creating a back-and-forth between working memory and long-term memory by investigating a situation, looking up existing standards, thinking hard about the gaps and what happened, and trying various solutions. The investigation effort, which is easier and more engaging, is what produced the learning itself.

If the investigation reveals no standard pertaining to the current situation, a new standard can be written on the spot for further reference. Standard learning and standard production are not a static activity to be done offline but, rather, a key part of on-the-job development for anyone seeking excellence in her work. Problem solving is not about solving all problems in the hope that one day all processes will run perfectly—that's silly. Problems are the result of friction in the environment, so clearly no matter how many problems are resolved, more will appear. The aim of problem solving with standards is to develop every person's competence and autonomy in dealing with a wide range of job situations and learning from them (Table 4.4).

Working with standards (detailed knowledge about specific elements of the job) and standardized work (mastery of job element sequences and underlying basic skills) is the real source of quality and productivity. Real-life cost is the result of large numbers of people performing routine tasks every day, all day. Every time a single task goes wrong, the cost consequences grow exponentially, from the time it takes to fix it locally, to the customer lost if the defect makes its way all the way to the final customer, to the tremendous expense of a legal claim if things go really wrong. Inspecting for defective work, isolating defects, and correcting them are huge macro-level costs generated by our inability to get all work right the first time on the first pass. Working with standards is the fundamental countermeasure to overcosts, but it is difficult to execute because it cannot be imposed on employees.

Working with standards is a mindful professional attitude that requires motivation and discipline, regardless of the work being done or

Problem Solving	People Development
Problem	Learning to formulate problems is a key skill that involves focusing on outcomes, recognizing that things didn't turn out well, and facing the fact that a mistake or mishap created the missed performance, without stigmatizing the person.
Cause	Looking for the proximal cause is an exercise in observation of what really happened and investigation of existing standards, both crucial disciplines in developing programmed knowledge and insight inquiry—the building blocks of action learning.
Countermeasure	Looking for immediate countermeasures to return to in-standard conditions exercises both creativity and competence. Finding smart countermeasures is an exercise in fighting functional fixedness and causal thinking, thus leading to identifying the true point of cause and start of the five "whys?"
Check	Studying countermeasures to evaluate their impact is essential to critical thinking and gaining a deeper understanding of the root cause of the problem, leading to both new standards and further investigation of "why?"

Table 4.4 How Problem Solving with Standards Helps People Develop

the educational level of the worker. This is why engaging employees in daily performance problem solving is such a powerful approach—not to solve all problems but to take the time to investigate problems one by one and, progressively, build mindfulness about the job and an understanding of the importance of standards.

Kaizen

In the Toyota tradition, *kaizen* comes essentially in two forms: (1) problem solving to return a situation to standard and (2) studying a process to improve on the standard. Having established the link between problem solving and standards, we will delve more deeply into self-study and actual improvement. Toyota's basic tenet is this: "No process is ever perfect so there's always room for improvement." Kaizen is about seeking that room for improvement and, in doing so, learning how to better perform both one's own job and one's relationship with others.

The process of kaizen is just as important as its output in terms of actual improvement. Kaizen is also about strengthening the *human capital* (knowledge and skills) and the *social capital* (relationships and trust) of the group. Of course, if the output is not a visible improvement, the process becomes a sham and the positive energy is lost, so both must be considered side by side. For instance, if we take the classic six steps of a Toyota-style kaizen activity described by Toyota veterans Art Smalley and Isao Kato, we can look at the developmental component of each step (Table 4.5).[9]

Most classic Lean tools, such as the *single-minute exchange of die* (SMED), *total productive maintenance* (TPM), or problem solving (A3), are in fact specific applications of the generic kaizen to recurring topics. For example, the SMED method centers on a specific study method of tool changeover, focusing on distinguishing *external* (machine is still operating) from *internal* (machine is stopped) tasks during the changeover. Similarly, TPM starts with the study of basic causes of machine time loss, such as downtime, setup and adjustments, small stops, slow running, start-up defects, and production defects. Although the TPS is explicitly a learning method and not an organizational blueprint, its use in Toyota over several decades has had a definite transformative impact on management

Kaizen Step	People Development
1. Identify a performance improvement opportunity.	Deepen the understanding of outcomes in terms of safety, quality, cost, variety, and energy performance by focusing on one specific performance measure and aiming to improve it visibly.
2. Study current work method.	Clarify the current work approach, and identify the standard sequence, the various standards required on difficult points, and the obvious problems and ideas for quick improvement.
3. Investigate new ideas.	Develop creative thinking by coming up with several alternatives for doing the job differently, exploring new ideas and different perspectives gleaned from other contexts.
4. Propose a new method and a way to test it, and get it approved.	Deepen the understanding of the organization and how to set up quick experiments, as well as learning whom to convince and how to get the green light, if needed, to implement the new method.
5. Implement the new method, and track results.	Learn to change how things are done, and measure carefully to see whether the new method really leads to improved performance.
6. Evaluate the new method.	Keep the outcome in perspective, and listen to various points of views (particularly other departments affected) to get a full idea of how the new method performs and what else should be changed to make sure the new way will not revert to the old habit.

Table 4.5 The Classic Six Kaizen Steps

practices. Managing the workplace to encourage the kaizen spirit has had, in particular, two radical effects:

1. *The pull system manages the flow of work rather than frontline managers.* In a traditional workplace, the prime directive is to keep workers busy no matter what and adapt to the daily scheduling changes generated by the planning system. The frontline manager's job is mostly to decide who does what, and then control that the work is being done. The manager easily becomes the decision bottleneck of the workplace, and she can be so focused on output that any interest in outcome or on people is lost. With a pull system, teams are stable, and the flow of work follows the flow of kanban cards, with as few schedule changes as possible, so that workers are autonomous in knowing what to do.

2. *The role of frontline managers is to instruct and improve, rather than to decide and control.* As the process is scheduled by the pull system, the frontline manager's job shifts from "decide and control" to "instruct and improve." The first responsibility of any manager in a Lean system is to train his subordinates, and jidoka and just-in-time conditions create the environment for it. The management role is to make sure everyone knows and maintains the standards and supports kaizen, whether as individual suggestions, daily performance problem solving, or self-study group activities. Control is built into just-in-time and jidoka because if a cell falls behind or hits quality issues, it will create visible disruption in the pull flow. Hence, the manager's attention is focused on supporting problem solving along the manpower, machine, material, and method dimensions.

To Be Lean, You Must Think Lean

There is no avoiding it: if you want to learn how to think Lean, you have to master the Lean learning system and the interactions between customer satisfaction, jidoka, just-in-time, and standard work-kaizen. Over the years, we have seen many people try to sidestep the learning effort by latching on to one specific aspect or tool and reducing the system to a single element, They have indifferent results at best, and disastrous failures at worse. The system is a system because it creates a specific thinking space in which to frame our challenges in a Lean way (Figure 4.2):

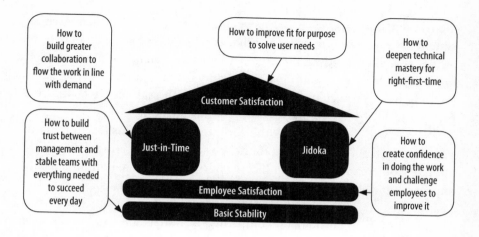

Figure 4.2 The Lean Learning System

- How to improve fit for purpose to solve user needs

- How to deepen technical mastery for right-first-time

- How to build greater collaboration to flow the work in line with demand

- How to create confidence in doing the work and challenge employees to improve it

- How to build trust between management and stable teams with everything needed to succeed every day

The system was developed over decades of trial and error, and it is manifest by specific tools one needs to learn and master, not just in his operations but in his purpose as well.

Executives who have made the learning effort to practice expressing their business challenges in terms of the Lean system are constantly impressed with its power to get them to see clearly things that were under their very noses and they could not grasp before.

In Lean thinking, leading from the ground up by practicing "go and see" at the gemba and learning to lead kaizen firsthand guides us to discovering our real problems first and then facing them through creating the key performance indicators that will help us communicate these challenges to the rest of the organization. Then, we use the frames of the Lean learning system to progress from facing our challenges to formulating them in Lean terms, as well as building the organizational learning conditions needed to seek people-centric solutions. The beauty of this approach is that since learning by doing occurs at the workplace, with real people facing real problems, short-term results are forthcoming all along.

Small "wins" should mark the early trajectory of this learning path. Focusing each person on caring for her customers better and solving operational problems will yield significant short-term results, both financially and in people engagement, even as the full picture remains unclear. The Lean strategy balances the needs of today (visible short-term results) with those of tomorrow (sustainable competitive advantage). As one sensei once said: if you take care of only today at the expense of tomorrow, you won't have a tomorrow—but if you take care of only tomorrow at the expense of today, you won't have a tomorrow either.

After finding problems, facing challenges, and framing them in a Lean way, the next step is engaging the whole organization in creating new collective solutions for competitive advantage. To take an organic metaphor, if performance results are the fruit of our labor, then the Lean frames of customer satisfaction, built-in quality, just-in-time, and standard work-kaizen are the branches; and the trunk is what Toyota veterans call "basic stability" (the bedrock on which the Thinking People System lies and where the roots, the capabilities drawn from individual competencies, feed the rest of the tree).

Toyota's specific solutions may not be right for your own department, company, industry. Toyota's set of improvement frames may not be either, but they are an incredibly powerful place to start. When it's hard to know what's what, Toyota's Thinking People System provides a solid place to start the exploration and inquiry into building our own learning frames— the alternative being making very large, untested gambles. You may not find immediate answers when applying Toyota's Lean learning frames to your situation. But you will be forming a foundation for learning.

In every case the four of us have seen, this approach proves to be invaluable as the leaders who adopt these frames and make them their own by working with them on their gembas grow and learn to develop their unique, gemba-based way of thinking. Trusting and practicing this approach has proven to be a better way than the conventional models of success. Knowing the Lean learning frames inside out is not an end in itself. Instead, it's a necessary first step to acquiring Lean thinking and, ultimately, developing one's own learning frames to form solutions with all employees.

MID TERM

LECTURE ON

MONDAY —

MIDTERM HAS

WEEK.

NOTE:

INCLUDE CHAPTER

5 QUESTIONS IN THE

MID TERM.

Lecture this chapter

Organize for Learning

Leaders can create the capability for step-by-step change throughout the organization.

As Jacques and Frédéric Fiancette progressed in their understanding of Lean, they saw how the principles of the Lean system provided them with practical dimensions to explore their own shop floor and in so doing, reveal their own blind spots about their operations. They learned through experience how the dynamic of kaizen and standard work surfaced new ways of solving old problems. The progress they enjoyed created a new problem: some departments progressed much faster than others. The puzzling part was that, on the surface, all department managers seemed equally committed to kaizen and improvement. Some of the managers who talked most about it still moved the slowest. At first, the sensei gave them a hard time for not doing enough kaizen. They defended themselves, and they demonstrated kaizen after kaizen, and still, overall performance did not improve.

Eventually Jacques and Fiancette were able to see how individual gains, personal insights, and local improvements were all enhanced—or obstructed—by the design of the organization. Some of their managers were able to learn from the kaizen their teams were doing, and they drew upon the lessons to change their department's procedures. The common mindset among managers who learned beyond any tangible improvement was a willingness to ask why this work was necessary in the first place. They came to view waste, or defects, or problems, as the outcomes of wrong-headed (or simply ignorant) policies, procedures, and practices. And they built upon the conclusions from repeated kaizens to change the way they managed.

Jacques's background in organizational learning led him to gradually shift his values as a leader. The ability of his managers to solve problems in a variety of situations—as a result of doing repeated kaizens—became a priority, as opposed to their ability to put out fires. Jacques started to see

117 to 140

that the more fires his best firefighters extinguished, the more fires broke out. Failing to work on fundamental improvement merely led to survive another day, then another, without a hope to make things better. And in order to create a setting that truly valued this shift, he needed the company to organize around shared competencies: on developing all individuals as well as improving the procedures that connect their work. Fiancette turned out to be a natural at this, patiently guiding his shop managers to face their area's weaknesses and work together better throughout the pull system.

Jacques discovered the pleasure of seeing people develop through their kaizen journeys personally (some faster than others), while tempering his patience in terms of expecting everyone to draw managerial conclusions from kaizen. He became somewhat discouraged with the whole notion of kaizen from these results. But above all, he recognized the difference between forming new solutions with the people doing the work themselves and dealing with the consequences of execution of decisions from up high. He saw his own organization adapt and evolve from the kaizen and learning energy, rather than resist reorganization or tightening the process discipline.

One thing that is not often discussed is the fact that an organization cannot go from "traditional" to "Lean" overnight. Some parts of the organization will progress faster than others, and this uneven pace creates significant pressure on the company's support systems. For example, at Wiremold, during the first couple of years, some parts of the production process had converted to flow and pull scheduling, while others were still dependent on MRP for push scheduling of batch production. During the transition, the company needed to straddle two different ways of operating, and the company found itself creating "work-arounds" in the legacy system to accommodate both methods. Needless to say, this created a short-term condition that some might describe as organized chaos. Moving equipment to create flow and pull felt easy when compared to changing the computer and other systems that supported the traditional batch processes. In the end, the computer, business, and accounting systems became the biggest impediment to becoming Lean.

As the pull system developed from end to end, from leveling customer demand, transforming it into takt time, and pulling work through the production cells to smoothing the order messages to suppliers to make their work easier as well, Jacques and Fiancette now saw the importance of teams and teamwork on the shop floor. Suggestions and kaizen ideas emerged out of performing teams, which were supported and encouraged by the managers who "got it." The new knowledge would apply at the department level as managers drew the lessons from the kaizen and changed their own procedures. The flow of ideas transformed into a flow of changes.

There is no such thing as learning, Jacques now saw clearly; there is only proof of learning. Proof of learning meant change for the better. This more effective way of working and abandoning wasteful ones needed to build up point by point and not, as he had previously believed, through global change born out of out-of-work "aha!" moments. Change was a work of learning, not a mysterious phase transition. For each department, the CEO and COO established a clear change framework, as shown in Table 5.1.

Department	Which department does this concern? People are organized by departments, and they're concerned only with what happens in their own department: what work habits will be changed and who will get which responsibility. Change happens at the departmental level.
Challenge	What is the overall challenge, why is this the clear and present challenge in the current business context, and what is the direction for improvement?
Measure	What indicator can best capture this challenge and measure whether, day after day, we're getting better at solving this problem or, on the contrary, matters are getting worse? One indicator only.
Previous changes	List the previous changes at a macro-level, typically, one per year: • Four years ago we changed this policy. • Three years ago we reorganized this work flow. • Two years ago we acquired this new technology. • Last year we changed how we worked with suppliers. • And so on.
Current change	What change is the department currently working on, from "before" to "after"? Why is the department making the change, and what does the department hope to gain?
Remaining issues	Listing the remaining unsolved problems with all previous changes carried out in the department, including issues that were never fixed fully and need some further kaizen for the changes to be stabilized to everyone's satisfaction.
Next change	What change do we envision making next, once we have successfully achieved the current one?

Table 5.1 The Framework for Change

After finding one's problems, facing them, and framing them in a way that all in the organization can grasp, how is change then formed with the employees themselves? One simple way of looking at this is through cultivating good "habits." As an individual, for instance, you can assume that you have effective habits that boost your performance and ineffective, wasteful habits that hinder it. Since these habits are yours, the difficulty is that you're likely to be attached to all, even if you have the clear-mindedness to recognize one of your own habits as bad. Changing *any* habit is hard.

Some habits are purely individual, but, particularly at work, habits tend to evolve at the team level. Team habits are a local interpretation of company habits, company habits stem from industry habits, and somewhere along the line, industry habits will reflect national culture (although with more and more transnational firms, industry habits or even company habits can largely transcend national cultures). Lean sensei would argue that this entire pyramid rests on a solid common ground: human nature.[1]

Since habits are hard to change, where should we apply the fulcrum of change? Personal habits are incredibly hard to change on one's own. At the other end of the spectrum, human nature (or even national cultures) is not likely to change much. Teams, however, are the place where most work habits originate, precisely because of human nature.

Human teams are naturally defined by the following:

1. *Boundaries:* It's important to understand who is part of the team and who is not. Project groups where some people show up only occasionally aren't teams. They're groups. Teams know how to draw a boundary around themselves separating those who are part of the team from those who aren't (which is a big reason why being accepted in a new team can be such hard work).

2. *Leaders:* Any team of human beings will have a leader. Leadership in a team typically expresses itself on the twin dimensions of competence and confidence. A leader who's perceived as knowing her stuff is seen as strong. A leader who doesn't know what to do in challenging situations is seen as weak (it doesn't matter that much if they're right or wrong as long as they make sense and are sure of themselves). A leader who inspires confidence that he is looking out for each individual team member and cares deeply about what happens to them

is seen as warm. A leader who uses people for her own ends (be it the organization's mission) is seen as cold. These two dimensions have a tension: too-strong leaders come across as cold; too-warm leaders come across as weak. Natural team leaders are people perceived by their teammates as both strong and warm. They don't need to be the most competent people, but they do need to be seen as knowing their stuff. They also need to get along well enough with all, and they need to be seen as taking care of the interests of each individual member of the team while still putting the common good of the team in front of personal issues.

3. *Habits:* Any human group naturally produces habits, mostly arbitrarily, that distinguish one group from the next one. Habits (or norms) are what groups and teams *do*. Habits can be productive or unproductive. Habits are more often inward looking, but they can be directed outward toward customers and partners. Habits are sticky, but they can be changed precisely because they're mostly arbitrary. Changing habits within a team leads to personal habit changes in a rather unconscious way (which is what happens to people when they change teams or jobs), but every habit change needs to be argued and pushed through.

4. *Atmosphere:* Teams are made of people, and people have moods, either individually or collectively. Individual energy often translates into team vitality or the reverse, despondency. As with personal moods, atmosphere can be distinguished into traits—that is, stable tendencies, such as the positive trait of trusting each other at work and feeling that one can be one's own person, or the negative trait of experiencing systematic put-downs by other members of the team. Traits often result from habits, but they can just as well be borne out of interpersonal dynamics. Moods are more superficial and change more quickly, but they affect high-performing teams as well as low-performing teams, and even the best teams have bad days. It might seem silly to consider moods, and they might seem to be beyond the pressing concerns of senior management, but they very much constitute the daily reality of teams and are worth paying attention to.

Returning from the Christmas break in early 2008, JC Bihr had a serious problem. Actually, he had several serious problems. After completing a

PhD in metallurgy in the mid-1990s, Bihr had been approached by Swiss watchmakers to create Alliance MIM, a start-up to develop cheaper parts with a new technology: *metal injection molding*. MIM is cheaper and more eco-friendly for precision parts because it's an additive technology (metal powder is mixed with plastic powder, mold injected the way plastic parts are, then baked to take away the plastic, and finally polished) rather than subtractive as normal machining is (cutting the part out of blocks of metal). Because his shareholders were looking essentially for price advantage, Bihr sought other avenues of development, and he had found the perfect application: telephone keypads for luxury phones. He got lucky when he convinced a major luxury phone maker that he could make the digits for the keypad, and he suddenly experienced annual two-digit growth. He convinced his board members (mostly watchmakers) to keep investing in the company, and he struggled to structure a supply chain that could deliver. He reached a point where his order book contained more than a year of production, and no order due in January had been delivered by July, with deteriorating quality—close to a 20 percent return rate.

From 2002 to 2007 the company grew exponentially, multiplying sales by a factor of 6. During the last months of 2007, Bihr worried about two distinct issues. First, operationally, he simply could not keep up with demand. On-time delivery improved 30 percent, and they held 36 days of sales in finished parts inventories, 26 days of sales of work in process (WIP), and 53 days of sales in molded parts—it was an operational nightmare. Bihr's second major worry was Apple's introduction of the iPhone. His main client was a daughter company of Nokia who famously didn't feel threatened by the iPhone, which it didn't see as a "real" phone (legend has it, it didn't pass the infamous five-foot drop test). A keen technologist, Bihr worried and worried. After all, his own business model was substituting MIM parts for traditional machined parts—he understood what substitution meant.

Feeling the heat, Bihr turned to Lean manufacturing to solve his quality and supply chain issues. He found a Lean sensei who immediately focused him on quality, establishing a daily discussion on returns to solve quality issues one by one. His management team discovered that many issues could be resolved simply by discussing them with the operators themselves. The process being complex (with presses, ovens, polishing, and so on), it didn't lend itself easily to flow, but by increasing flexibility where he could, he succeeded in catching up with deliveries, and by the end of 2008, the company was making money and delivering better—when the crisis hit and orders fell by 70 percent in eight months.

With the advent of the iPhone, this business would be irrevocably changed. Keysets for phones disappeared, and the rest of the business shifted to the Far East. The company had to reinvent itself completely by manufacturing other kinds of products, and it had to try to avoid falling into the one-dominant-customer/one-product trap again. Bihr sought markets in medical appliances and aerospace where focus on details was essential, and here again the growing experience with Lean thinking and collaboration between engineers and operators made the difference. At this stage, the company's survival was driven by the engineers' ability to innovate and convince new customers, and production's focus was simply to catch up and survive.

After two years of intense collaboration with customers and engineers, Alliance had recovered financially but with more customers and a wider range of products that made both kanban and SMED (batch reduction) the mainstays of the company's strategy. The only way to satisfy a wider range of customers and parts on the same equipment base was to become flexible quickly. Quality began to improve, and the return rate was now down to 5 percent. At this point, the CEO decided to aggressively expand the early kanban experiments in the hope of liberating enough space to bring in the specialist machines for the aerospace parts.

Just-in-time was introduced in a top-down manner by the logistics manager who, having trained herself, introduced all the tools, explained them to people, and pushed the process hard—creating internal pushback even though she was steadfastly supported by her boss, the operations manager. Still, return rates fell by half every year, and delivery performance increased to 92 percent. WIP inventory was divided by a factor of 6, and stocks shrunk to less than three days. These spectacular results can hide the amount of internal pain the just-in-time created in terms of production stress to support the frequent changeovers. There were constant crises and a growing need for greater teamwork, which was simply not happening in a company that remained very siloed.

Moving from large batches to a system where operators prepared parts for pickup every half hour had implications that echoed throughout the entire organization. Previously, the factory had been run by technicians who set the tools, ran initial tests on the parts, and then let production run for batches that could add up to months of customer demand. Now, operators had to learn to take on much of the setting and preparation tasks in order to run much shorter production runs. This meant modifying the existing tools, changing how manufacturing engineers designed the tools, and training everyone to better handle standards.

To create the organizational structure to support the pull system, Bihr and his HR manager took a page out of the Toyota handbook and reorganized the factory in production cells of three to five operators, each with a team leader. The team leader (TL) had no hierarchical power. She was the person who was the most knowledgeable on the process and products, and her goal was to help operators to know if their quality was OK or not. She was the first line of defense in quality. If the TL didn't know, she called the product manager directly or the quality manager. Around this team, experts who had some knowledge on the machines themselves were at the team's beck and call. They tuned machines when a new part started production, and they made the maintenance. For every department, trainers were designated to create *dojos* (operator motion training) and realign all drifts from standard jobs.

Bihr and his teams took inspiration from chef schools where all recipes are broken down in 40 basic motions. Previously complicated standards were now modified to fit within single sheets (Figure 5.1).

However, although the need to focus on people had been very clear since the early steps with the pull system, the CEO knew that Alliance remained an engineering-driven company, and as the changes rolled out, he recognized the increasing tension within the teams and between production employees and engineers. Absenteeism, which was historically low, doubled, and tempers were running high.

Taking a step back and discussing the problem with his HR manager (she changed her job title to "people manager") and the rest of his management team, Bihr recognized the tension the pull system and the andon were putting on the shop floor by creating a sense of urgency and importance to every single internal part delivery: right quality, right time. They also saw that in creating the stable team structure to support the move to pull flow, they had picked the best technical people for team leaders. One of their best operators suddenly announced she was giving up the team leader role, which was a real wake-up call.

"We shape our tools," Bihr is fond of saying, "and then our tools shape us." In facing his problem, he saw he needed to reframe the team leader job

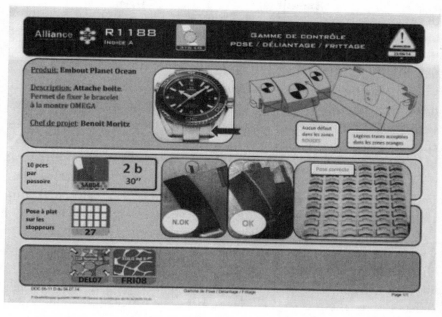

Figure 5.1   Complicated Standards Modified to Fit Within a Single Sheet

from "the most competent person to solve the technical problems to enable the pull system to run smoothly" to "natural leaders who could support the team in both day-to-day work and improvement." In a moment of profound insight, the CEO realized the progress driven by the pull system had been so huge that he didn't need it to run perfectly as a machine every day—it wouldn't make such a big operational difference at this stage. What he did need to do was to stop and uncover previously hidden problems that could now be explored in depth in order to reduce the production of defects still caught at final inspection and the tooling difficulties in production change. Stops and hiccups in the smooth running of the pull system were not to be shunned or avoided but embraced and explored. With hindsight this sounds pretty obvious, but for such a gifted and brilliant technologist, shifting from a mechanical view of the pull system to a more organic one that considered people in their people dimension was a true mental revolution.

Following on his insight, Bihr now understood that all the dojo training of operators made sense within relationships and that he needed to progressively find team leaders who were OK technically but, more importantly, who had an easy relationship with their coworkers and earned their respect for their human qualities: it had to be a compromise between technical and, well, leadership skills.

In the end, Bihr now has had one year without a work accident and 210 days without returns from his medical clients (who are highly demanding). On-time delivery is up to 94.2 percent versus 89 percent last year. New customers are now 15 percent of the customer base. Internal defects have been cut by half. Sales are up 10 percent with 10 percent fewer people overall. Bihr attributes all these results to the pull system, with a clear understanding that it had to be supported by strong teams and astute team leaders to be sustainable. Yes, the pull system is an organizational tool to improve coordination across departments and to reveal problems for managers to solve to give the means for each team to achieve 100 percent of their hourly schedule. But this architecture for improvement, this spine to the plants, only works if the organic, people-centric development of teams follows pace. The people themselves make the process; the pull system reveals it.

Bihr started his company to change the story of metallurgy and convince the world to switch from extractive metalworking to additive processes. Bihr originally built a company around his own engineering decisions. Project managers were there to run projects. The plant was there to execute his design. This worked fine as long as he dealt with a few, very profitable parts, but as the world changed around him, Bihr had to change himself to be able to grow through a wide mix of products and wild variations in volume. This meant radically changing as shown in Figure 5.2.

Clearly, this change emerged from practicing Lean thinking, but as JC Bihr discovered the hard way, applying Toyota techniques can be double-edged without a deep commitment to understanding their real purpose. The sensei's problem is that (1) leaders learn only if they start by doing hands-on, but (2) applying the tools without constant self-reflection ("hansei" in Lean language) will lead to painful mistakes and disappointments. In Bihr's case, he learned that just-in-time's main purpose is to *reveal* problems—not to solve them per se. In the early days, such obvious problems appear that, indeed, they can be solved through direct pressure on engineering and production. But as low-hanging fruit are gathered and the most obvious issues in the overall process resolved,

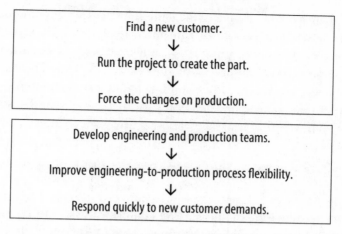

Find a new customer.

↓

Run the project to create the part.

↓

Force the changes on production.

Develop engineering and production teams.

↓

Improve engineering-to-production process flexibility.

↓

Respond quickly to new customer demands.

Figure 5.2 Growing and Adapting

the nature of the problems changes, becoming more varied and more detailed. At this stage, Bihr and his management team learned the hard way that the team structure—and the team development process through constant training of all operators and writing standards by team leaders and production managers—is the key to success.

As one ex-Toyota sensei once phrased it simply, Lean is about "continuous flow—stop to solve a problem—continuous flow—stop." Organizing for learning means setting the team-based structure to support the problem solving to respond in real time to all the issues uncovered by the pull system, which can then be tightened progressively to get as close as possible to customer takt and fully continuous flow.

And so Lean change occurs organically in companies in what is an identifiable arc:

- Teams generate work habits.

- Groups of 30 generate procedures to streamline those habits.

- Clan (300 and beyond) leaders establish policies mostly during crises when normal procedures are changed due to exceptional circumstances.

This process is never a natural trend. Leaders often change policies to improve situations or better suit their needs (often both), which drives a need for procedure change management at the frontline management level. Resistance can be found from team habits that are too sticky to budge much. A top-down approach would force these procedural changes through expert change enforcers, on the basis of efficiency studies.

Lean thinking, on the other hand, is about embracing both stability (standards) and change (*kaizen* literally means "change for the better") at the team level, where work really happens. The Lean change engine works as follows:

1. Leaders frame the problem that needs to be solved (but not the solution) in terms team members can understand.

2. Frontline managers encourage and support teams (led by team leaders) in exploring new habits accordingly and adopting more effective (less wasteful) ways of working.

3. Frontline managers draw the conclusions from these innovations at team level and change their departmental procedures.

4. Leaders investigate all such procedural changes, highlight those that better answer the problems, and ask frontline managers and teams to study the most interesting answers to try something on their own and make it better.

As this process of distributing knowledge through copying and improving (*yokoten* in Lean parlance) occurs throughout the company, organic change builds up into performance-driven transformation, something that is often described from the outside as a performance-based culture.

Kaizen and Respect for People

The deeper point of kaizen is employee satisfaction. Sure, kaizen is the key to lowering the overcosts caused by misconceptions, but the real challenge of Lean leaders is to engage all individuals in their work so they feel better about their day. Lean executives commit deeply and with true intent to developing people to the fullest of their abilities. This, however, means expecting people to change.

Change is both exciting and scary. We all know that the interesting stuff is to be found out of our comfort zone, and yet, leaving the comfort

COMFORT ZONE IS MOST INTERESTING -

zone is . . . uncomfortable. When trying something new, people can easily feel that the challenges this involves are beyond their internal resources to deal with—a sure sign of stress and anxiety. Furthermore, enduring frustration easily leads to anger and occasional acting out.

Leadership is essentially about turning down the fear and cranking up the excitement. This means reinforcing constantly that failure is fine, and actually to be sought out as part of the learning process, and that the changes will happen with the people, not against them.

From the person's own point of view, there are four hurdles to overcome to effectively take the next step:

1. *Taking responsibility:* No one would walk past a child looking into a well without pulling the child back. However, it's easy to walk past trash on the street and not feel responsible to pick it up and dispose of it because it's too trivial or, at the other end of the spectrum, to feel that acting effectively against global warming is beyond us. The first step to change is taking responsibility for change, which inevitably feels either awkward or daunting. How do we make taking responsibility easier for people?

2. *Exploring uncertain avenues:* Complex problems tend not to have simple answers, and finding the right way to solve the problems is likely to entail a fair bit of exploration to look into possible solutions. This, in itself, is not natural because it often feels like wasted effort to invest time in looking into options that are not likely to pan out. Exploration can be fun, but it can also be frustrating and somewhat whimsical. The second question is how to make exploration rewarding, even though the early and obvious answers are unlikely to be the right ones.

3. *Overcoming setbacks:* Successes are fun, but setbacks can be very painful. When trying something new, setbacks are unavoidable and, in actual fact, part of the learning process: finding out what doesn't work is as valuable as being lucky in finding the way that does work. However, there is no denying the emotional cost of failure (particularly public failure), and the temptation to give up quickly is always there. The third question is how to keep the person focused on the next try, and then the next try, and technically learn from the previous failure while sidestepping the pain of it by already playing the next point.

4. *Anticipating the next step:* Because sustainable results are dynamic, always looking at the next step is a key motivational element to getting this step done. For instance, one of the early mistakes in Lean was to consider that the pull system was a "final step"—this idea made it almost impossible to go to pull. On the other hand, when leaders such as JC Bihr realize that pull is the start of the "perfection" journey, they go there quickly because they have their eye on what the pull system will teach them to continue their journey. If people think that what they're working on is going to be it, they'll take forever and come up with something disappointing. The joy of looking for the next challenge needs to be supported all the time.

Kaizen occurs within relationships—no one is an island. A few people actually innovate on their own—sometimes spectacularly so—but they have to fight against the pressure of conformism in their own times. No matter how celebrated they get, even within their lifetime, the pressure to conform to current group norms never stops *at the same time as these same innovators are changing the group norms.* Very few people have both the creativity and resilience to be such transformative figures. For most of us, standing up to our peers to effect a change is hard indeed. Since the Lean learning system is built entirely on exactly this—small, ongoing changes— we need to understand the team-kaizen structure to make these changes easy for the people themselves.

There are pragmatic ways that Lean leaders at all levels support this change. Above all they make the notion of discomfort familiar and almost comfortable. By expecting every team to always work on an ongoing kaizen topic, leaders establish small-step change as a team *norm.* Improving within a team removes some of the pressure of having to fight the entire universe to push one's ideas, particularly when the team is tasked (and recognized) by its management to come up with new ways of working.

Leaders also recognize that mentors are immensely important for any learner. Mentors can be the team leaders, or they can be trainers on specific skills. Clearly, having someone recognized in your professional environment who genuinely cares about your development and can both encourage you and give you tips about how to overcome difficulties makes a huge difference, both in terms of motivation and progress. In Lean thinking, mentors coach in problem solving not as much for error reduction (the obsession of any traditional operational excellence approach) as to support new insights.

Team leaders also use Lean tools as coaching mechanisms. These tools are designed to break down typical problems into simple steps that facilitate team efforts in solving problems. Teams tend to work better at producing new ideas. The back-and-forth that occurs within a team that has set itself a new task is the key to serendipity and the sudden connection of dots that will change the game.

Team-based kaizen rests on mutual trust. In order to perform in large organizations, you must know how the organization works, know whom to talk to and know that you can trust them to do their part of the job. If you don't trust the organization in place, you will naturally second-guess it and try to achieve what you need through parallel routes, thus creating further organizational chaos and pushback. Without some degree of institutionalization of improvements in the organization, the situation will reverse to the mean sooner or later. How can such trust be achieved? By relentlessly focusing managers on practicing respect for their people.

Respect in Lean terms is not about being nice or polite (being nice and polite is great, but not all managers can be both nice and drive change). It means deeply caring about every customer's satisfaction and every team member's success. In practical terms this means committing to the following:

1. Keeping people safe from physical injury or harassment

2. Making sure they understand the purpose of their job and have the means to do the job well

3. Making one's best effort to understand their point of view, see obstacles as they see them, and help them resolve them

4. Train, train, train to develop both basic skills and problem-solving skills to increase people's autonomy in doing their job better

5. Create concrete opportunities for people to act on their ideas and improve the way they work both individually and in teams—from individual suggestions, to team-based quality circles to management cross-functional improvement projects

6. Help people navigate the organization in order to support them in their career evolution and personal success

The Lean idea of respect for people means showing one's absolute confidence that all employees can reach their full ability provided that one gives them the cognitive and noncognitive basic skills they need to get the job right and then constantly challenging them to think more deeply about what they do (while supporting them when they hit snags they find overwhelming).

As Akio Toyoda has noted, however, the irony of a system based on people development is that respect for people starts with challenging them, which is often perceived as criticism. Without such criticism, there is no problem awareness, no healthy tension to resolve issues, no struggle to figure out a better way, and no progress. Mutual trust is vital precisely because this first step is so challenging, and criticism is OK within the bounds of a strong relationship where the genuine intent to make people progress is recognized and accepted. Without this bond, many will react badly to criticism because they will view it, unfortunately, as disrespectful. In order to help avoid this, it is important that any challenge or criticism is aimed at the system or process being analyzed, not at the people who are doing the work.

Growth occurs when you meet resistance. Athletes train. Innovators tinker until they make it work. Kaizen combats organizational inertia. Organizing for learning means creating the social structure that will support individuals and teams in facing the resistance from the status quo. The team leader is the cornerstone of this effort.

Team Leaders

"How are you organized?" is a question Freddy Ballé often asks managers on the shop floor. When managers start detailing the organization's chart, he corrects: "I meant, how are your operators organized? How is this gentleman or this lady organized? Are they part of a stable team? Who is their reference point? Who is responsible for their success?" His inquiry invariably reveals how people-free organizational thinking creates the best organizational chart possible, and then staffs it as seems best with the managers on hand. Few organizational charts go all the way to the people who actually add value. They're considered a "department," a "resource," but not people. In Lean thinking, however, both kaizen and respect for people rest on the team leader and the frontline manager.

The team leader is the cornerstone of getting the team to perform. Team leaders have no managerial responsibility. They're regular value-adding employees with a bit of an extra mission. They're the individuals who will lead, by stepping in and doing it first, the rest of the team on their mission with the team-level Lean tools. Team leaders make an extra point, for instance, of the following:

- *Responding to team members' calls:* There is one person available to turn to whenever one runs into trouble. However, employees will turn to the team leader if he or she is seen as both competent and caring, if they see their own interest in asking for the team leader's help or advice.

- *Respecting safety procedures:* The team leaders can explain the safety procedures and communicate constantly about safety awareness. Team leaders point out the difference between good and bad habits, as well as discuss recent accidents. Each team member is responsible for his or her own safety, but the team leader has an important role to play in sustaining *attention* to safety.

- *Knowing standardized work for the tasks in their area:* The team leaders are able to demonstrate how standardized work supports specific quality points for both the final customer and the next person in the process. Standardized work is not about creating habits but, rather, about having a clear method to test one's habits against a standard, as a reference point. By demonstrating standardized work in their own practice, the team leaders establish this reference. By explaining specific points on how to keep to the standardized work, team leaders develop quality awareness in their teams.

- *Encouraging the fourth S of the 5S plan:* Team leaders lead each team member in keeping to the work environment standards decided by the team as a basis for standardized work. Team leaders play an essential role in the relationship between how the work environment is organized and everyone's ability to maintain work standards.

- *Highlighting areas for further kaizen and leading the improvement activities:* The team leader role originally developed at Toyota as Taichii Ohno took the operators who did the best kaizen and staffed them in other cells to act as kaizen leaders. Over time this role evolved more toward sustaining work standards and training, but a core mission for the team leader remains spotting waste and leading improvement.

Lean teams and team leaders operate within the context of just-in-time and jidoka conditions, which determine how each cell operates very precisely. Still, it's important to realize that the tension created by the pull system will resolve itself in actual improvement only through the leadership action of team leaders. They're the guys on the ground, while management is making important decisions in management meetings. Team leaders are always there when managers are not. They are the ultimate caretakers of both standards and kaizen. By modeling standardized work in practice (and being able to explain it), they give other employees a reference point to depend on. By seeing and pointing out waste and leading waste reduction activities, they create the thinking space for other employees to join in and be creative. Team leaders have the essential function of making respect for people a reality within the day-to-day grind of operations.

Basic Stability

To be able to support each employee as an individual, teams and team leaders must find their rightful place in the value stream of the organization: who works with whom to serve which customers? The purpose of value streams is to eliminate the labyrinth, to create less stagnation in parts of the system, and to help make it easier to see which products need to come out of the line after the first production instruction from customer demand. In a mainstream organization, each process is optimized daily by the central management system. This means that a team might see its internal customers and suppliers change as work is routed through one sequence or another. This is destabilizing and makes it very hard to build up good working relations with colleagues across the boundaries of teams. A typical work routing flow might look like the one shown in Figure 5.3.

To stabilize the work of teams across functions, we want to, as much as we can, create *value streams*: baskets of products that go together and flow through the same teams. This means establishing which team does what work. This apparent loss of flexibility is in fact a gain. As long as any team can take any work, the IT system can always reroute when there is a

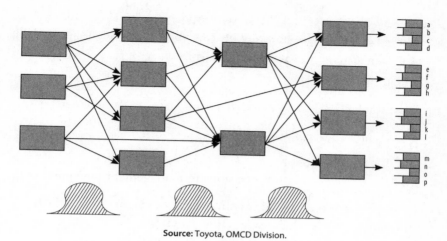

Source: Toyota, OMCD Division.

Figure 5.3 A Typical Work Routing Flow

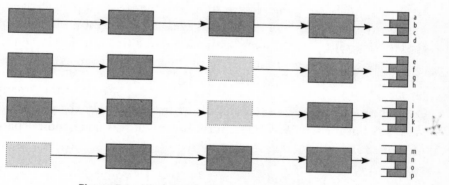

Figure 5.4 Work Routing Flow Using Value Streams

problem, which takes away the pressure to solve the team's problems. If the routes are set, management must give the teams the means to work, and management must support daily problem solving. Flexibility will develop as the teams themselves learn to deal with more product within their stable flow, as shown in Figure 5.4.

Value streams, however, do not eliminate the need for specialty silos. Functional departments are essential to sustaining and growing specialist learning, and attempts at "reengineering"—that is, organizing around process rather than technical specialty—have largely failed. The flow of work between teams is stabilized, however, so that each team works daily with the following:

1. A stable list of products

2. Known internal suppliers

3. Known internal customers

4. A stable list of equipment

The department works as a competency center, with the department head's number one responsibility being to train each member of the team, with the support of the team leader. The team leader needs to both master work standards and be well regarded by the teams.

Promoting Managers on Their Ability to Learn

To sum up the Lean dynamic, we start with the leadership challenge to improve the flow. This will reveal blockages and highlight problems that need to be resolved. By installing just-in-time conditions and jidoka conditions, these problems are framed in a concrete way that enables employees at team level to face the problem:

- *Just-in-time:* A job is being pulled, but it is not ready yet, or a job is ready but there's nowhere to put it because it was done before being pulled.

- *Jidoka:* Stop, point, and call out rather than let a dubious piece of work move on to the next step, or if you have a doubt while working, or if one of the components being brought to you looks dodgy. Responding immediately connects analysis much closer to the actual point of cause.

- *Production analysis hourly board:* Team leaders describe the obstacles stopping the team from reaching hourly objectives to clarify the issue and share it with management so that we can all agree on problems before trying to resolve them.

Having framed the problem in this way, the teams themselves express what it means at their level through the production analysis board, and they can take up resolution by either (1) problem solving and reducing the gap to standard when the standard is known or (2) engaging in kaizen when a new standard needs to be developed. In both cases, the team will in all likelihood come up with new ways of working and change its habits.

This change of habit, however, is only possible and sustainable if the frontline managers support it by solving the environmental issue that makes the new habit possible. Furthermore, this new habit will truly benefit the company as a whole if and when the area managers ultimately change a department-level procedure in order to take into account the new, better way of working and support it.

Managers are therefore expected to jump in and point out problems to their teams and team leaders. They are then, of course, expected to support the team leaders and the teams in their efforts to solve the problem. But, at the end of the resolution, managers must also be able to learn from the problem solving or kaizen efforts and improve their own ways of working. Without this last change, many of the shop floor improvements will peter out very quickly. Managers need to attune the system to support the new way of working, both in terms of procedures and incentives. This is a complete change of posture, from telling people how to do their job better (on the assumption that one knows) to discovering with them what "better" means in the current context (and making the new, better way possible and sustainable).

To succeed at Lean, managers must be able to teach because developing their subordinates is their number one responsibility, but they must also be able to learn. If not, the benefit from all kaizen efforts will simply disappear as the pushback forces of existing procedures and incentives reassert themselves. Change is hard. Any new way of working must be supported through many, many cycles of practice until it becomes a new habit. This is the manager's essential mission in Lean thinking. Becoming Lean is not about changing per se but about creating the capacity to change again and again.

To get changes started, managers must build engagement carefully, step by step, through making things better, identifying clear spaces for autonomous thinking, and encouraging people to take responsibility:

1. *Supporting visual management:* For both motivation and autonomy, employees must know at one glance whether they're succeeding or not. Visual management is enriched by kaizen, and it is a technique that must be learned by the hierarchy, as part of the jidoka principle. Before

we try to improve the line, we will visualize what is OK versus what is not OK so we can create a space for discussion with the operators. Again, visual management is not a people-free solution. It's a people-centric approach with the aim of having better observations and better discussions with the teams themselves.

2. *Engaging individuals in solving daily performance problems:* Similar to medical training, the most powerful way to engage experienced employees in their own self-development is to have them solve daily performance problems. Careful, the idea here is *not* to solve all problems in the process so that, magically, someday the process will be efficient because it is totally problem free. This is wishful thinking at its worse because most problems come from environmental changes, and no process will ever be free of problems; it will just have new ones. The aim to solve problems, one at a time, is to develop people's understanding of their own jobs, by expressing the problem, thinking about root causes, trying countermeasures, and studying carefully the impact of their initiatives. The true goal of daily problem solving is the individual suggestion where one person comes up spontaneously with an idea to improve work that she can share with her colleagues and get accepted by them—the ultimate proof of professional recognition.

3. *Supporting team study of their own work methods and improvement initiatives:* Any team will naturally produce norms—ways of behaving within the team, which, on the one hand, regulates how team members interact and, on the other, distinguishes this team from others. Ask each team to pick one kaizen subject at a time to steer the norm-production process. Teams are asked to (a) spot a performance improvement potential; (b) study the current work method (there are several Lean tools to do this case by case such as 5S, flow and layout, statistical process control, or SPC, SMED, and TPM); (c) think of new ideas; (d) come up with a plan to try them out and involve the necessary stakeholders in the organization to get expert input, authorization when needed, and so on; (e) try and measure as a way to capture the impact of the new ideas; and (f) evaluate to adjust the idea further or change the standard if it works. This ongoing system of having each team grapple with their own work methods is the fundamental engine for making things better, as it simultaneously builds team unity and

competence, and it develops autonomy and the motivation to be part of a performing team. (One note of caution, however: these teams are not "self-directed." They are part of a just-in-time flow, and they have objectives from their hierarchy. They are self-improving.)

4. *Leading end-to-end value stream improvement projects to form new solutions*: End-to-end just-in-time projects often go beyond one department, or even one site when we're looking at whole supply chains. Just-in-time projects offer opportunities to cooperate beyond organizational boundaries and establish a commonality of purpose on the entire supply chain, which, in turn, leads to much better win-win deals and lower total waste. Increasing the level of just-in-time through an end-to-end flow has three effects. First, it often *increases* costs in some areas—for instance, with creating a repacking unit in receiving to dispatch supplier containers into smaller units to deliver with the train on the line. Second, by increasing costs, it *reveals* waste: why can't the supplier supply in the correct packaging to go to the line in small containers? Third, the combination of local raising of costs and revealing waste highlights kaizen needs in no uncertain terms. The inherent tension of just-in-time also leads to shortening the kaizen lead time, therefore further developing human resources.

Organizations should support learning, not hinder it. And yet most organizations are generally designed to reflect the strategy-and-execute, command-and-control nature of mainstream thinking. What kind of organization can we build to reflect Lean thinking and Lean strategy? As we've seen, there is no reason to abandon the natural way humans organize, with hierarchies, specialties, and frontline teams. But we can interpret them differently to sustain Lean thinking:

- First, as a leader, you can learn to go and visit every work site and encourage and support flow improvement from frontline teams. It doesn't have to be very structured or particularly effective at first, but it's important to show people that things can be changed right away with a try-and-see approach.

- Then, you can progressively establish visual management and the corresponding workplace measurement wall-to-wall. This requires more of a personal investment because these techniques need to be learned (Toyota has a 60-year tradition in such tools) and taught. Visual management is the physical aspect of the Lean principles of value, jidoka, and just-in-time, and it creates the right kind of scaffolding to have kaizen from teams across the board, every team, every day, every place.

- The improvements generated from supporting kaizen and directing it by visual management will then open up larger questions and new opportunities for learning and taking the business somewhere else. For example, in order to create flow and productivity improvements, physical change is necessary. At this stage, the key is to work with local leaders closely to see where they would want to take things, how this fits with your own improvement dimensions, and what specific steps forward can come out of these debates. This people-centric improvement approach will simultaneously open the organization to new challenges and intensify the corporate structure through closer collaboration and mutual trust.

Here again, the crucial step is to change one's own vision of oneself: from the user of other people as tools to achieve specific results to the grower of competent and autonomous colleagues who will help you in forming the solutions to achieve the goals you have framed. Yes, superior performance is born from dynamic progress rather than static optimization, but this also means letting go of the need for direct control and seeking instead to be in control of the dynamic. As a leader, this means finding the excitement of learning from one's own team's learning. As they find local ways of doing things better, what change challenges (and improvement opportunities) does this open up at the leadership level? This is where the real fun of Lean can be found.

CHAPTER 6

A New Formula for Growth

A Lean strategy compounds value dynamically over time.

Now that we've examined how Lean thinking shapes the way organizations are managed and led, let's examine how Lean presents a fundamentally different way to think about strategy—the decisions and actions companies make, as well as the accounting and finance systems used to support these actions and that serve as a proxy for what the company values. As Toyota and other Lean exemplars reveal, the Lean strategy operates by an alternative formula for growth over time—a compounding of both top-line growth while systemically reducing bottom-line expenses, creating dynamic opportunities that others can't match.

The counterintuitive aspect of this approach becomes clear when compared to traditional views that leaders must plot grand strategies to conquer new markets. But in fact, the key to Lean growth is having a foot both on the ground and in the clouds. One senior U.S. executive commented about learning to work with his Japanese boss, "When I answered a specific problem with a specific solution, he asked me: 'What is the general principle at play here?' But then when I answered with a general solution, he would ask: 'What is your specific solution?'" This interplay between detailed, specific problems and countermeasures and high-level thinking about principles is something Freddy Ballé learned from his own sensei. Deep learning, it turns out, occurs during this exercise of moving from the finest detail to the most global vision and then back down—from surface features to theory and back.

Learning from the ground up means working from specific problems, looking for local countermeasures, and thinking through the wider implications with the people themselves, through repeated improvement experiments. However, these kaizen, small step-by-step efforts, are not random walks. They are part of a larger strategy: a Lean strategy.

A *strategy* is a high-level plan to achieve competitive advantage in conditions of uncertainty. In this sense, the Lean strategy to grow a business is clear, and it rests on three main strategic intents:

1. *Challenge yourself to halve the bad and double the good.* Whatever the current situation is, challenge yourself to find the operational levers to improve the performance of your business radically. By facing key problems and choosing dimensions for improvement, we can offer customers and society at large attractive alternatives competitors will have to follow. Challenging oneself beyond the minimal need to "stay in the game" is the key to managing one's own learning curve, and putting pressure on competitors in the process (as they have to catch up, they'll find managing their own learning curve harder and costlier).

2. *Create a culture of "problems first."* Problems are the day-to-day material that Lean managers use to run their area, from business-level problems expressed as challenges, to detailed, workplace-level obstacles that employees encounter. Problems are what Lean works with. Managers are taught to go to the source to find facts and listen directly to what customers and employees have to say. They have to admit that they don't know everything, and they have to be willing to have their long-held assumptions about how things work overturned. They are also taught how to visualize issues and ask "why?" repeatedly until root causes are surfaced and countermeasures implemented. This means that unfavorable information must be welcomed rather than concealed, and managers must thank employees for the problems they bring to light rather than blame the messenger and dismiss or ignore people's concerns. This also means that improvement initiatives must be nurtured and supported and that managers must learn to learn from them.

3. *Free capacity to develop new products and/or services.* By solving problems that create waste, you free up capacity (people, machines, and spaces) to be able to grow without adding new capacity. As the business grows and that growth is satisfied with existing resources, the only significant added cost of the next unit of sales is its material content. The traditional *return on investment* (ROI) calculation multiplies

operational efficiency (that is, margin) by *capital efficiency* (that is, assets used to create output). A Lean strategy changes the financial frame of how to improve the ROI by solving problems through continuous kaizen experiments, which leads to continuous learning, which leads to continuous simultaneous improvements in both operational efficiency and capital efficiency. This freed-up capacity creates space in which to introduce new products and try innovations without carrying the financial risk of dedicated production facilities. Eliminating waste from increasing flexibility (and solving all problems that entails) is the key to concretely sustaining growth with a steady stream of innovative new offerings.

When Art Byrne joined Orry's old company, The Wiremold Company, as its CEO, he stated the strategy, in part, this way: "Become one of the top 10 time-based competitors in the world." He also set the following metrics and stretch goals:

- 100 percent customer service

- 50 percent annual reduction in defects

- 20× inventory turns

- 20 percent annual productivity gain

- 5Ss and visual management

The point of such a challenging approach is to spur kaizen. Indeed, kaizen is the engine of the Lean strategy, and time is its currency. Achieving these extreme stretch goals would not happen as a one-time campaign, simply by optimizing the current situation. They would require a different, ongoing way of thinking and acting. These challenges, however, are not dreamed up out of thin air. Kaizen is not a random walk. With Lean thinking, you can't know the shape of the solution to come, but you do know where to start looking. There are 25 years of Lean initiatives that confirm Toyota's own approach:

- Increased perceived quality drives sales (and reduces costs).

- The intensity of kaizen efforts reduces total costs.

- New product introduction (from freed-up capacity and higher flexibility) is the key to sustainable growth.

- Reduced lead times increase margins and generate cash.

By using these four assumptions as a starting point, Wiremold succeeded spectacularly. Its enterprise value increased by 2,467 percent in 10 years, sales more than quadrupled, gross profit improvement jumped from 38 to 51 percent, inventory turns increased from 3× to 18×, and earnings before interest, taxes, depreciation, and amortization (EBITDA) increased from 6.2 to 20.8 percent. These spectacular financial improvements were driven by concrete shop floor efforts—for instance, increasing machine changeovers from 3 per week to 20 to 30 per day and improving productivity through continuous flow cells by 162 percent. The sum of shop floor and engineering improvements reduced lead times from 1 to 6 weeks to 1 to 2 days (customer service improved from 50 to 98 percent), which in turn drove the financial improvements.

These bedrock assumptions are not strategies to execute. They are signposts to sponsor kaizen from the teams. The big mental step management needs to take to achieve these kinds of results is to see that executive decisions are not meant to "make the numbers" as they currently stand on the books but, rather, to create (and nurture, and support) opportunities for kaizen. Right at the start of Lean thinking, puzzling about how to achieve hugely ambitious targets, early Lean engineers realized they needed to accelerate kaizen from the teams rather than look for more perfect solutions. This, in turn, led them to make some fairly counterintuitive calls from a static optimization point of view:

- Stop the whole process rather than let dubious parts go through and be checked at final inspection. When one workstation encounters a problem, all others are stopped as well. Surely, it would appear to make more sense to keep working, pull the problem parts apart, and check them later, when it would be more convenient. Sensible, yes, but in the Lean frame of improvement, there would be no real pressure to look at the issue right there and then, figure it out, and get back to normal production once it had been fixed. By stopping the entire line, one can learn from the situation by deeply investigating the real problem conditions where and when they have occurred—and all the people concerned are far, far more likely to appear quickly on the spot.

- Schedule engineering changes according to what production can absorb, and schedule new products on existing lines to be able to make different models without needing to gamble on taking all the market with one big new product introduction. It would seem to make more sense to aim for large sales volumes right away to recoup the development costs, but large volumes means dedicated production resources and making large gambles on fickle customer tastes, as opposed to introducing many varied models assembled on the same production facilities and waiting to see which models customers like (and which they don't).

- Run the smallest production batches possible by working hard to reduce all production changeover times in order to have short lead times and low inventories. Although it might seem more sensible to run equipment as fast as possible to lower the part cost, then store the parts in warehouses to be used when needed, Lean pioneers figured out early on that reducing inventories systematically was conducive to more kaizen because all blockages to smooth flow had to be resolved and machines had to be improved to be both more reliable and more flexible.

- Multiskill all employees through constant training with standardized work to create continuous flow lines and not be dependent on expert craftspeople who specialize on the "difficult" issues. Training everybody all the time rather than hiring already trained people might seem like an unnecessary expense, and yet this allows for just-in-time (JIT) production and lower total costs throughout the entire flow.

- Cooperate more intensely with suppliers through the just-in-time pull system to reduce total costs and share the savings in order to build trust from win-win solutions, which pays back in collaborative innovation with key suppliers. Of course, this bucks the notion of always finding the lowest-cost supplier, and double, or triple sourcing to drive prices down, but the benefits of seamlessly integrating innovations, having no quality issues, and ensuring prompt deliveries largely compensate for whatever price advantage is obtained by strong-arm purchasing practices.

All Lean business decisions make perfect sense through the simple frame of "encourage kaizen." If people agree on the problem on the basis of facts seen together with customers or at the workplace, they will come up with a better way of doing things, and, overall, this will increase sales by increasing quality perception. Developing flow will generate cash by reducing inventories and backlogs, thus lowering total costs by taking away a layer of waste, which will lead to smarter technology investments by understanding the real need, not the maximum need, for capital expenditure. The kaizen spirit drives the find, face, frame, and form cycle that shapes smarter solutions together. Management choices, therefore, should logically create better situations for kaizen.

We are not, in any way, suggesting we should abandon financial accounting. Instead, we should frame it in different terms. Rather than look at financial elements independently of each other, Lean thinking highlights the dynamic relationships between those elements, and the physical quantities that underlie them.

Every Lean leader we've known has had to convince financial managers who believe that by reducing the unit cost of anything, the total cost will go down. These managers hew to a number of conventional wisdoms about finance: they believe that by controlling costs line by line in the budget, the bottom line will improve, and that lowering prices and commoditizing products will improve sales (and volumes, thereby lowering unit costs, thereby increasing profitability). They see people as a cost to be replaced by automation. In their world view, there is always somewhere cheaper somewhere around the globe to outsource productions to, to lower unit purchase costs.

At the end of the day, they believe that operations don't really matter as long as costs are continually reduced, because value, as seen by the share price, is created by financing mechanisms and not grown from within by satisfying customers and doing the work well. However, Lean thinkers know from experience that (1) higher sales are driven by higher perceived quality, (2) more cash is driven by faster flow, (3) lower total costs, by the spread and speed of kaizen, and (4) more effective use of capital, by constantly reducing lead times and freeing up capacity.

We're seeing here two very different world views. One is the Lean view that the total costs of doing business will go down as a result of the energy and dynamism of kaizen by everyone, everywhere, every day. The other is financial management by which the costs of products and services will be reduced if they are controlled line by line in the accounting systems.

These two views oppose themselves all the way down to the detailed level, such as the cost of correcting every defect on the spot as opposed to inspecting it out at the end of the batch; at management level, such as the cost of investing time in training employees all the time and having them participate in kaizen efforts, as opposed to treating people as a cost to be optimized at all times; and at the investment level, such as using small flexible machines to follow demand as closely as possible as opposed to buying ever more powerful machines to reduce the unit cost by running them full speed for short periods (and making long batches). Differences exist even at a philosophical level as Lean thinking sees the company as a collective team effort to be grown from within to satisfy customers, engage employees, and benefit society as opposed to financial management that sees the only real purpose of a company as making money for shareholders. These represent two radically different approaches to "value": loyal customers from education and innovation versus increased share price from financial engineering such as share buybacks, mergers and acquisitions, and changing tax jurisdictions. Lean leaders must learn to navigate both world views. Lean production managers have financial controllers. Lean product design managers have to deal with financial purchasers. Lean COOs have financial CEOs. Even Lean CEOs have to deal with financial board members. The Lean strategy is clear: fix quality, improve cycle time, and increase flexibility in order to provide value that competitors cannot. But it needs to be explained in financial terms.

Through trial and error, Toyota has created a concrete method to pursue this, which it explains as market growth by earning customers' smiles through offering them the product they look for at every stage of their lives and peace of mind; productivity from building in quality (and avoiding rework and other nonquality costs); and seeking capital efficiency from just-in-time (better coordination of sites, equipment, and people to create value while generating less waste). This is achieved through engaging people in striving to follow standards and engagement in kaizen. It works because dynamic progress sustains superior overall performance—but how to get it across to a financial manager who is seeking point optimization for next month's accounts?

The most common response when presented with the scope of Lean results is, "What kind of investment does this require, and what are the returns on this investment?" Most executives will be convinced by nothing but a precisely calculated return. True to the Taylorist assumptions on which most businesses are designed, what their leaders seek is to invest in an implementation project that will deliver higher margins by reducing costs, ideally in such a way that one can see the cost impact of the budget line by line. The map has become the territory: management accounting is no longer an accountant's method to calculate the bottom line but, rather, the reality most managers subscribe to.

At the business level, Lean's promise is that if you engage people in improving the flow of work and getting rid of stagnation by reducing batches everywhere, both cash and margins will improve—to be bold, let us say double the inventory turns every two years and aim toward doubling margins. This promise, however, doesn't make much sense when one is looking for line-by-line cost reductions in the accounts. As a financial manager, at some point, you've got to change your mind—which is exactly what happened to one of us (Orry). The Wiremold story is well known, and it has already been discussed in Dan and Jim Womack's seminal *Lean Thinking*, but the unique perspective of the financial director has so far been largely missed. As an accountant and chief financial officer, Orry testifies to how practicing Lean on the shop floor radically changed his vision of accounting and finance and, in the process, led him to cofound the Lean accounting movement.

In 1987, as its chief financial officer, Orry was glad to report the best year in Wiremold's 87-year history by any traditional financial metric—sales, profits, ROI, and any other measure. As the company looked at those results, leaders realized that one of the contributing factors was that they had no foreign competition to challenge their position as the market leader in their product category. However, they could see that was going to change, and they assumed that when the products from new foreign entrants were introduced into the market, they would probably put price pressure on their products and if they wanted to maintain their level of profitability, they had to improve quality and cost. Although the quality out the door to customers was high, that was the result of strenuous inspection and a lot of internal scrap. They were far from being a low-cost producer.

As a result, when the company decided to implement just-in-time in 1988, like most western companies at that time, people believed that this was an inventory management program used to improve working capital turns that "somehow" would have a positive impact on costs. However, they really didn't know what they were doing when it came to implementing JIT.

Orry has recalled, "We were so ignorant that we were implementing a new MRP scheduling system at the same time we were trying to implement JIT, not realizing that they were incompatible—MRP being a 'push' scheduling system [make to the forecast] and JIT being a 'pull' scheduling system [make to actual demand]." They began to reduce inventory by changing the formulas in MRP to reduce safety stock levels and lot size calculations. Since they hadn't changed anything operationally, they started having higher levels of out-of-stock instances, and on-time delivery performance to customers started to decline from its historical level of 98 percent to less than 50 percent. As a result, customers were not paying on time, and the company was losing market share.

Wiremold, like most manufacturing companies, used *standard cost accounting* as its management accounting system. Standard cost accounting is a management accounting system developed at General Motors in the early 1920s, and it was heavily influenced by the organizational structure created by Alfred Sloan (divisions and departments) and the engineering work of Frederick Taylor (engineers determine the "best way," managers enforce, operators execute). The focus at that time was for accounting to keep track of inventory and to report on the cost of products that were produced in high-volume/low-variety batch factories, in order to set selling prices and determine the "profitability" and the return on investment (ROI) of those products and factories.

A *standard cost* is developed for each element of a product's cost (material, direct labor, and overhead), and then through a complex transactional reporting system, each month the deviations from the standard (called *variances*) are calculated and are supposed to represent deviations from the *ideal* (that is, the standard cost). Orry had learned this as part of his accounting education. It was something that he had audited during his years in public accounting, and it represented what he believed was the accepted way. Even though the financial statements this approach produced were unintelligible to anyone without an accounting degree, he assumed that was OK because that's what he was there for. His "job" was to "interpret" the statements to the rest of the management team. This is the way the world of accounting worked.

What Orry didn't realize then was that from the time he had joined Wiremold in 1978 until 1987, when each year was better than the previous one, he had never tried to use the financial statements to analyze why that was happening. They were simply box scores of past victories with little diagnostic use. The "bottom line" confirmed that they were getting better, and that was enough. Now that things were going downhill fast, when he tried to use the traditional financial statements to understand why that was happening, he discovered that they were totally useless. As he dug into the variances from standard costs, he discovered that they revealed no useful information.

In order to deal with his frustration of not being able to understand what was happening in the business, he began to experiment with alternative presentations of the financial information. Initially this experiment was an attempt to simplify the presentation of the information and make it more transparent. Each month the executive team members would receive both the traditional financial statements and the simplified financial statement, as "supplemental information," and they were asked to give their feedback on the new format, especially about what was not clear to them. These new statements began to give them a clearer picture of how bad they were and why. In the world of Lean accounting, this is now called the "Plain English P&L" (Figure 6.1).

In one of their first meetings in 1991, Art Byrne said to Orry, "Standard cost accounting hides problems and will hide the improvements we will be making. We need to stop using it." Orry pulled out the Plain English P&L and said, "How about this?" They started using it as their primary financial statement from then on, which was the first step in a multiyear process of dismantling the standard cost accounting system and abandoning the process of calculating the "standard cost" of individual products. From that day forward, they used the Value Stream Plain English P&L to understand their profit picture. This became their primary tool for "accounting for Lean."

Every metric that a company uses reflects the problems it chooses to face. The implicit message embedded in every metric is, "I, as the boss, think that this is important, and you, the employee, should pay attention to it and make it better." In companies managed by traditional financial-thinking managers, most of the key metrics (sometimes referred to as *key performance indicators*, or KPIs) are financial. Orry realized that when Byrne had established the high-level metrics and stretch goals described earlier, none of them were financial metrics, just operational ones. The first, and most important, was focused on the customer. The second one, productivity, was a key driver to improved profitability. Years earlier when

Plain English P&L*

	This Year	Last Year	+(-)%
New Sales	100,000	90,000	11.1
Cost of Sales			
Materials:			
Purchases	28,100	34,900	
Inventory (Incr)Decr: Mat'l Content	3,600	(6,000)	
Total Materials	31,700	28,900	9.7
Processing Costs:			
Factory Labor	11,400	11,500	(0.9)
Factory Salaries	2,100	2,000	5.0
Factory Benefits	7,000	5,000	40.0
Services & Supplies	2,400	2,500	(8.0)
Scrap	2,600	4,000	(35.0)
Equipment Depreciation	2,000	1,900	5.3
Total Processing Costs	27,500	26,900	2.2
Occupancy Costs:			
Building Depreciation/Rent	200	200	0
Building Services	2,200	2,000	10.0
Total Occupancy Costs	2,400	2,200	9.1
Total Manufacturing Costs	61,600	58,000	6.2
Manufacturing Gross Profit	38,400	32,000	20.0
Inv Incr(Decr): Labor & Overhead Content	(2,400)	4,000	
GAAP Gross Profit	36,000	36,000	0
GAAP Gross Profit %	36.0%	40.0%	

*By Value Stream

Figure 6.1   Value Stream Plain English P&L

working on his master's degree, Orry had written a paper on the subject of productivity and had been calculating it annually for Wiremold at a macro-level ever since. Because of that, Orry clearly recognized that productivity is a physical concept. Even though his education and training focused on financial analysis, he realized that financial numbers (dollars, euros, and so on) are, in the end, merely the product of a physical quantity times a price ($ = quantity × price). Sales are the product of the number of products sold multiplied by their unit price, labor costs are the result of the number of people employed multiplied by their wages, and so on. And productivity is the relationship between the quantity of output and the quantity of resources used to create that output.

Orry then made the connection between Lean and productivity, and he realized that most of the metrics that Wiremold should be concentrating on were those that focused on the "quantity" part of the equation since everyone could affect that. One truism is that since productivity is a physical concept, if you want to improve it, you have to physically change the relationship between input resources and output. The price part of the equation for sales and any input (materials, wages, and so on), called the *price recovery*, was controlled by relatively few people, and it is different from resource consumption. From that point forward, the discussion regarding metrics centered on the questions, "Are we doing the right things, and how do we know that they are creating improvement?" rather than the traditional question, "Did we make enough money?" As demonstrated by their results, they did lots of the "right things."

An important financial metric for most companies is the ROI, which is the measure of the *operating efficiency* (calculated as earnings as a percent of sales) multiplied by the *capital efficiency* (turnover calculated as sales divided by total investment). It is an attempt to capture, in a single number, how management utilizes investments to achieve maximum benefits. The most used ROI calculation is depicted in the classic DuPont Model (Figure 6.2).[1]

This model is a sensible breakdown of the components that make up the financial return on investment.

However, this way of framing return on investment easily encourages taking each block item by item. System costs and impact on qualities like one-piece flow are discounted if not ignored. Sales, for example, can be considered independently of the cost of sales. Many companies give discounts for bulk buys to encourage sales, without taking into account the impact on the cost of sales of holding inventories in terms of (1) creating peak demand on critical equipment, (2) storing products or other references as a consequence, or (3) organizing the transport, holding, and all other non-value-added activities related to holding inventories. Similarly, focusing uniquely on the cost of sales, such as purchasing uniquely on the piece price without taking into account quality, delivery, or batch, can lead to delivery and quality issues at the customer, thereby lowering sales.

Lean thinking, by contrast, looks at the *dynamic* relationship between these various elements. Sales and cost of sales move together if you consider that sales are driven by perceived quality and that quality is achieved by building quality into the process, which also reduces cost of sales.

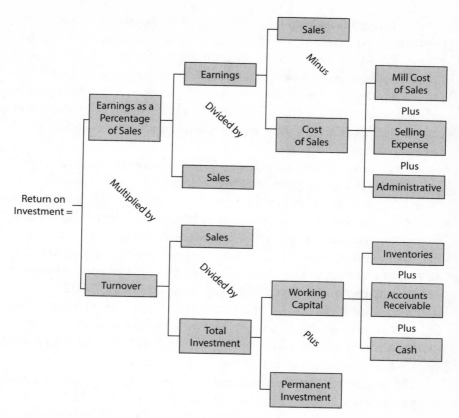

Figure 6.2 Relationship of Factors Affecting Return on Investment

Then, lead-time reduction affects the capital efficiency ratio (turnover = sales/total investment) by both sustaining sales and reducing the need for working capital (less inventory, less accounts receivable) and permanent investment.

Margin Increases Through Built-In Quality

The financial argument that kaizen leads to greater margins and profits is compelling for those who understand the Lean strategy, but much less so for those who think in traditional financial management terms. The reality is that kaizen, done by the people doing the work using a learning-based approach, is central to improving a company's financial performance. In short, creating more value by the systematic application of kaizen inexorably leads to . . . more value. The practice of kaizen and jidoka don't change the ROI formula, but they do dramatically change the way we think about how to positively influence it. A Lean strategy acts in ways that influence multiple elements for the good (for example, it improves quality to both increase sales and reduce costs and it creates flow to increase sales by reducing lead times, while simultaneously reducing the need for capital investment).

Using the largest database they could find, holding the records of more than 25,000 U.S. companies, and measuring performance as *return on assets* (ROA), which is an alternative to ROI, researchers Michael Raynor and Mumtaz Ahmed identified exceptional performers and sought statistical rules to explain why some companies stood out over time against the other "average Joes." Exceptional companies, it turned out, came in all shapes and forms. After submitting the data set to various statistical tests, they came to three conclusions about what distinguished superior performers from the rest: (1) better before cheaper—they competed on differentiators other than price; (2) revenue before costs—they prioritized increasing revenue over reducing costs; and (3) there were no other rules—change anything you must to follow rules 1 and 2.[2]

This seems straightforward enough. Yet, Michael Raynor has pointed out a core problem with this approach: it's hard. In his words, "Rules can work their magic only if you follow them even when, especially when you don't want to, when you can come up with reasons to do something else because you're pulled in other directions by other desires or other considerations." Finding ways to be better to increase revenue, he has argued, is "messy, strange, and dicey." By contrast, lowering prices or cutting costs is "tidy, familiar, and reliable."[3]

Moving up the hill is a messy problem with strange solutions, and it's hard even knowing where to start. It feels dicey. On the other hand, to financial managers familiar with price pressures from customers and competitors and cutting costs budget line by budget line, rolling down the path of least resistance by reducing price and cost is a tidy, known problem with a familiar solution. Lean thinking is a structured approach to keep struggling uphill by seeking higher revenues through better products, but it feels messy, strange, and dicey.

The Total Cost Basis Diminishes According to the Intensity of Kaizen

For the past hundred years or so, manufacturing has been driven by Taylorism, characterized by the narrow division of labor and belief in economies of scale. Both of these ideas have been codified in the modern standard cost accounting system that most manufacturing companies use. The economies of scale thought process says, "If we can produce more units in less time, we can reduce the cost of the item and therefore justify a lower selling price."

In order to achieve this, companies must invest in bigger and bigger machines capable of running at faster and faster speeds. When these machines are installed, a standard cost is established for the parts being made on each machine with the labor and overhead rates driven by the machines' rated output-per-hour specification. In order for operations to avoid unfavorable labor and overhead volume variances (a very bad thing), the company must keep the machine running, even when there is inadequate demand. The company creates inventory that must be moved, stored, insured, and so on, with the related cost spread across all products through overhead rate allocations. This inventory must also be paid for, but the cost of money must be treated as a current period cost, and it never shows up in the cost of the product.

Lean thinking, on the other hand, argues, "Let's build only what we need, only in the amounts that we need it, and only at the time that we need it, and let's do it in a flow that avoids work that doesn't create value for our customer." When we think this way, we realize that most of the large machines (affectionately called "monuments") are overkill for the task at hand. We realize that engineers (at Wiremold they were referred to as "catalog engineers") love to buy or build overly complex machines with many bells and whistles. We also realize that we should have machines that are designed to do only the task at hand and nothing more, thereby reducing capital investment.

During Wiremold's Lean journey, it encountered many examples of investment overkill. In 1995, it acquired a company in China that made surge suppression products. It had a very large wave-soldering machine for soldering PC boards, a component in every surge suppressor, and it had to be in a separate climate-controlled room. The PC boards were first assembled in another area, boxed, and transported to the wave-soldering room in which they were stored.

When needed, the PC boards were removed from their boxes, processed through the wave-soldering machine, re-boxed, and moved into inventory. Some time later, they were moved from inventory storage to the assembly line, taken out of the boxes, and installed in the final product. Only one type of PC board could be made at a time to accommodate the settings on the wave-soldering machine so there were big batches of PC boards stored everywhere. Manning the wave-soldering process took four to six people because people were required at both ends of the 12-foot-long machine, plus some material handlers. In order to provide flexibility, reduce inventory, and have better productivity and better quality, the company built its own small (about two-by-five feet), one-piece flow wave-soldering machines that could fit directly into the flow production line.

As soon as the PC board was stuffed, it could be placed directly on the wave-soldering machine and then assembled into the finished product in an uninterrupted flow. These small, right-sized machines were built in-house at a cost of about $5,000 each. They allowed the company to make and solder multiple products at the same time on different lines, resulting in vastly increased flexibility, significant improvements in response time to their customers, improved quality, and reduced inventory and space requirements. In addition, fewer people were required in this process, thereby freeing them up to handle the increase in customer demand that was taking place.

One of the fallacies that exist is the belief that a Lean transformation is very capital intensive. In fact, this is what Orry initially believed based on a prior bad experience. Wiremold had attempted to adopt just-in-time before, erroneously thinking that it was an inventory management technique. It knew that JIT involved buying and making a product just when it was needed (by whom was a mystery since production was still scheduled by MRP), so it began to reduce the batch size calculations in its MRP system.

Naturally, when it did so, that effort necessitated more frequent change-overs of the machines because the production runs were smaller. It also had heard that setup time on the machines should be reduced to allow for the more frequent setups. When it asked its manufacturing engineers how much it would cost to equip the machines for faster setups, they referred to their vendor catalogs and came up with an enormous price tag since the company had lots of machines. This was much more than the company could afford to spend, so nothing was done. As a result of the smaller batch sizes, more frequent, but still long, setups, and the fact that they discovered that the machine tools had been poorly maintained and were not capable of more frequent setups because of required triage work on the tools between production runs, they began to experience severe stock outs, and customer on-time delivery fell from 98 percent to less than 50 percent.

When Art Byrne took over as CEO, one of the early kaizen improvement events had the goal of reducing the setup time on a punch press from 90 minutes to 10 minutes, and he asked Orry to be part of that kaizen team. Orry, at the time, was still under the impression that you had to know the technical work being done in order to improve it, and his reaction was, "But I don't know anything about punch presses. I can't contribute anything to that team." However, he did join the team, and having reached the goal, Orry realized afterward that kaizen is a learning activity. It teaches, among other things, teamwork as well as the principles and tools of improvement.

Before, engineers proposed expensive solutions to reduce setup. Through repeated kaizen and giving all members of the team the space to think things through together, the team reduced setup time on that punch press from 90 minutes to 5 minutes and 5 seconds . . . and spent $100 in capital. This helped teach Orry how "solutions" proposed by "catalog engineers" were the result of wrong thinking. Contrary to popular belief, the real cost of becoming Lean did not involve significant capital spending.

Wiremold's main plant in West Hartford, Connecticut, manufactured wire management systems made of steel. Each system consisted of various size channels, called *raceways*, and a family of fittings consisting of electrical boxes (round and rectangular), *elbows* to install the system around corners, and so on. The production of the round boxes, one of the highest-volume fittings, was typical of overinvestment. Table 6.1 shows a summary of the series of improvements that were made over several years.

This doesn't mean that improvements are "capital free." As can be seen from the round line example above, over a period of several years Wiremold spent $72,000, mostly on substituting right-sized equipment in place of oversized equipment. However, this investment facilitated significant productivity gains (eight people to one), improvements in quality,

	Before Kaizen	After Kaizen 1	After Kaizen 2	After Kaizen 3	After Kaizen 4	After Kaizen 5
No. of operators	8	4	2	2	1	1
Setup time	5 hours	2 hours	45 minutes	30 minutes	30 minutes	15 minutes
No. of SKUs per day	1	5	5	5	9	10
Area, square feet[a]	1,116	1,116	340	459	459	459
Quality checks	0%	100%	100%	100%	100%	100%
WIP inventory (pieces)	1,750	1,610	10	5	9	9
Die rack distance (steps)	Next building	50	50	55	55	55

Notes:
Before kaizen, blanking, paint, and assembly were done offline.
Kaizen 1: Move blanking and draw in line. Reduce setup time.
Kaizen 2: Right size (that is, smaller) presses costing $65,000. Reduce setup time.
Kaizen 3: Move packaging in line with new shrinkwrap machine costing $7,000. Reduce setup time.
Kaizen 4: Use prepainted steel, eliminating offline paint operation. Add transport mechanism linking in line machines.
[a] Not counting area of offline processes.

Table 6.1 A Summary of the Series of Improvements Made at Wiremold's Main Plant

reduced space consumption, reduced inventory, and reduced lead time allowing for improved customer service on a real just-in-time basis.

One of the big misunderstandings about Lean is an assumption that all of the improvements from kaizen will immediately appear as a benefit in the company's financial statement. They will not. Some types of improvements such as reduced scrap, reduced energy consumption, or reduced supplies will appear as immediate cash savings. However, the increases in productivity that free up capacity will not result in an immediate improvement to profits because the people and machines are still part of the company's cost structure.

In order to actualize these gains into additional profits, management must build on this new structure by increasing sales, reducing overtime, holding on to employee attrition, insourcing things that are now being outsourced, and more. Many Lean transformation efforts fail because management gives up after falsely concluding that the gains reported by the kaizen teams were all smoke and mirrors. No one has taught them what they need to do to actualize the productivity gains created by the people doing the work into improved profit.

Future Sales Are Supported by New Product Introduction from More Flexible Investments

Lean is a growth strategy, not a cost reduction strategy. In hypercompetitive markets, the growth strategy is to convince more loyal customers to work with us. This means (1) convincing existing customers to continue to work with us and repurchase our products or services when they renew them and (2) persuading new customers to give us a try. Growth, in this sense, comes from seeing customers as friends we help with solving their problems (and not as customers we "acquire" so that we can fleece them), supporting them as they go through good and bad times, and demonstrating that they'll make more money working with us than with any of our competitors.

Growth is best driven by the regular, and relatively rapid, introduction of new products. Although growth can be achieved by winning market share from competitors (an expensive method since this can lead to price wars), the preferred method is to increase the size of the market via new products of higher value to customers and capture all of that market growth. When Art Byrne came to Wiremold, one of the first things he did was to establish several goals, one of which was to double in size every three to five years—half by organic growth and half with selective acquisitions. In reality, the company doubled in size in four years, and again in another four years, and was on its way to doubling a third time when it was sold in 2000. Wiremold focused on improving simultaneously production and product development. It realized that if customers didn't believe that it could fulfill its promises of quality and delivery, they would not listen to stories about new products.

The goal was to "fix the base" (that is, customer service, production, logistics, and so on) and accelerate new product development. By "improving the base," its quality improved, and on-time delivery of less than 50 percent improved to over 98 percent. Its customers were then willing to listen to its new product stories. By adopting *quality function deployment* (QFD), its new product introduction cycle went from years to months.

Along the way, it decided to introduce the concept of *cost planning* by incorporating the tool of *target costing* into the product development process. The traditional method of developing products did not get accounting involved in the process until after the product was designed, which was when its cost would be determined. And if the cost was too high, a period of redesign followed. Target costing acknowledges the reality that the majority of the cost of any product is determined by its design and therefore requires that the desired cost be determined at the beginning of the design process (target selling price − desired profit = target cost). This target cost became part of the engineering specification. Thus, design engineers now would be designing for fit, form, function, and cost simultaneously.

Over time, Wiremold improved its new product introduction rate from two to three per year to four to five per quarter, and those products were designed in a way that ensured the desired level of profit. Wiremold went from a historical growth rate that was geared to GDP growth (typical of the U.S. electrical industry) to accelerated growth. It made the size of the pie bigger. And yes, it also took some market share from competitors by developing products that offered more value for its customers.

A good example of using a Lean strategy to achieve competitive advantage is when the National Electrical Code changed the specification of poke-through electrical devices for safety reasons, but the code set the implementation date two years into the future. Orry's company saw this as an opportunity. It was already a very profitable product for them, and the company was the market leader. The company decided to accelerate the development of a revised product and introduced it to the market long before the required date, which it could do because of its improved product development process.

The newly designed product (1) met the new safety requirement, (2) was better looking and had new features, (3) electricians could install eight of their units in the same amount of time it took to install one of the competitor's products, and (4) the cost was lower due to a new design that required two-thirds less labor for assembly. Even though they more than doubled its price compared to the product it replaced, the company began taking market share from competitors. Architects preferred the new look and features, design engineers were reluctant to specify a competitor's product when they now had one that met the new safety requirement, and the electricians could complete the job in one-eighth of the time and move on to the next job.

Orry's firm taught its salespeople to sell the "installed cost" of the product, not the cost of the unit itself. So in spite of the higher purchase price, the installed cost to the building owner was less than any competitor—a case of win-win-win.

Sales and Inventory Turnover Increases from Increasing Quality and Flow and Reducing Lead Times

Both the China plant's PC board example and the West Hartford plant's round box example illustrate the approach that Wiremold used repeatedly to reduce inventory, thereby increasing its working capital efficiency. When like machines are grouped together in functional work areas (such as stamping, milling, drilling, painting, and assembly) and have long changeover times, lots of inventory is created and moved between functional areas. When the functional areas are dismantled and the necessary equipment is moved into flow lines (that is, closer together), and changeover is reduced, the need for inventory is reduced at the same time that lead time is reduced. In 10 years' time, inventory turns in the West Hartford plant improved to 18.0 turns. However, the progression in turns for the first five years was as follows:

- 1990: 3.4 (that is, pre-Lean)

- 1991: 4.6

- 1992: 8.5

- 1993:10.0

- 1994: 12.0

- 1995: 14.9

This progression in improved inventory turns followed the improvements, through repeated kaizens, in creating flow. Lean is not a "no-inventory" strategy. But it does create the conditions, through improvements that come from repeated kaizen, for improving sales through improved quality, creating flow to reduce lead times and the cost of waste, freeing up capacity to support the increased sales, and generating additional cash by reducing the need for inventory throughout the process.

Organizations are dynamic. And virtually everything in the organization is interconnected in some way. However, traditional financially oriented managers make decisions as if changing something (a procedure, a policy, or something else) is a stand-alone decision. The interrelatedness either is not recognized or is ignored. As a result, making changes in a vacuum constantly creates suboptimization at best and negative unintended consequences at worst. A Lean strategy works to avoid these pitfalls by acknowledging the interrelatedness that exists, believes that nothing is "sacred" and everything is subject to improvement, and actively seeks out problems that create work that does not add any value for the customer. In addition, a Lean strategy recognizes that it is the knowledge of the people doing the work that represents the most powerful force for improvement, that learning is primarily by doing, and that investing in its people to improve their problem-solving skills is the best way to create competitive advantage.

The Lean strategy, in the end, is one of creating *reusable learning*. This is not so much about finding gimmicks that work somewhere and then replicating them across the board as cookie-cutter methods as it is about learning how to approach typical problems in a typical way to find local Lean solutions. To do so, you need a starting point, a direction for progress, repeated workplace experiments, and a management focused on learning from these experiments.

The starting point is given by the Lean tradition—wherever you are, you can challenge yourself to increase safety, quality, and delivery consistency by reducing lead times. Improving the flow of work at the process and individual levels will reveal all problems in operations. This will allow you to focus on the real technical issues you need to improve in order to put pressure on your competitors. The Lean learning system we discussed in the previous chapter will allow you to bring these questions into the day-to-day work so that the employees themselves start asking the question, "What does this improvement mean in my daily job?" If you are organized for learning with managers who spur, encourage, support kaizen, and draw the right conclusions from it, local learning will progressively be embedded into products and procedures, making the company as a whole stronger and stronger.

CHAPTER 7

Reusable Learning for Continuously Growing Value

Learn to learn by starting at the right point and following a clear improvement direction.

Lean, as the previous chapters reveal, embodies a fundamentally different way of thinking, a cognitive revolution that changes how one organizes, finances, and acts. The elements of a Lean strategy differ radically from conventional wisdom in everything from a different formula for growth to a different way of leading and managing. In particular, the elements of a Lean strategy include the following:

1. Increased perceived quality to drive sales

2. Intensity of kaizen efforts to reduce costs

3. New product introduction pursued as key to sustainable growth

4. Reduced lead times as key to increasing margins and generating cash

Now we will look at the Lean strategy in practice. We will see how Fabiano and Furio Clerico, two brothers who run a sales and service operation, turned catastrophe into opportunity as they navigated a restructuring of their customer base from oil companies to independents through practicing value analysis and value engineering—an approach that allowed their sensei, Evrard Guelton, to turn around the industrial part of their corporate group. With the FCI, Pierre Vareille and Yves Mérel radically changed the story of a 1 billion euros electronics company by reducing operational costs through increasing quality and trebling the value of the company as a result. Finally, as we've seen in Jacques's own company case, the strategy was to pull a wide variety of models, mostly achieved through kanban, some SMED, and quality problem solving—the remaining question is "*how?*"

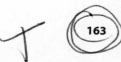

Above all, we will see the dynamics of a Lean strategy in orienting a company to navigate complexity, first, by aligning all the elements of the organization toward value and, second, by constantly embracing rather than avoiding the tensions required to be responsive and oriented toward outputs rather than outcomes. In the following chapters we will share cases of how companies practice Lean at a high level (oriented toward True North) and from the ground up simultaneously. The constant challenge for people using the full TPS as a system is going from the concrete to the abstract and back. You can't separate the tools, but the point is that there is, on one hand, the learning strategy (high level), and then, on the other hand, the discovery method (the tool) to get you moving from one idea to the next.

Using Lean Strategy to Develop the Learning Capability to Respond to Uncertainty

Lean thinking is in essence a structured method to *learn to learn*. We accept that there are never the same conditions twice, so there are no replicable solutions. There are, however, replicable ways to tackle certain typical problems: knowing where to start, looking for some typical solutions, and then exploring by repeating try-and-see, try-and-see. A Lean strategy is about knowing where to look for learning moments to create the conditions for kaizen so that the improvements will benefit customers, unburden employees, and lower total costs. As leadership teams encounter such different situations at different levels, whether at corporate, small business, or departmental, it can be hard to know where to start with such a Lean strategy.

This approach acknowledges that the first real step to transforming the organization by transforming yourself is to find a sensei you can work with. Sensei are rare—true sensei are usually part of a student-master chain tradition that goes back to the team of engineers surrounding Eiji Toyoda and Taiichi Ohno at the birth of the TPS. Sensei have learned Lean judgment as well as the rigorous application of the Lean tools from their own apprenticeship, and they are part of an oral tradition of interpretation of various situations in Lean terms, which makes them uniquely valuable but often hard to follow (sensei, funnily, have lineages, with different emphases according to who their masters were).

As part of the Lean teaching tradition, sensei will typically start by having you solve small, very concrete problems that don't seem to relate much with the larger problems you know you have. To many, this is very disconcerting—and often frustrating. To the sensei, this is a test of your resolve, your ability to progress on pragmatic problems, and it is a way to reveal your level of understanding of the situation in real terms. The sensei then will teach you to use a few concrete Lean tools and help you build the entire Lean system tool by tool, but without necessarily giving you the overall destination beyond very high-level explanations of Lean principles. To truly learn by yourself, you need to learn by doing. If we look back at the various cases we've studied firsthand, where are the sensei taking us? They are not teaching solutions. They are teaching how to learn:

1. *Clear the window.* Start by solving immediate customer and employee issues to figure out what the deeper problems are. As you do, set up the visual basis of the Lean learning system to create the conditions for on-the-job learning by the teams themselves.

2. *Build the Lean learning system to improve the flow of quality work (to accelerate kaizen).* By focusing on the four basic strategies of (a) increasing sales by reducing defects through building in quality, (b) reducing the cost base by accelerating the rhythm of kaizen and training people to solve problems, (c) making space for new product introduction by freeing up capacity, and (d) reducing lead times to increase inventory turns, you reveal both detailed and high-level problems to be solved.

3. *Conduct repeated experiments to learn more about key technical processes.* A competitive edge accrues as key technical problems are solved better than the competition does. As these problems highlighted by the Lean learning system get clearer, so do original solutions from the teams themselves as long as management is on the lookout for these new ideas and knows how to nurture and support them and then change the organization accordingly.

Lean thinking produces *reusable learning*: generic ways to go into a problem and look for a unique solution, built on the ideas and experience from the people on the ground. This technique, however, can feel uncomfortable to managers who are used to the idea of reusable *knowledge* (or, in many cases, opinions) and replicate what they know in every circumstance.

The difference lies largely in the philosopher David Hume's fundamental question: "How many instances should I have seen firsthand before

QUESTION # 5 QUIZ
CHAP 7

allowing myself to generalize?" Lean thinking is profoundly empirical and requires repeated practice before generalizations can be trusted. The role of the sensei is to deepen thinking by pointing out problems that had not been seen before (*find*), insisting that they be acknowledged (*face*), discussing a Lean way to approach the issue (*frame*), and challenging the kaizen teams to continue to try until a solution emerges (*form*). How, then, can we acquire these new learning skills? How can we get started precisely when we don't know where to start?

From Clearing the Window to Improving the Flow of Quality

Fabiano and Furio Clerico, respectively, CEO and COO of the Italian sales and service branch of a large gasoline dispenser business, turned to Lean when they saw they would lose a significant chunk of their business in the near future and had no idea how to avoid it. Their company sells dispensers to gas stations in Italy, as well as the service maintenance contracts that go with it. Gas station networks traditionally belong mainly to oil companies, in a hodgepodge mixture of directly owned gas stations and franchises, then some large independent companies such as supermarket chains, and finally fully independent owners running one to five or six stations.

The company's main business was with the oil companies, with extensive service contracts negotiated centrally with the oil company's purchasing department, mostly on price and service-level agreements. Oil companies were spread wide over a range from low price, minimal service to premium priced with very high service expectations. At the time of the financial meltdown, the Italian service market started changing rapidly. The low-cost oil companies increased further pressure on prices by setting up a system of open bidding (at least one of the service companies who won the contract during one such bidding situation subsequently went bankrupt), and the premium oil companies started divesting from the station network altogether. With one thing and another, service sales to oil companies dropped by 30 percent over four years. The situation was dire.

Fabiano and Furio had been interested in Lean for several years and had tried several consulting projects without ever finding an approach that truly fit the service business. Mostly it seemed that consultants applied standard tools, and they took a lot of time from everybody for rather indifferent results. Still, when they first felt the price pressure in earnest and could not see any obvious opportunity to further reduce costs without hurting the business, they asked Evrard Guelton for help. Guelton, recently retired, was the manufacturing business unit director who had turned around the design and production of dispensers (produced in Scotland and in France) with Lean thinking. As distributors for the dispensers, the Clerico brothers had witnessed the improvements in quality and delivery, as well as the 4 percent annual transfer price rebate they had on the equipment for the previous several years. They were convinced Guelton could help them as their sensei.

With no previous experience in service, Guelton convinced them to approach Lean thinking by finding out what the problem truly was first, by improving things as they were, rather than trying to respond to the low prices by cutting costs line by line: what were the most obvious sources of waste? From walking the workplace, three improvement opportunities came to light right away:

- Dispatch was a critical activity to send the maintenance technician to the right station to do the right job, which could change according to the nature of the contract and, of course, what was discovered once the machine was opened. There was great opportunity to learn from tackling problems in this area. When asked, the dispatchers immediately said that the stupidest thing that could happen was to send a technician to a site and then find him unable to do the job, for either lack of parts, information, or wrong specialty.

- The various operational centers were clogged up with old machines in various stages of disrepair that had to be held there for customers under various contractual arrangements. This hid all sorts of other mess resulting from working with maintenance, as well as hiding the need for stripped down parts to replace components that were no longer manufactured. Reflecting on the dispatch issue of getting the right part to the right technician, it turned out that service of components to technicians could be haphazard and that they used their vans to store "just-in-case" parts.

- Salespeople were used to deal with the oil company's purchasers, but they rarely went to visit station owners themselves. Service was seen through the prism of contracts rather than actual maintenance or building work on the station. Similarly, service agreements were looked at statistically rather than as tools to understand deeply how customers used their stations and what they really needed.

The CEO, Fabiano, began visiting client stations to see what sales opportunities the company could be missing. The COO, Furio, jumped into the problems of improving the physical flow of components through the business and benefiting from technicians' visits. They started facing their issues by measuring parts service to technicians locally, progressively narrowing the internal delivery window, while looking into every customer complaint in the dispatch offices. Rapid improvements in these issues in the first year of kaizen with the teams opened up intriguing possibilities, while the price pressure from oil companies continued to increase and more competitive bids were lost due to rock-bottom prices. The Clericos' company ended up doing work on a contract they'd lost at bidding because, after all, gas stations need to be maintained.

Independent station owners, it turned out, largely preferred to work with small local operators because they felt that the "corporate" approach of the bigger business would not suit them. They felt they were not listened to by the technicians, their specific concerns were ignored by salespeople, and "quality" meant just so much more paperwork. Conversely, it emerged from the work with dispatchers that quality concerns with the oil companies were mostly about contract interpretations than what really happened in the station. The Clerico brothers were discovering that different customers valued different things:

- *Premium oil companies:* Service agreements were what mattered most with respect to planning and procedures.

- *Low-price oil companies:* These companies wanted to reduce the endless—and expected—point-by-point negotiations about what was contract work and what was not.

- *Independent station owners:* The station owners wanted individualized care to ensure that their stations operated well and continuously to run their own business.

The brothers built a new set of indicators clearly separating the equipment sales from service in terms of total sales, safety issues, customer complaints, inventory turns, inventory in the service vans, delivery lead times, and cost of components. In doing so, they realized that by following their corporate clients, they had never clearly separated the business models of selling dispensers, on one hand, and running the service business, on the other hand, because contract negotiations often mixed both. As they progressively built up the Lean learning system to solve daily performance problems, conducted kaizen team study groups, and rethought full processes (particularly concerning invoicing, a specific Italian issue), they progressively narrowed down improvement dimensions as needing to do the following:

- Listening to the specific needs and styles of independent station owners and building trust relationships with each of them, recognizing that independent station owners had different ideas of how to run their business and different preferences.

- Developing the flexibility of the technicians to be less hampered by the fact that an electrician would not touch mechanical work and vice versa. By setting up dedicated training areas and programs in each operational center, they focused on the mastery of the most frequent operations, which led to possibilities of crossover—for instance, electricians could learn to change filters—which, in turn, meant less travel to stations for lack of multiskilling.

- Accelerating the flow of parts through the business continuously by learning to supply just-in-time, which, unexpectedly, led to developing a parts distribution line to other maintenance operators.

- Developing a new offer of "full station" work, including building in work and system checks to offer the station owners looking for a "one-stop shop."

While they continued to lose oil company sales, a result of their efforts in patiently building competencies with dispatchers and technicians was that independent revenue more than doubled over the period (Figure 7.1).

Furthermore, as the inventory turns doubled from 7 in 2011 to 15 in 2014, so did the margins, improving from 8 percent in 2012 to 15.6 percent in 2015 (see Figures 7.2 and 7.3).

The Clerico brothers' business learned that the "independents" who had been purely ad hoc had become a key growth area and, equally importantly, a profitable one. Sales in the independent sector did not grow from a more streamlined sales process and pipeline management (though no one argues against that) but from a different understanding of value. The Lean

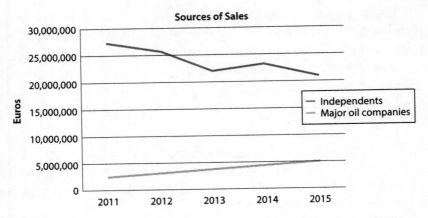

Figure 7.1 The Doubling of Independent Revenue Between 2011 and 2014

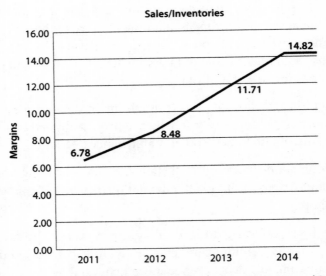

Figure 7.2 The Doubling of Inventory Turns Between 2011 and 2014

learning system enabled a customer-by-customer investigation of the customers' lifestyle, the value the company could deliver to customers, and the best ways to engineer that value (Table 7.1).

For the CEO, the breakthrough was the shift from thinking about sales by generic type of contract (the products we have to sell) to solving

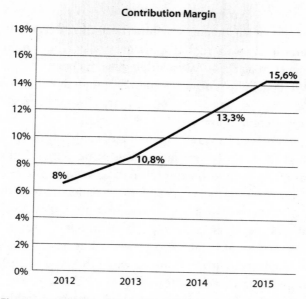

Figure 7.3 The Doubling of Margins Between 2011 and 2014

problems for individual customers (offering and delivering value). This insight radically changed how he looked at the business as a whole: let's start with the customers rather than worrying about markets, fronts, resources, and the usual vocabulary of twentieth-century military thinking. Customers enjoy their lifestyles because they find convenient products and services to help them solve their problems. The reusable learning was to look at each customer as an individual rather than think in terms of "customers" in general and to develop flexibility in the delivery process to adapt to specific customer lifestyles rather than streamline generic processes.

Customers' Lifestyle	Value Analysis	Value Engineering
How do the customers run their stations, how do they make money with them, and how can we help them achieve this and respect their preferences?	What can we do to further help customers within the existing contracts and in the existing work, and how can we reduce our own cost by eliminating waste?	What new features should we offer customers to further help them develop their businesses and improve our own performance?

Table 7.1 Investigation of Customers' Values

In Lean, the Clerico brothers found a way to stay focused on what matters as leaders of the business without becoming overwhelmed by the flurry of operational issues that crop up every day. They could reflect on core questions such as these: What value does the company provide, and to whom? What challenges do we need to face to deliver that value? What advantage do we offer our customers compared to our competitors? How do we help our people doing good work every day? Which technologies should we invest in? And, overall, what kind of company do we want to be?

Most of their competitors facing the same pace of change were struggling simply to adapt to external market factors. The Lean strategy helped the Clerico brothers learn to be more agile and lead their people to change more quickly. During this transformation, they needed to keep the company as stable as possible to continue to operate service contracts day in and day out without major disruptions while having everyone in the company be in contact with customers, while they were developing new skills and adopting new attitudes toward the work to be done.

In hindsight, Fabiano and Furio have highlighted several key practices that had a deep impact on the way the company worked:

- *Customer gemba visits: staying in touch with customers one by one.* By following a regular schedule of visits at customer sites, they could connect with individual customers and see the facts directly, which informed an opinion independent from that of their middle managers. This also helped them realize they had been intent on delivering a generic service, and they had found it difficult to adapt to personalized customer demands—or indeed even to hear the requests for what the demands were.

- *Technical dojo training: refocusing on the job one person at a time, on what needed to be nurtured and what needed to change.* The brothers asked managers to regularly ride shotgun with technicians for a day to see how the work really presented itself, and they created dedicated rooms for training, with a regular training plan for each technician. At first, they focused on rare or exotic operations, but then they realized there was more to learn from the most frequent operations instead. This way, they were able to narrow down needed changes of practice. This also opened the way to limited cross-training between specialties to reduce the number of unnecessary trips to customers.

- *Daily problem solving: continuously establishing the line of sight between personalized customer value and solving obstacles in our own processes.* Team leaders were asked to investigate a customer or technician field problem daily. The idea was not to remove all problems from processes (an impossibility) but to learn to better explore problems and solve them. This practice allowed people to continually clarify their understanding of how the value they sought to provide to customers translated into everyday work decisions (mostly mundane problems such as expediting shipping of rare parts or billing issues and so on). This practice converted lofty goals into daily actions.

- *Ongoing team kaizen: developing team ownership and confidence and encouraging teams to keep trying harder.* In the end, the people themselves solved most of the leaders' problems. At the strategic level, they understood what they were seeking to be able to survive the industry's restructuring. But most of the process-level solutions were found by the teams themselves in each center as they conducted kaizen after kaizen and discovered new ways of working. The teams found clever ways of better responding to customer issues, while simplifying their own internal processes (sometimes with astonishing results). The Milan center, for instance, moved to a new location with half the surface (creating a quarter of the cost) that still felt less crammed than the old facility—simply as a result of ongoing kaizen by the teams themselves.

- *Suggestion system: accelerating the flow of ideas and recognizing each person's contribution.* By teaching their middle managers to support the suggestion system and by systematically highlighting a suggestion of the month in each of their centers, they were able to cut through some of the fog and start recognizing the real contributors to the business. Celebrating suggestions (the company was able to respond to 98 percent of those submitted) allowed the leaders to accelerate the flow of ideas throughout the company and to develop a much clearer understanding of which teams worked well, with an open, friendly atmosphere and easy initiatives, and which teams remained problematic and were not great places to work.

"We believe our Lean practice was the key to our success in turning the company around," they have said. "Over this period of upheaval, not only did we succeed in maintaining our overall turnover but we also increased our EBITDA by 70 percent, due to our kaizen results in reducing finished goods inventory by 50 percent, maintenance spare parts by 30 percent, and technician van stock by 35 percent. We halved the square meters occupied by finished goods and spare parts in all of our five distribution centers, and we reduced the sales delivery lead time from eight weeks to six weeks and the spare-parts delivery lead time from 15 days to 5 days. Our on-time intervention record grew from 80 to 95 percent. If we hadn't learned Lean thinking on the gemba, we're not sure the company would even still be here today."

Using the Learning System to Reduce the Cost Base by Intensifying Kaizen

Once the problems of the business have been clarified in one local area, lean workers can now focus on how to lead improvements across a large base of operations. This is where a dynamic Lean system creates the scaffolding for across-the-board learning. Pierre Vareille is a strong advocate of Lean being the business strategy. He took over as CEO of the FCI group, a 1.3 billion euro connector business of 14,000 people across the world, after the company was acquired by a private equity firm. His job was to turn it around for resale. In four years, he increased sales by 40 percent, reduced manufacturing costs by 7 percent of sales, and increased profitability spectacularly mainly by instilling a culture of built-in quality in the company (Figure 7.4).

Profitability progressed while the company was dealing with the aftermaths of the 2008 financial meltdown, multiplying the value for the investors (Figure 7.5).

Vareille was known in his previous company, an automotive parts supplier, as the CEO who personally walked through inventories and looked at labels on rolls of steel and asked "why?" every time he found material sitting there for more than a month (sometimes, actually, years). He had worked with Freddy Ballé as a sensei before, and together they had developed (with Lean Director Yves Mérel) the Lean system of his previous company. The Lean initiative in FCI would start in the best conditions: a CEO experienced with Lean who was committed to learn more, an experienced Lean director committed to improving from past experience, and a sensei steeped in the Lean tradition (his own sensei worked directly for Taiichi Ohno). Vareille took over as CEO in 2008, just a few months before

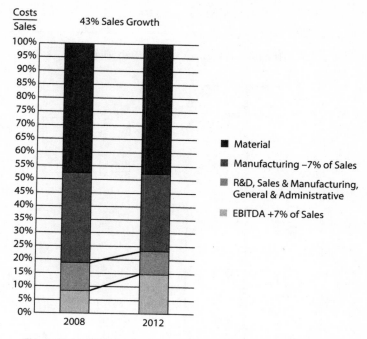

Figure 7.4 FCI Sales Increases, Manufacturing Cost Decreases, and Profit Increases from 2008 to 2012

the financial crisis was about to hit the worldwide economy. And still, in four years, by which time the equity firm sold the company, he tripled the group's overall value.

How does one Lean such large companies? Where does one start? If Lean is an antidote to big company disease, isn't it much harder in global corporations? With 20 plants over four continents and several development centers, where do you start? The answers are specific to every company, but the questions remain the same: how can we improve value for customers right now, and how can we build in value for the customer in the next-generation products? A study had shown that FCI had a mediocre ranking in customer perception, and Vareille told the group's managers in the spring of 2008, "Our goal is to become the benchmark in our industry in terms of market share, growth, profit, and people empowerment." Sure, every CEO says this on his first day on the job. The question is, "how?" Again, where do you start?

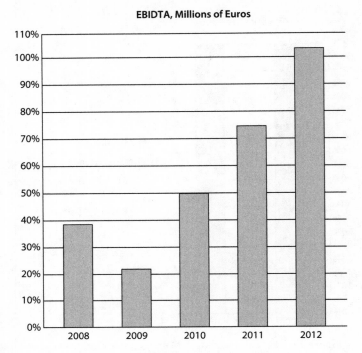

Figure 7.5   FCI EBITDA Increases from 2008 to 2012

Vareille started by visiting each of the 24 plants and the R&D center in the first year of his tenure. Common knowledge in the connector industry was that differentiation came from innovation rather than operational capabilities. Yet, as Vareille met employees, from operators to plant managers, he came to the conclusion that the industry was changing as new entrants were increasing competitive pressure on the established players. He reached the conclusion that quality and customer service were now key drivers in addition to innovation.[1] His main difficulty was then to make his managers operating in Asia, America, and Europe face the issue.

To do so, Vareille put together a few key performance indicators (KPIs), and he told his direct reports he would simply ignore all others the business had previously used (most of which varied from business unit to business unit). He also told them that he would not be managing the business from its financial reports but from operational performance improvement. His goals were as shown in Table 7.2.

More importantly, each plant had to measure these results monthly. The challenge was not to reach a goal in the end but to do so levelly, step by step (Figure 7.6):

- 3 percent reduction in the number of accidents every month on every site

- 2 percent reduction in the number of quality complaints every month on every site

- 2 percent reduction in the number of missed deliveries every month on every site

- 2 percent inventory reduction every month on every site

Not all sites started at the same level, obviously, but that was not Vareille's point—he was after speed of learning and improvement, not static optimization. And sites reacted very differently from one another. On a compound measure of continuous improvement (CI) speed, Figure 7.7 shows what the picture turned out to be.

Value, from the customer perspective, has three dimensions: first, performance, which is the functionality promised to the customers (most

Focus	First-Level KPI	Target	Second-Level KPI
Customer satisfaction	Quality (complaints)	Cut customer complaints by half	People in quality wall
			8D audit compliance
			Plant Int Parts per Million (PPM)
	Service to customer (management processs management, or MPM)	Cut missed deliveries by half	Sales and operations compliance
			Procurement batch size (receiving frequency)
			Production batch size (every part every interval)
People empowerment	Safety (accidents)	Cut accidents by three-quarters	Suggestions
			Absenteeism
			Team-based organization compliance
			Turnover
Cost and cash improvement	Supply chain (plant flow time)	Cut flow time by half	Aging of inventory
			Indirect delivery
			Distribution center flow time

Table 7.2   Vareille's Goals and Key Performance Indicators (KPIs)

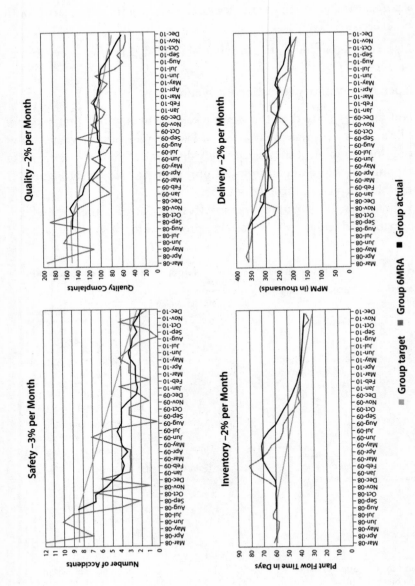

Figure 7.6 Key Performance Indicator Monthly Results for FCI

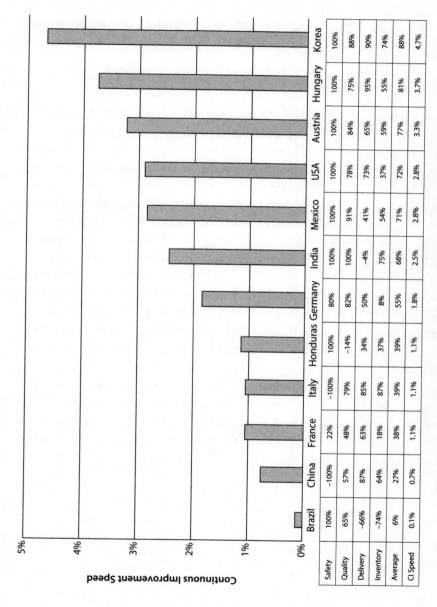

	Brazil	China	France	Italy	Honduras	Germany	India	Mexico	USA	Austria	Hungary	Korea
Safety	100%	-100%	22%	-100%	100%	80%	100%	100%	100%	100%	100%	100%
Quality	65%	57%	48%	79%	-14%	82%	100%	91%	78%	84%	75%	88%
Delivery	-66%	87%	63%	85%	34%	50%	-4%	41%	73%	65%	95%	90%
Inventory	-74%	64%	18%	87%	37%	8%	75%	54%	37%	59%	55%	74%
Average	6%	27%	38%	39%	39%	55%	68%	71%	72%	77%	81%	88%
CI Speed	0.1%	0.7%	1.1%	1.1%	1.1%	1.8%	2.5%	2.8%	2.8%	3.3%	3.7%	4.7%

Continuous Improvement Speed

Figure 7.7 Varying Speed of Continuous Improvement Across FCI Work Sites

competitors have similar levels of promised performance); second, quality, which is the degree to which we achieve this performance over time for the customer; and third, cost of use, which is the total cost of using the product, from acquisition to use and maintenance, to disposal at the end of the product's life cycle.

Start with Delivery

Early feedback from customers was that FCI's most failed promise was delivery. Customers had to hold vast inventories of connectors just to cover for the unpredictable nature of shipments. To improve quality to customers, the first issue Vareille had to tackle was the quality of service.

Vareille and Mérel needed to make plant managers understand how vital the issue was for the company as a whole, so they focused on a simple tool to help their managers understand the detailed issues in delivery: truck preparation areas. A truck preparation area (TPA) is a square painted on the floor in logistics to prepare each truck's load in advance of the truck's arrival. When the truck arrives, all parts are there, physically, and the truck can be loaded, after which it can leave right away. Truck preparation areas are a simple device to control whether all the parts are in the truck before customers find out what is there and what is missing at their receiving dock.

A simple board goes with the squares painted on the floor, as shown in Table 7.3.

Truck preparation areas sound ridiculously simple, but it turns out simple is rarely easy. Plant managers and their logistics managers are often reticent, not to say resistant, to organizing TPAs because of the immense complexity and sheer friction these will reveal. In most companies, humans have lost control of shipping, which is driven through the MRP. Trucks are

Destination	Departure Time	Preparation Zone	End of Preparation Time	Status	Comments

Table 7.3 Board to Accompany the Squares Painted on the Floor

ordered when the system says the parts are in stock, the parts are in stock when the system says they've been produced, and on-time delivery is the outcome of a mishmash of feedback loops of scheduling and rescheduling—none of which is understood by a single person.

Truck preparation areas are a visual example of the Lean notion of visual control. Parts are no longer controlled through numbers on a screen but physically, box by box: the parts are either there on time, or not. Shipping dock personnel are asked to count "good" trucks (all boxes are there, exactly, with no boxes missing or extra) from "bad" (a box is missing, or one is extra). At first, the rate of good trucks is appalling, but step by step, people learn to improve. Each truck is looked into, one at a time, by the shipping employees themselves.

Visual control structures the physical environment in such a way that anyone can understand what needs to be done at any time. Plant managers didn't need to be personally present every second of the day to tell people the trucks should be exactly completed on time—the truck preparation area did it for them.

The ground rules of the truck preparation area are: *save the truck*. When a truck is seen to be incomplete at the trigger point of the "end of preparation time," management must step in to save the truck, which means going back into the production area and stopping whatever else is being produced on the process to make the missing box (if components are available). Then, management needs to conduct a "five whys?" analysis to figure out why the problem occurred in the first place and kaizen the operational procedures that led to the problem.

This was a struggle, but overall, plant managers got to it, and results started improving (Figure 7.8). During his biyearly visits, Vareille always started by going to the truck preparation area to show his interest in service to the customer and to challenge people to do it better, listen to the obstacles they encountered (many obstacles came from other areas in the company they didn't have access to, but he did), and support their improvement initiatives.

Build Quality into the Product

In similar fashion, the second, deeper quality problem Vareille heard about from customers was the high rate of defects. Certain markets, like Japan, simply did not tolerate defective connectors, and the cost of nonquality could be immediately seen in the roomful of operators bent over magnifying glasses to identify and separate all suspect products—the costs of which were directly taken out of profit margins. Other markets just complained.

Vareille and Mérel adopted the same approach of visualizing quality problems so that people on the lines could become aware of the problems they created for their customers. The first step was to systematize the final inspection at the production cell itself with an on-the-spot analysis of every defective part. The job of the team leader was to conduct an immediate analysis and check the entire container to save the box—in the save-the-truck spirit. The team leader would also call management as soon as a real problem appeared.

Checking every single part was costly, and it needed to be done only when warranted. The real issue was teaching people when to use a 100 percent checking rate and when not to:

1. If a cell created a complaint at a customer

2. It installed a wall with 100 percent check

3. Check placed at the end of the process to feed back results immediately to the cell

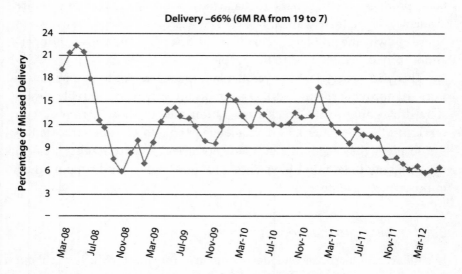

Figure 7.8   Improvement in FCI Delivery Results from 2008 to 2012

4. Until no defects were caught at the 100 percent inspection rate and the wall was taken out

5. Until there was again a customer complaint, and so on

The aim of this tool was to develop employees' sense of responsibility for their own work and to investigate further bad parts immediately. In many plants the quality walls led to in-depth reflection on how bad parts could be spotted within the process and what to do about them.

The next step to built-in quality was to *stop-at-first-defect*. In one pilot plant, Mérel took the first three machines out of the 50 in the shop, and he asked the plant engineers to reprogram them so that they would literally stop at every single defect. This had the immediate effect of lowering the overall equipment effectiveness (OEE) from 80 to 30 percent, with significant impacts on production. Having faced the problem, Mérel assigned all three maintenance engineers to just these three machines, hoping the rest would continue to produce for the time being. The engineers first cleaned up all the small issues that fed into the stop-at-defect, bringing the OEE about halfway up, and then they tackled the bigger problems, learning as they went. After a month of hard work, these three machines were back at their initial OEE with radically better quality output. Mérel then tackled the next three and so on until the entire area was covered.

To be able to replicate this experiment across the group, he then devised a system for all the plants in the group where a machine would earn a green badge (a sticker) if it was reprogrammed to stop-at-every-defect, a red one if not, and a yellow one if it stopped at the first defect in some cases but not in others. Plant managers now had to come up with a plan to move all their machines from red and yellow to green, in a classic implementation of jidoka—improving detection first in order to improve capability.

In this industry, improving delivery and quality had a radical impact on sales, with an increase of over 40 percent in this period—simultaneously, the learning system led to local learning, which overall decreased costs and supported sales.

Support Local Learning with the Lean Learning System

From the top, looking down, the Lean program that Vareille, Ballé, and Mérel ran could be described as follows:

- CEO visits to show commitment and learn from the specific problems encountered by the teams in different locations and situations

- Key performance indicators (nonfinancial) to challenge the speed of the continuous improvement process

- Visual control systems to share shop floor problems with everybody and allow quick reactions

- Management routines to decentralize the management at workstations

- Problem-solving workshops to see the wastes and launch the continuous improvement

From a traditional management mindset, the Lean program is very easy to interpret as a straightforward control process: to avoid errors and control operations more tightly. In actual fact, it is nothing of the sort. It's an *education* program where every person in the company can orient themselves and understand (1) how the score is kept, (2) that the CEO really cares about performance and is there to help, (3) how the playing field is set up, (4) the ground rules to avoid errors, and (5) that they're expected to scratch their heads and come up with ideas and initiatives to make things better.

What does this look like from the ground up? The plant manager of an FCI site in China described how he was inducted into the Lean program.[2] After a personal visit from the CEO outlining what was expected from the site—quick learning, particularly in the matter of safety improvement—the plant manager (PM), a veteran of 13 years in the company in various positions, took a standard nine-day course organized in three sessions of three days in India, the United States, and China. He was then asked to find someone for the full-time job of coordinating with the small central Lean team run by Yves Mérel (seven people for the entire FCI group).

After a kickoff event, the PM's first task was to set up the visual management—and, in doing so, fix many of the safety issues that plague operations anywhere. As the PM trained his direct reports to implement these visual standards, he realized that he needed to answer confidently recurring questions such as these: What is Lean for? What immediate targets are being pursued? What are the benefits to the site of learning Lean?

Each visual standard required that new management routines be put in place, and again, this required a consistent training effort from the PM. The core of these management routines was the Daily Flash Meeting at every production cell to discuss the day's objectives and yesterday's problems. The PM now found himself spending a third of his time on the shop floor, confirming that his line managers had all the resources they needed to achieve their goals. His main problem was to get his own managers to grasp the new thinking on quality, which he now understood as, "If you identify a defect, stop producing. Think about what you did and how to improve it," which ran against the plant's existing habits. The teams needed to learn that (1) in case of defects the reflex should be to stop producing and think, and (2) managers had to go to the shop floor to check things physically and not rely on what they saw on their computer screens.

As he conducted various workshops with Mérel, the PM came to realize that the point of these workshops was not to implement a new way of working but to teach him a new way of analyzing his operations (see Table 7.4).

Having grasped this fundamental shift in focus, he now realized he had to use the program as a learning approach, using the improvement workshops as the fundamental tool to involve his own teams to understand what was expected of them in terms of waste elimination and "five whys?" thinking. With the area's Lean manager, the PM devised a plan to make sure that every employee in the plant was involved in at least one workshop a year—which led to a considerable increase in the number of kaizen workshops, as shown in Figure 7.9.

At the beginning of the program, there had been an accident in the plant, customer complaints were averaging one and a half per month, missed deliveries were at 4 percent, lead time was around 65 days, and the time between parts changed was a week on average. Two years later, the plant had had no accident since the start of the program, complaints were down to 0.6, missed deliveries 0.5 percent, lead time was down to 26 days, and the time between production changes was down to 2.5 days.

This illustrates the change process of Lean thinking: the tools are there to help each local leader change her own story as she better understands her situation and problems and she starts relating differently with her value-adding team. As each individual manager changes her area's story, new opportunities appear globally to accelerate the learning at full company level. The intensification of the kaizen events is typical of a plant that progresses quickly within the Lean program. However, the workshops do not deliver performance in themselves if they don't create reusable learning.

	Analysis	**To Understand This**
Layout and 5Ss	Cycle time variation analysis to visualize the main sources of variations in the layout disposition, in the daily control of the zone, and in the balancing of operators' work	The main source of waste is the friction from multiple sources that stops people from seeing clearly how to organize themselves for smooth, continuous production.
Quick quality response	Analysis of defects one by one by listing potential factors, testing every hypothesis to improve work standards	Any defect is put into the product by a mindless action or technical misconception, and only rigorous hypothesis testing can surface quality problems.
SMED	Video analysis of tool changeovers to distinguish external steps (machine is still operating) from internal (machine is stopped) and reorganize the change to externalize activities and reduce final adjustments	Large batches are the second source of all evil (after letting bad work pass) because the larger the batch, the more difficult it will be to spot defects, and inventories ultimately clog the system and slow on-time delivery.
TPM	Daily analysis of the production run by causes of production losses such as stoppages, slowdowns, changeovers, defects, and so on to improve machine use through better maintenance	Equipment is a major source of variation in the cycle time if poorly maintained and understood. To support people's success, we have to free them from equipment constraints by separating human work from machine work.

Table 7.4 Operations Analysis to Trigger Learning

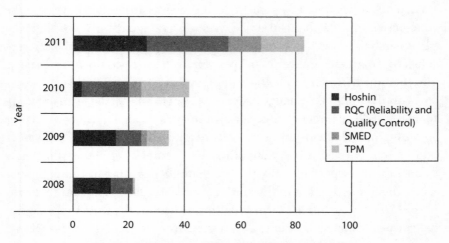

Figure 7.9 Increase in the Number of Kaizen Workshops

Old Habit	New Habit
Run the plant from the boardroom, making decisions from reports with the management committee.	Run the plant from the shop floor by challenging work-level teams to solve specific problems and get senior managers to support them in their efforts.
Tell customers, "This is how it is, and we're doing our best to service you, so just be patient."	Listen to customers' complaints, do what it takes to solve their immediate problems, and delve into the root causes of our internal operational problems.
Solve quality issues by paying for batch inspection while running production full tilt.	Solve quality issues by paying for stopping at every defect and challenging frontline management to solve problems as they appear.
Achieve delivery by holding large inventories of finished products and components.	Achieve delivery by making the supply chain more flexible through small-batch production and milk runs to suppliers.
Train people by sending experts in who will enforce new processes and demand discipline of execution from middle management.	Train people by involving them in improvement activities, and demand rigor of hypothesis testing and asking "why?"

Table 7.5   Changes Necessary in Problem-Solving Habits

Overall, FCI's plant managers had to change their problem-solving habits on a number of topics such as shown in Table 7.5.

Because people cannot be convinced but will make up their minds on their own, the only thing management can do is create repeated opportunities for the "aha!" moment to occur. A more intense rhythm of kaizen events, initiated by the manager himself or herself, usually corresponds to a quickening of his or her understanding of the need to learn (and teach) by doing.

Vareille states, "Lean is not only a way to improve operations, it is a way to think about all aspects of business. Even more it is a complete strategy and it has been my strategy to turn around four companies during my career. What I found in Lean is a way to blend strategic thought with concrete action to lead large-scale transformations by developing all the people in the company."

Conducting Repeated Experiments to Grow the Learning

In Jacques's old company, the COO, Frédéric Fiancette, and the continuous improvement director, Eric Prévot, had successfully worked with their sensei and implemented many of the aspects of the Lean learning system, such as focusing on reducing defects and accelerating flows. Indeed, although in 2009 the volume (hit by the Lehman Brothers crisis) went down to 79 million euros, the inventory was only 8 million euros (Table 7.6). If the turns had remained at the previous year's six turns, the inventory would have been 13 million—the simple change had released 5 million euros in cash from the production process (at a much needed time).

To make the pull system work, Fiancette, Prévot, and planning manager Matthias Fumex struggled with leveling customer demand and learning the discipline of takt time. Fiancette and his team were not looking yet at actual product takt time by product, but they had established the need for a set cadence to produce a fixed batch of high runners every day. This batch would have to circulate at the same cadence across the process steps throughout the factory, which created a smooth flow of products from castings to packaged goods. This quantity was specific to product types.

It became quickly apparent that operations had cumulated all the usual syndromes of (1) large batches, (2) no clear idea of the sales pace, (3) complex overlapping of production flows, and (4) poor internal conveyance and logistics. (Indeed, the logistics department had been largely overlooked over the year and was in a disastrous state of both competence and morale.) To better grasp the problem, Fiancette and his continuous improvement director Eric Prévot calculated that, as is often the case, less than 10 percent of the thousands of products made 50 percent of the total monthly volume. They drew up a short list and decided they would look at them one by one, starting at the higher runners. It turned out that as few as two or three high runners made the bulk of the production in each assembly cell. Without actually simplifying the flows, they could now investigate the path of a few products before fixing the system as a whole.

Year	2004	2005	2006	2007	2008	2009	2010	2011	2012	2013
Sales, millions of euros	65	69	73	80	83	72	75	79	79	78
Inventory, millions of euros	14	15	11	16	13	8	7	6,5	6,6	6
Turns	2.7	2.7	3.5	3.4	3.4	4.8	5.5	6.5	7.2	8.0

Table 7.6 Sales, Inventory, and Turns from 2004 Through 2013

In pulling one product after the other, they structured their learning curve as each new attempt created the opportunity to start from scratch and check what worked and what didn't, much in the way Mérel implemented stop-at-defect on three machines at a time. Chunking a repetitive problem in small steps rather than going for broke is an essential part of managing learning because it allows for repeated plan-do-check-act cycles on the same topic—and so, learning. For these few products, they decided to adjust batch sizes to exactly the demand volume—the idea was to make every day, on a few very high runners, exactly the demand from the previous day. Their thinking was that if these high runners made, on the whole, a cumulative volume equivalent to half the plant's demand, they should stabilize flows considerably. The question then was: what should be the batch size?

Fumex, the planning manager, then looked at the behavior of the highest runner and saw that the law of large numbers did apply: variation as a proportion of volume was indeed much smaller than on other types of products. As a result, they decided to plan for each week the averaged daily demand from the previous week, and they would then force the production cells to produce exactly that quantity every day. In just a few months, on-time delivery improved by 20 percent. By the end of the first year, inventory turns had improved by more than 40 percent.

The fixed list of products going through a set process (set list of equipment) made a *value stream*. A value stream is in fact represented by its overall takt time, and product-by-product takt time. This cadence changes everything because processes are now dimensioned to deliver regularly. Cadence creates a capacity plan around the recurring jobs, and it lets one-off fill in the rest of the available time. Cadence has the further advantage of revealing more starkly the products that do not conform to a regular pattern. Working with the general concept of a regular cadence, the planning manager embarked on a learning journey of trial and error that would continuously improve the plants' performance, as shown in Figure 7.10.

These results were, however, not achieved as mechanical approaches that rolled out new processes without regard to the input of people by applying Lean logistics from the start. Companywide results appeared as a result of careful progress by both Fumex in product planning and Prévot in production, followed closely by Fiancette as COO—interest is what

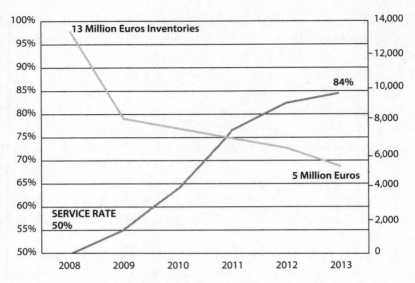

Figure 7.10   The Plants' Continuous Improvement

made the whole thing work, interest and discovery. Through repeating experiments on the same theme for over several years, Fumex learned the following:

- *Year 1:* Focus on a few high runners and pull them through the production process. In a few months, the finished goods inventory is divided by an order of 3 and on-time delivery improves by 20 percent. Yet, although having a regular production of high runners works (due to the law of large numbers, what customers don't buy this week, they will next week), some products fall short because customers buy these at infrequent intervals but in large quantities.

- *Year 2:* The production capacity dedicated to high-running products is enough to produce the average day's demand, but it is not enough to fulfill an unexpected large order of products sold infrequently to large customers. Create a new category of "middle-runner" products, which will be held in inventory and produced as soon as a customer asks for some. Since the demand is infrequent, production can level the inventory reconstitution. As a result, stock value goes back up some, but on-time delivery improves by another 15 percent. However, it is now apparent that this approach does not work for the Russian market:

there is a marked seasonality, and the inventory needed to satisfy the upsurge of summer demand is considerable—as well as always short.

- *Year 3:* Since the leveled pull principle is now confirmed by many cycles of experimentation, the idea is to treat the Russian market as a "perfect customer" that would order all year round the same amount— thus creating a stock calculated to correspond to the lowest historical sales in Russia. In this way, as the summer season starts, the factory needs to make only the extra parts for Russia as opposed to producing it all at the expense of capacity for the other markets. Weekly scheduling of quantities during the low-demand season, and then according to real demand during the high-demand season. On-time delivery increases again by 20 percent as inventory values hit an all-time low. However, leveling production schedules reveal that components arrive in large irregular batches, causing production interruptions and huge component inventories.

- *Year 4:* Apply pull principles to the supply chain in order to level frequent smaller deliveries. Renegotiate contracts with suppliers to better level shipments, use regular milk runs, and so on. This is a continuing effort through years 5 and 6, with experimentation with cross-docking and relocalizing parts closer to production, both of which progressively radically change the entire supply chain.

Learning accrued by extending the same practical experiments with takt time to increasingly difficult cases. Fumex didn't learn from his first attempt but from the deeper understanding of working the same problem time and time again in different conditions. As he did, he both became more autonomous in solving all kinds of unexpected real-life situations and developed a much deeper understanding of his job as planning manager— some with organizational consequences as he moved most of the forecasting staff to reinforce the procurement office and level the demand on suppliers. Writing after the fact makes this learning process seem smooth and reliable, but that is a hindsight illusion. In truth, at each stage, no one had any idea what to expect. Fumex's learning curve had to be sustained. Several mechanisms were at work:

1. *The pull system itself is a harsh master.* The original researchers looking into Toyota's pull system thought Lean was "fragile"—meaning that it would fail whenever any accident introduced a large variation in

the system. This very fragility is the strength of the pull system, which is rather like turning a plate on a stick: if you stop turning the stick, the plate falls. Matthias Fumex had to face his pull system crashing time and time again, and he had to figure out which mindless decision had led to the problem every time, and which hidden misconception explained the decision.

2. *The leader cared.* Fumex was never alone in his experimentation—both the CEO and the COO were curious about what could be eked out of the current systems and they came regularly to see progress, discuss, hear, and learn. If people don't feel that they're covered in case of a problem and that they have the freedom to experiment with their management watching their back (the plant manager carefully monitored what happened both with the delivery performance and inventory levels), they'll be overcautious, toe the line, and keep their heads down.

3. *The leader supported (and encouraged).* As Fumex learned to change both scheduling and procurement habits, he kept hitting barrier after barrier, both from unexpected issues, functional resistance from other departments, such as sales or production, and internal resistance from his own teams who didn't want to change the way they did things or think about new possibilities. Any pragmatic manager will deal with some of these issues, but rarely all, and top leadership support is essential to remove obstacles from the path and solve issues out of the manager's zone of influence that only the leader can solve (many things are easy for the leader to do but almost impossible for someone in the system). Top management support is also much needed recognition, particularly when something new is being criticized or resisted by colleagues—learning takes time, and motivation needs to be maintained over the duration.

4. *The focus remained on what worked and what didn't work.* A key role for leaders is to help managers take a step back and constantly ask the key questions: What worked? What didn't work? Managers naturally get carried away with the narrative argument of what they want to do, the barriers put in their path, and how this is all so unfair. The leader needs to constantly reaffirm the rationality of learning: some things work, some things don't, and many are indifferent. The challenge is to continue with hypothesis testing, even though the spot situation can be confusing or frustrating.

Throughout this extended learning process, Fumex learned to see his job differently and to work with his professional tools such as the MRP, as well as develop specific tools to level the flow of finished products and schedule production. He also learned to work better with purchasing and procurement to solve problems across the supply chain, and so there was a spillover effect of new tools and techniques from the upstream to the downstream, and one day, it is hoped, to suppliers. From an a priori Lean principle, and through careful parsing of cases in which each experiment worked and cases where it didn't, the scheduling office developed unique case-by-case knowledge that sustained a continuous improvement curve, with a cash conversion ratio of 200 percent.

Lean breakthroughs hinge on the quality of the kaizen efforts: ask the right questions, and the teams will come up with new, unexpected ways of cracking difficult problems. The executive challenge, obviously, is to learn what are the right questions to ask—which is precisely what the sensei teach. Although no two situations are truly alike, the Lean thinking space is still structured with reference points, like visible buoys on a bay, defining the racing area, as shown in Table 7.7.

Of course, it matters where one is sailing toward. In the next chapter we will see how the Lean strategy builds on this type of flexibility and innovation by continuously feeding back into the makeup of the organization at all levels.

Where to Look for Results	How to Create the Conditions for Kaizen	Develop Each Person's Autonomy in Problem Solving
• Faster delivery improves sales. • Reducing defects improves sales and lowers total costs. • Reducing lead times improves use of labor and equipment and frees up cash. • Freeing up capacity improves the introduction of new products.	• Stop and investigate every defect—don't work around problems. • Improve flow of work: activities, individual operations, and information. • Explicit standard work so everyone can compare what they do to a reference. • Support teams and the basic stability of their working conditions.	• Challenge people to find their own problems and will to improve. • Support them to face the difficulties and carry on against obstacles. • Teach them to frame issues in terms of the Lean learning system. • Encourage repeated exploration by taking action on their experiments and forming larger solutions together.

Table 7.7   Reference Points in a Lean Thinking Space

CHAPTER 8

Accelerate the Gains

Gains can be accelerated by reinvesting learning from operations into product improvement, and then vice versa.

After Jacques's company was sold and he had retired, he pondered a key question: *how sustainable is Lean?* Fiancette and Prévot had continued to pursue Lean learning, and they enjoyed impressive results for several years, but over time the increased pressure from the new owners to return to traditional financial decision-making forced both to give up and move on. Naturally the company rapidly returned to its pre-Lean performance levels. Interestingly, the acquiring company saw itself as committed to Lean (part of the reason why they acquired Socla) in terms of optimizing flows to get short-term accounting results.

The new owners asked expert "Lean guys" to accelerate the rollout of flow optimization according to corporate roadmaps, using kaizen events to impose the corporate story rather than genuinely seeking to tease out ideas and initiatives from people on the ground. Without ever realizing it, the new owners killed the magic of kaizen; and the so-called optimized flows stopped working as they were supposed to without being sustained by the kaizen spirit of every team, every day.

Wiremold too was acquired by a large industrial company in 2000. At the time it had strong Lean leaders at least two layers deep, but even this strength was not enough to survive the non-Lean thinking of a new leadership team put in place by a new non-Lean-thinking owner. Within two years after Art Byrne and Orry retired, the entire senior management team was gone . . . not because they were fired but because they could not tolerate the non-Lean things they were being forced to do (for example, increasing production batch sizes, building inventory, and selling on the basis of price rather than value). The golden rule is alive and well: he who owns the gold makes the rules.

Unfortunately, traditional Taylorist companies and consultants have misinterpreted Lean, largely missing what is innovative, new, and frankly, exciting, and they have reduced it to just another operational excellence program based on three broad operational efforts:

1. A program of specialist-led improvement activities, frequently aimed at "reducing cost through removing waste," rarely at improving quality or reducing lead time, with the twin purpose of (a) generating savings and (b) training work-level teams to manage their performance and solve problems

2. Mindless (that is, not mindful) overuse of management routines such as daily five-minute stand-up meetings and workplace maintenance practices such as 5S (keeping the workplace organized at all times)

3. Progress reviews and maturity audits to measure both accrued savings from cost-reduction activities and progress in acquisition of "best practices" across the company

Although now commonplace, these "Lean" programs have the confusing distinction of being criticized by the founding Lean thinkers as modern extensions of Taylorist management (and therefore missing the key aim of improving customer experience by flowing work better across the organization and engaging frontline workers—as opposed to staff specialists—in improving their own work). They are also criticized by TPS veterans from Toyota itself as irrelevant management rain dances far removed from the gemba where work occurs and where customer satisfaction and profitability are created by how mindfully employees understand the "point of process"—where the tool touches the part to actually add value (as opposed to the many various tasks necessary to achieve this point of process that don't actually add any direct value to the functionality of the product or service). Yet, as these programs have become prevalent, and as their shelf life is generally limited to two to four years, they have spread the notion that Lean is fundamentally unsustainable.

Is Lean unsustainable then? Clearly, there is no such thing as a Lean company. There are only companies led by Lean thinkers. This is a battle of ideas. When these people leave and are replaced with mainstream financial managers, not surprisingly, old thinking reinstates old ways of working. The promise of Lean, nonetheless, is one of sustainable growth. Toyota has continued to "Lean" itself through thick and thin over the past 60 years. It is, as we speak today, still relying on its Thinking People System to improve car performance while spectacularly reducing the cost of new production facilities by 40 percent, making them smaller and more flexible (up to eight car models per line assembled at the same time on the same line) and improving their energy efficiency. Toyota has achieved this with continued Lean leadership at the top.

How can this be maintained beyond the individuals who make the system? Discussing this with Fiancette, Jacques realized they held the answer to this thorny question, but in the end, they lacked the time to fully implement it. Sustainable competitive advantage happens only when you close the loop—when the value you've freed by eliminating waste is given back to customers, through product and service improvements. By building on learning, Lean establishes three dynamic virtuous circles: higher customer satisfaction from better products, better products from improved production processes, and improved production processes from tighter connections with suppliers and their innovation capabilities (Figure 8.1).

Right from the start of his interest in Lean, when he had traditional consultants carry out productivity projects, Jacques had been interested in seeing the impact of Lean on product development. One of the projects had been a value analysis initiative to redesign a key product. This project had been carried out with the traditional view of optimizing an existing project through an in-depth analysis of "value" with many drawn-out meetings between engineering, production, and supply chain. The effort had been extremely energy- and time-consuming and disappointing in terms of

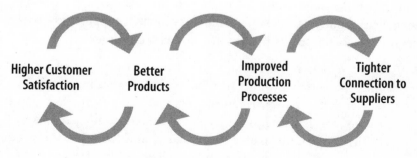

Figure 8.1   The Three Dynamic Virtuous Circles of Lean

results, delivering a 5 percent cost reduction to an objective of 20 percent—but it had been very interesting in revealing how little the company silos agreed on what constituted value.

After they started working with a sensei and clearing the window in production, the sensei pushed them to restart the value analysis project. Using the same *find* logic as he had used on the manufacturing process, he suggested focusing on a few immediate improvements to better understand the product in practice. Each of the functions (engineering, production, and purchasing) initially looked at things they thought could be improved immediately on the product from their specialist perspective, and then they came together to see if they could agree on obvious candidate features for improvement.

The sensei told them to limit the number of changes to the product to limit the real-life risk for customers, so they quickly agreed on a short list of changes that would benefit each function and were unlikely to affect either performance or quality (in fact, the changes should improve both). The sensei made the further suggestion of trying things with mock-ups and trials rather than solving all problems on paper and then making prototypes. Engineers produced a set of prototypes testing different approaches that were discussed by the project team. In six months' time, the project team finalized a better product with a 23 percent cost reduction. A key part of this success was based on the engineering changes on the shop floor and the value analysis improvement achieved in production.

Unfortunately, Jacques had retired by then, and although Fiancette realized the importance of what had happened, he lost the political fight with corporate sales to approach the entire catalog in this way, rather than making financially based decisions on which products to keep and which to dump. Still, Jacques and Fiancette saw the answer to the question of Lean sustainability. Sustainable, profitable growth is supported by a regular stream of better products that hit the spot with customers:

- *Seeing products as a stream of value:* Rather than pursuing the goal of selling one perfect product that will take the entire market, deliver at a regular cadence improved products that will put pressure on competing offers. Each iteration tackles a limited number of changes to avoid risking performance and quality, and it makes the product evolve according to what customers like or dislike. At Wiremold, the company's leaders described this thinking as having our competitors "chasing our tail lights." By the time a competitor was copying Wire-mold's latest iteration, the company was already introducing the next one.

- *This evolution of products is supported by evolution of technical processes:* The improved features of the new product would have been very difficult to manufacture if the processes of assembly and paint had not radically improved as well, allowing engineers to make smarter design decisions.

 A company is little more than the sum of the products and/or services it offers to its customers. The true aim of Lean thinking is to reinject the value garnered from waste elimination in production processes into better designs and more value to customers.

Lean thinking is the key to sustainable growth as it creates the basis for these:

- Better individual products that are more robust and include more features as they evolve organically by improving the same product base step by step at a regular cadence, in step with what customers go for (or don't)

- The opportunity to push some really innovative features (as opposed to innovative "products" as a whole) on stable products and thus create original offers to customers that are new and reliable

- A wider, clearer range of products where customers can find what they need according to their use (the same customer can well buy several distinct products) without cannibalization and with the protection of the margin of each individual product

In his insightful book *How Toyota Became #1*, researcher David Magee explained the fabled Toyota Production System in manufacturing, yet he emphasized something else as the secret to its enduring success: better cars. "When buyers get more for less," he wrote, "they are typically happy. Many industry observers say Toyota gives customers an average of $2,500 more in value per vehicle compared to competitive vehicles from the same class."[1] The stunning thing is that Toyota actually profits more per car as customers are willing to pay for perceived value and demand fewer rebates. According to the *Detroit News*, based on earnings before interest and taxes, Toyota earns on average $2,700 more per vehicle sold than its competitors. Toyota's consistent delivery on its quality promise keeps customers coming back again and again, which sustain its real price, while the constant kaizen efforts deliver space for real innovation and lower the total cost basis.

In his autobiography, *Toyota: Fifty Years in Motion* (Harper & Row, 1987), Eiji Toyoda, the architect of the Toyota we know, rarely mentions the Toyota Production System. His entire focus was on designing and building cars that people would buy because they offered good value for money. Not that the TPS is unimportant. Eiji Toyoda himself added to his great-uncle Sakichi's (intelligent automation so that the machine stops at every defect) and cousin Kiichiro's (complete elimination of waste by building only what is needed, when it's needed in the quantity needed) revolutionary ideas by introducing the creative idea system inspired from Ford's suggestion system. Toyoda constantly backed (and often protected) Taiichi Ohno in the development of his concrete approach to "making things" in Toyota's unique way, which became the bedrock of the TPS. He promoted the philosophies of "daily improvements" and "good thinking, good products."[2] His main concern was always to develop better people to make better cars. The Toyota Production System is a companywide education system to teach people how to improve technical processes to give engineers the concrete tools to make better cars.

Most companies treat knowledge and learning purely as a collective process—it is assumed that the company, somehow, "learns." This is just sloppy thinking because there is no evidence whatsoever to argue that case. A people-centric vision of a business sees it as a collection of individuals who work together (more or less) to achieve a common aim: helping customers with some problem or other, charging for it, and making a living out of it, more or less profitably. Each of these individuals can learn quite quickly, both technical facts and practices, and each can also learn to work better with colleagues to coordinate efforts involving new knowledge. To the outsider looking in, this might look like the business is learning . . . until one key person leaves or loses an internal political battle and all the so-called learning is lost. After all, Xerox invented the mouse and never used it, Kodak perfected digital photography and never used it, and so on.

People centricity is particularly important in product design. Every era has its gifted and visionary engineers who invent great devices and then entrepreneurially build companies around their inventions, and we see what generally happens when they leave: the company reverts to design-by-committee and very quickly loses its edge, and eventually its relevance. You need a human mind to integrate the fast-moving zeitgeist of consumers and the technical processes capable of delivering new products that *fit*.

Toyota has long understood this and has, from very early on, given the full responsibility for any new product to a single person, a "chief engineer" (CE) whose responsibility it is to capture the heart of the segment's consumers by designing the right concept and product architecture to fit with the times. The chief engineer is a single person with the whole responsibility for the product's success (including the product's design architecture, not a "project manager") but no authority over any of the engineers under the authority of their functional boss.

Because a person learns much faster than a collective, this system enables Toyota to continue to rapidly offer fresh new products while maintaining quality and continuity in its product range. Eiji Toyoda believed that only one person could hold final judgment on technical decisions in order to make an outstanding car. He built on a system established by Kenya Nakamura, Toyota's first chief engineer who developed the Crown, the company's first successful passenger car in the 1950s. Like Taiichi Ohno, Nakamura was known to be irascible and demanding, and he was sponsored by Eiji Toyoda. Toyota's leaders trusted individual engineers to capture a gut feel for customer experience and turn it into design parameters.

Chief engineers are first and foremost technicians—they personally design the product's architecture. They have immense influence but no direct authority over other engineers (beyond a small team of assistants). The idea is that they're entrusted with designing a winning model and have to use specialist functions as contractors. As a result, the chief engineer also has the responsibility of setting the key milestones of his project, using the milestone management method (as a result, different projects can be managed differently). Chief engineers need to handle the tough trade-off between incorporating new technology (when they feel it's ready) and reverting to standard, well-known but boring solutions. Functional leaders have the complicated task of balancing experiments in new technology and training all their engineers to known standards.

As a result, Toyota models have a far more idiosyncratic evolution than other automakers. (Some other Japanese automakers, such as Honda, follow the same approach.) The chief engineer is first supposed to practice "genchi genbutsu"—go and see the facts at their source—at the customer's gemba, where customers buy, use, and store the products and make choices about where to add value and what to ignore. Chief engineers are expected to know existing products inside out in order to establish a clear short list of what issues must be fixed (often, production is also working hard at the same time to fix these issues) and where value can be improved.

A classic Toyota story is that of Chief Engineer Yuji Yokoya who, tasked with designing the 2004 Sienna (SE) minivan, decided to drive the existing Sienna and other minivans in every U.S. state, every Canadian province, and most of Mexico. In the course of his 53,000 miles, he concluded that several features had to be improved such as deciding to put much more value in seats.[3] Or realizing that American families drive long distances with their kids in the car, so interior design really matters. The next-generation Sienna, however, was given to a new chief engineer, Kazuo Mori, who thought that the car needed to turn more crisply. For the 2011 version he concentrated on a more sporty and cool feel to the minivan ("From a driver's standpoint, the SE is downright cool," as confirmed by a journalist[4]) by focusing on some features such as suspension tweaks to give drivers and passengers a crisper feel.

Consider the Takt Time of Product Evolution

The other key component of forming value to sustain sales is to see every project not as a single event but as a *value stream of products performing a service for customers*. Fundamental value to customers evolves as products and services themselves evolve. Forming greater value first means establishing a disciplined rhythm of product evolutions, in the same way that Apple regularly releases a new iPhone. This "takt time" of product evolution is the backbone of forming value. Each new evolution is entrusted to a chief engineer whose job is to deliver a product iteration that people don't just like but love.

A glimpse into how enmeshed chief engineers and product models are at Toyota can be seen through the evolution of one of their star products: the Corolla (Table 8.1). The overall strategy for the car, across 11 model generations, has been to equip it with features of the next range up while keeping it a family car—this overall concept has not changed since the very first model in 1966. Nonetheless, every chief engineer is asked to find a new

Generation	Chief Engineer	Quote	Context	Concept
First, 1966–1970	Tatsuo Hasegawa, was previously the chief engineer (CE) of the Publica and the engineer who first codified the expectations and roles of a CE.	"80 Point Doctrine + α Concept." Failing one score is not acceptable, nor is achieving 80. Without a +α feature to reach 90 points in some areas, you can't capture the public's heart.	Motorization is booming in Japan.	Toyota is adopting technologies never previously used in a domestically produced car. New features and equipment are comparable to those found in higher-grade models.
Second, 1970–1974	Tatsuo Hasegawa, while developing the second-generation Corolla, became responsible for managing CEs.		There is rapid economic growth, and Japanese customers are beginning developing discerning tastes.	Toyota focuses on "the feel." It aggressively expands the line of sporty models.
Third, 1974–1979	Shirou Sasaki, after taking charge of the chassis division, worked for Hasegawa in the product planning division and supported Corolla development until becoming CE.	"Do not strive to be the honor student in the area of costs." Cost planning will lead you to a cheap, shoddy product. A car is an investment for customers, so a better product will be happily purchased even if it is slightly more expensive.	There is growing export popularity and strict emission standards for environmental pollution in line with the Muskie Act in the United States.	Toyota creates a solid basis for further brand development by improving driving performance, function, interior comfort, and quietness. The company develops a wider vehicle with greater interior quality. The focus is on feelings that passenger experiences.

(continued)

Table 8.1 The Evolution of the 11 Models of the Toyota Corolla

Generation	Chief Engineer	Quote	Context	Concept
Fourth, 1979–1983	Fumio Agetsuma, body design expert on the Corona and Mark II, participated in the Corolla team until becoming CE.	"An appealing design is a design with high-level originality that is ahead of its time." Designs must have originality and express a clear message.	Japan is recovering from the oil shock, and the focus is on the quality of life.	Toyota is producing a top-range family car: "Luxury car status and features with excellent fuel economy." Toyota's international perspective and outlook in styling are growing.
Fifth, 1983–1987	Fumio Agetsuma, after developing the fourth-generation Corolla, stayed on to tackle the fifth.	"The Corolla has a continuous responsibility of being the 'bread and butter' for various people in nations throughout the world." He emphasized the basic areas that have the greatest impact on passengers, even though they might be low-key.	Richer lifestyles in Japan have led to a taste for higher-grade products. The younger generation explores a wider range of lifestyles, and consequently their sense of value diversifies.	Toyota pursues front-wheel drive to "strive to ensure its status as a worldwide strategic vehicle that is a high-quality, high-grade family car and to reinforce its international competitive strength." "FF designs to pursue straight line stability at high speeds, handling performance, and a spacious interior."
Sixth, 1987–1991	Akihito Saito was involved with vibration testing and chassis design before joining the Corolla fifth-generation development team, before taking charge of the sixth-generation Corolla development.	"Provide high quality time." Customers seek thoughtful attention, ample room, driving excitement, and family time. Experience focuses on the senses—sight, sound, touch, and smell—to create high sensitivity to quality.	Customer needs have been changing from satisfaction of ownership to enjoying life and using possessions to enhance their personal lifestyle.	Self-fulfillment is part of the product's performance, beyond transportation. The CE sought a level of quietness and riding comfort found in the Crown (top range) by appealing in to the senses.

Table 8.1 The Evolution of the 11 Models of the Toyota Corolla

(continued)

Generation	Chief Engineer	Quote	Context	Concept
Seventh, 1991–1995	Akihito Saito, after successfully developing the sixth generation, stayed on to become the seventh-generation Corolla development leader.	"The impression that a car makes is first developed when its essential functions and performance significantly exceed expectations." Saito sought "impressions that inspire the soul."	The seventh generation reached the market as the Japanese economy took a plunge.	The Corolla series was the worldwide leader of family cars, and the team sought to once again be on the cutting edge. Saito focused his team on fundamental vehicle performance such as driving, turning, and stopping.
Eighth, 1995–2000	Takayasu Honda first worked with chassis, and he later became responsible for the Corolla and Sprinter. He became leader of the development of the eighth-generation Corolla after having worked on the four previous generations.	"Convey a slim, healthy image with a beautiful shape." He pursued significant weight reductions while ensuring safety, body rigidity, and improvements in quietness and fuel efficiency.	In 1995, the Japanese economy remained sluggish, and the focus was on environmental and economic performance.	The car was lightened to improve its efficiency, which meant improving body rigidity. Careful consideration was given to environmental aspects such as recyclability and cleaner emissions from the diesel engine.
Ninth, 2000–2006	Takeshi Yoshida started in body design, and he went on to be in charge of Corolla planning. After being CE of the Soluna in Thailand, he joined the Corolla team and became the ninth-generation CE.	"Start from scratch." The "can't fail" position of the Corolla made engineers overprotective of past designs. Yoshida stressed departure from the past to construct a "new global standard for compact cars."	In Japan, new car sales continued to fall due to the poor state of the economy. Customer tastes were shifting away from sedans toward minivans.	To respond to the drop in brand strength with a radical redesign, large-room development was introduced to challenge ingrained design habits and seek breakthrough packaging, style, and quality. Previous performance targets were attacked aggressively with new technology.

Table 8.1 The Evolution of the 11 Models of the Toyota Corolla

(continued)

Generation	Chief Engineer	Quote	Context	Concept
Tenth, 2006–2011	Soichiro Okudaira started at Toyota with functional parts such as wipers and locks, and he then moved to the United States to research trends in collision safety technology. After becoming CE to the Brevis and the Scion, he took charge of the Corolla tenth-generation development.	"Corolla's only adversary is Corolla itself." Always try and incorporate superior factors in a car that is already top of its class.	Toyota has become a truly global company, which changes the thinking of the Corolla 40 years after the first generation.	Focus was directed at the instantaneous good feeling when entering the car and starting off. Toyota was planning ahead for a global vehicle, with cabin space consideration for user-friendliness in the U.S. market.
Eleventh, 2011–	Shinichi Yasui, having worked in the body design division and the planning division, became the concept planner for Corolla's tenth generation and then CE for the eleventh.	"I believe this new model clearly breathes the Corolla DNA that has been inherited over a period of 47 years."	To compete in world markets, Corolla needs more excitement in the sense of meeting someone new, reaching the final points of a match, receiving something that exceeds expectations such as occurs when people watch an athletic event.	Toyota dramatically improved the dynamic drive performance (agility and fuel economy), and it achieved impressive value for the money.

Table 8.1 The Evolution of the 11 Models of the Toyota Corolla

concept to nurture the relationship between the car and its customers in their current context.

Each new generation of Corollas has to encompass more value to a baseline family car in terms of top-of-the-range attributes. Each chief engineer is also tasked to revitalize the brand with a new model within the same direction. Chief engineers are supposed to provide a "concept" for the car that will act as an intent statement so that any designer on the project can grasp the intent of the design. This chief engineer concept should somehow link the tradition of the car with the spirit of the times and become a North Star for each engineer.

Value is formed as each new generation accomplishes the following:

1. *Offers the same core value:* Every generation of drivers will look for an affordable family car with some luxury features.

2. *Improves by offering this value in different ways:* Features will respond to present taste and lifestyle preferences, which evolve unpredictably.

A product is a dynamic success if the yang of aggressive new features is balanced by the yin of stable design standards. This balance is easy to miss. One can lose the purpose of the product, as did one of Toyota's European competitors. An automaker renowned for its daring styling but under attack for quality issues chose to respond with a big improvement leap in quality—at the cost of styling. The car was definitely better on the quality front, but it was a spectacular flop for customers who were looking for the styling and did not find it, and those customers looking for quality had no reason to turn to this brand. One can easily get it wrong as well by introducing uncertain new features that are not convincing, as the VW debacle on cheating on emission standards has shown.

Value Is Formed by People-Centric Solutions

Toyotas are hardly recognized for their daring design or radical innovation. Indeed, robustness and quality remain the driving factors of the brand's strength. In fact, the car is the result of the blend between the chief engineer's dynamic vision and what the general manager of each function, such as body engineering, interior, chassis, and electronics, consider safe or practical. Although this looks like a classic organizational matrix at first glance, it isn't. Chief engineers have no direct authority over individual designers (although quite a bit of influence). Design engineers have only one boss: their department's general manager. The chief engineer is a client of each department and can't demand things to get done her way—she must persuade rather than impose. On the other hand, the chief engineer has the final say on every strategic performance and technology decision.

Any new development is truly people centric inasmuch as it is the brainchild of the chief engineer—yet it also benefits from the company's technical heritage because standards must be maintained. The product is therefore the outcome of a dialogue between the chief engineer's passion to improve and reinvent and the department head's caution to depart from standards. This is not a conflict as such because chief engineers well recognize the need to stick to engineering standards, but there is an ongoing discussion of what new features should be included in the new model, and which should not change.

A large part of Toyota's effectiveness at regularly hitting the market with successful products stems from the fact that this discussion occurs early in the development process, before even the drawing phase. The chief engineer and the department heads must agree on what will be flexible and what will be fixed before detailed design, mostly on the basis of experiments the chief engineer will have conducted with his team and suppliers in order to provide proof of concept.

Customers' lifestyles change, and industrial contexts change in the case of B2Bs; therefore, we should offer them help in solving their problems in each specific case. The dream would be a customized product for each person, but this is obviously hard to do at affordable prices. Still, hard or not, that's the ideal. The consequence of holding such an ideal is that rather than focus all efforts on the most profitable segments, a Lean strategy will have a response for every problem segment, and it will have an approach that makes this segment profitable (Figure 8.2). Every segment is considered worthwhile as long as it answers a customer problem. And the company will in fact deliver more value—a better solution—at a regular rhythm. Using our example of gas pumps, by imposing a tempo on new product releases, a Lean strategy structures engineering work at several levels:

1. Solving quality problems of products now in production through engineering patches (or adding customers' required options)

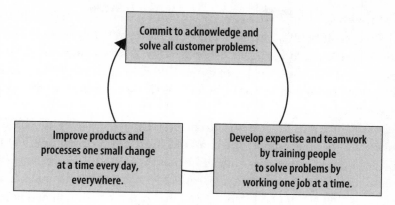

Figure 8.2 A Lean Strategy Response for Every Segment

2. Introducing regular product refreshes through engineering improvements to keep the customers (gas stations) interested in refurbishing

3. Reducing work content through smart engineering in order to drive manufacturing costs down

4. Making step change improvements to key functionalities such as the meter and the pump to keep market leadership

5. Making technological breakthroughs to invent the dispenser of the future, with technologies such as connectivity, VGA screens, and Big Data diagnostics

People-Centric Solutions Require Learning by Doing

Evrard Guelton, the sensei who helped the Clerico brothers turn around their sales and service business, had faced the same issue with his own sensei on the product side a few years earlier as head of manufacturing and engineering for the company. He took over the manufacturing side of the business as the company was stabilizing after mergers, acquisitions, and a streamlining of the product list—with endless trade-offs because no one dispenser could fully satisfy all world markets with their local and regulatory specificities.

An old hand at Lean manufacturing, Guelton had a clear idea of what to do in the factories: he somehow needed to fix quality and get work to flow through the confusion of option mix and volume. It wouldn't be easy, but he'd done it before. The questions that had him stumped were deeper: what did value mean for a fuel dispenser? And, how could they help the engineering department deal with the endless list of modifications to make, new options requested by the sales and services operations, and pressure to release new products?

For the previous three years, nozzle sales (how the company measured its unit sales because a machine can hold from one to eight nozzles) had been steadily retreating, reaching a low point in 2003. Common sense told the company's management that, particularly in the old, saturated markets of Europe, sales should be defended and that real expansion would happen in new Asian markets. The last "star" product had not been well accepted by the market, and engineering was swamped with demands for fixes and modifications from all over the world. And the sales and service divisions were asking for a 4 percent reduction in the selling price yearly. Guelton had never dealt with so much complexity before. He was confident that kaizen would reveal the real problems in the factory, but he was uncertain as to where to start in engineering.

Guelton was facing five different questions:

1. *Who are our customers?* Are the customers the final users who pick up a nozzle at the gas station and fill their tank? Are the customers the station managers who distribute and charge for fuel? Are the customers the oil companies that own a network of stations and defend their brand (the logo on the stations)? Are the customers the sales and service (S&S) outfits that need special features added to the product to sell on the local market? Is the customer manufacturing that requires design changes for cost-effective production? All of the above? Understanding the true customers without making rash choices is the first step in supporting quality.

2. *What do these customers say they want?* The sales and service regional leaders all had pressing requests with regard to what customers had asked for in order to put in a new order. These demands came in constantly, rather loudly, and they were never the same from one meeting to the next. What the S&S directors really wanted were lower prices. As well as full options. And fixing issues customers complained about in the field. The painful lesson was that once you had expended

engineering time to develop a new option the customers said they absolutely needed (and without it, wouldn't place the order), you often ended up . . . not selling it. What people say they want and what they actually purchase are often two very different things.

3. *What do these customers really use?* Most customers tend to value only a few things out of the myriad offerings any product or service is supposed to provide. The difficulty is in understanding which and when. Toyota, for instance, has bet the farm on mobility and peace of mind— their dominant assumption is that what customers most expect from a car is safety, ease of use, and reliability. These are very strong assumptions. Other automakers have gambled on styling or smooth rides or driving pleasure. Not that all functions don't matter, but products and services are complex undertakings, and trade-offs need to be made. Discovering what customers really use in a product is a huge step forward in understanding value.

4. *What do engineers want to do?* Engineers would not be very good at their job if they didn't have a strong sense of what kind of technologies they want to use to do what. The question, of course, is whether this is in the service of better value for customers or blind force of habit. Steve Jobs was obsessed with calligraphy, expressing technology through metaphors, and finicky design detail, and his obsessions translated into a lot of engineering time devoted to details that other engineers felt weren't that crucial to customers. After his death, iOS7 was received coolly by Apple fans who felt the new operating system was a step back from Jobs's relentless pushing of boundaries. What engineers want to do matters a lot because if they get a right feel for customers' evolving tastes, this will result in a leading product. If engineers make conservative (or worse, wrong) guesses about where customers are heading, this can result in a following product. As Henry Ford quipped, "If I had asked people what they wanted, they would have said faster horses." Ford wanted to make cars to ease the farmer's work. Gates wanted a PC on every desk. Jobs wanted to break down the barrier between technology and people. "Imputing"—that is, having the ability to form a strong engineering opinion from customers' reactions to a product or service—is a key feature or value. When Guelton envisaged a redesign of a new product that was faring badly with customers, its new product

leader had a strong sense of "simplification," which has affected the product design to this day.

5. *What does your environment want you to do?* Although it wasn't politic to say so at the time, one of the reasons the new product had so many issues was the emphasis on "good" project management—the emphasis on a bureaucratic "tick-the-box" approach to product development with the proper process, gate reviews, management go-aheads, and so on, and not enough customer or product focus. Regulatory changes also have a strong impact on product development, triggering sudden refurbishment campaigns and so on, as do some technological changes— including a degree of ethanol in fuel seems innocuous from the user's point of view, but it has a significant impact on hydraulics.

The Lean strategy starts with quality, then stabilizes cycle time, and then progressively increases variety. Guelton was dealing with a situation in which quality was hard to pinpoint, and cycle time to build a dispenser was impossible to stabilize because diversity was already huge as each market had different specific demands with no way of simplifying the problem. With no clear path forward, Guelton decided to bite the bullet and take up the challenge of quality by finding where his real problems were. His first step was to come to grips with the problem by starting a number of kaizen activities both in production and engineering to figure out what were the most fundamental issues. Out of this string of improvement activities, he made several, progressive changes to the business unit.

Change 1. Track All Quality Issues

The company's industrial base was a hodgepodge result of various acquisitions and rationalizations. Production was based in Scotland and France, while quality specialists sat in the Netherlands, with little love lost between all the groups that, not so long ago, had been competitors. Guelton's first task was to create a comprehensive database of quality problems both from customers complaining in the field and from inspections by the quality team—arrival quality that measured the issues encountered on dispensers that had been shipped as "good" from the factory, but that arrived at the S&S outfits with visible defects.

This first big change refocused manufacturing and then engineering on solving quality issues. The first visible impact of the change was a tightening of quality inspections at final control in the factories. What Guelton discovered when he delved into customer complaints was that problems with dispensers appeared infinite. The machine had to operate in a wide range of conditions, from cold northern seaside towns to subtropical African heat. Nevertheless, his first step was to work with the quality department in the Netherlands to systematically gather customer complaints and post them on a website. He also focused on the gap between reception inspection in the Dutch distribution center and final control in the main plant in Scotland. Rather than accept the focus on the elusive 20 percent "head of the Pareto" problems, he set up a rigorous measurement system for every quality issue.

Change 2. Clear the Window in Production

Guelton then hired a few consultants he trusted to start improvement activities in the factory. The aim was to eliminate obvious sources of variation and progressively move toward continuous flow. That apparently simple task was immensely complicated by the fact that the work content on each dispenser varied greatly by model. One model could have low work in, say, installing piping but needed a lot of work in wiring, while another would be the reverse. As the demand for specific models was volatile, organizing flow turned out to be far more complex than expected—but still, early gains were made. As cells would turn to improvement activities, quality issues started appearing more clearly.

As soon as a rudimentary flow was established on the shop floor, the production managers were asked to create rigorous "quality gates" within the process itself to get quality under control by segments of the flow (it looked far from a line at this time). This had the benefit of narrowing down quality issues by type of work and type of product. As they delved into the issues list, many seemed either unsolvable (rust issues in harsh climatic conditions) or unpredictable (one-off complaints that could affect many dispensers but arose in mysterious conditions—and disappeared as well). Every management team implicitly considers that some customers will have to live with some problems because (1) they've done so in the past,

(2) there are no easy solutions to these problems, and (3) it would cost too much to investigate. One thing became clear from mutual blame sessions around the report on the quality problems: production and engineering had to learn to talk to each other. In framing his industrial problem, Guelton set the collaboration between engineering and production as a key—and urgent— improvement dimension.

Right at the start of the redesign project to stabilize the high-profile product, Guelton set up a war room in the shop floor, and a Tuesday morning meeting (with free breakfast) for engineers to present to production what they had in mind for the product. Progressively, product engineers and the production manager's supervisors started working together on solving issues. Steve Boyd, the production manager, worked equally hard at improving the flow in the factory, which meant solving many quality issues. As in many industrial processes, products are assembled through a reasonably flowing sequence, but they are then put aside whenever a problem occurs, such as a missing part or quality issue. The product with a problem is then backflushed through the flow, causing havoc. Boyd took the built-in quality message to heart and started, step by step, fixing quality issues at every step of the process in order to improve flow. This, in turn, generated a flow of problems to fix in engineering, with engineers already immensely busy with new product design as well as customization for customers.

The question was framed as follows: can a machine be assembled from start to finish without a defect being spotted during assembly? In the early days, several defects were found for every machine. After a couple of years of hard work, machines went through with less than a defect per machine— then quality took up. Defects were then counted per 10 dispensers, and in 2010, per 100 dispensers.

Change 3. Attribute Quality Responsibility of Dispenser Models Nominally to Engineers

Engineering was typically swamped with demands from endless sources, from development of new products, to fix-it-now requests from S&S leaders with burning customer issues, to new features required by country managers without which such and such large order could never be closed, and so on. Guelton struggled with the complexity and the variety of demands on engineering, but he progressively created a chief engineer system in which engineers had nominal responsibility for a basket of products. The first request was that they coordinate factory support on "their" product even though this meant working with other specialty engineers—for instance, a mechanical engineer responsible for product A would have to field an electronics problem on his product to his electronics colleague and follow through the problem resolution.

Guelton found himself facing the thorny problem of organizing engineering demand. For some months, he had asked engineers to track their time to try to understand where they devoted their efforts, but that didn't seem to clarify the picture. Taken as a whole, engineering dealt with four fundamental types of requests: (1) product evolution to go to customers with totally new products, (2) new features to enhance existing products, (3) customizations according to specific sales and services demands, and (4) engineering change requests from production to improve assembly quality or simplify the supply chain. No matter which way Guelton cut the problem, he always found himself with an engineering workload greater than the available engineering resource. The time sheet exercise had shown one thing: the urban legend that said that loading engineering over 80 percent meant it simply stopped delivering seemed to be true.

In the end, Guelton simply organized engineering around product leaders. Senior engineers were given responsibility for a product line and had to balance the needs for product renewal, customization options, and production change requests. The dream of radically new products was put aside for the moment, and each was given latitude to make judgment calls. The intractable nature of the priorities problem soon appeared. According to who shouted loudest, what relationships the product leaders had, and which were their specific strengths and weaknesses, engineers made very different choices in terms of which problems they tackled and which they avoided. Contrary to how it sounds, this was not a bad outcome at all. Over time, quality problems were fixed (the production manager and his boss, the site manager, knew how to shout loud enough indeed), features were added or refined, and customization improved. Quality at the test bench improved radically, from finding several defects per dispenser to measuring defects per hundred dispensers. And sales followed.

Change 4. Integrate Purchasing in the Quality Effort

As the picture cleared, it turned out that many quality issues were due to changes at suppliers or miscommunication with suppliers. Purchasing was now asked to join the factory workshops and the factory support work at engineering and to take a far more active role in supplier development. Turning purchasing away from its traditional role of price pressure and understanding the hidden cost of missed deliveries and parts variation were no easy jobs, but compromises were now looked at part by part, according to how sensitive the component was to the quality of the full dispenser.

Change 5. Rebuild Hydraulics from Scratch

Over time Guelton and his engineering manager, Laurent Bordier, could see that through the systematic use of product standards and checklists and A3 problem solving, products were being enhanced as the difficulties that customers experienced with products progressively lessened. Yet, the fundamentals of the product didn't move much, and they were no closer to designing the "new" model that headquarters and sales and service outfits had demanded. By observing and discussing the dispenser's design architecture, they came to see the machine as, essentially, a meter (so that the gas station knows how much fuel you've helped yourself to) and a pump (to deliver the fuel at a good rate through the pipes and hose).

This may sound obvious, but when you're drowning in the million small issues customers complain about, the elephant in the room is not always easy to see. And elephant there was: Guelton and his engineering manager realized that the core hydraulics competency that was needed to address the product's core functionality had eroded to almost nothing in the due course of normal attrition, as well as the company's changing hands and its reorganizations. They had found a core problem, a hole in their core competencies that they needed to face. They then embarked on a project to rehire and retrain hydraulics specialists in order to radically improve the performance of the meter.

Over the years, due to retirements and various changes, and under continuous pressure to cut costs, the number of world-class hydraulics engineers in the company had been reduced to one, and then even he started working part time. Yet, this was typically a situation no one in the corporate management team was willing to face. Guelton progressively came to grips with the issue that if good dispensers were the fruits of his organization, the roots were withering, and something had to be done about it.

In the end he challenged the CEO on the issue, and in a series of very fraught discussions he succeeded in getting the CEO to sign off on the budget to reconstitute a hydraulics department, which meant finding and hiring hydraulics experts—in short supply on the job market. This new hydraulics team started working on improving the machine's meter—a fundamental function for the dispenser as it measured the fuel sold to car drivers. The hydraulics team eventually created a superior meter that gave visible competitive advantage to the company and boosted sales, but it took much longer than expected as problems resisted resolutions and Guelton had to hold firm while being constantly under attack for "not delivering."

Sales results followed the quality improvement, first with fixing quality issues and then with the impetus of performance improvement of the new "no-drift" meter introduced in 2010 (Figure 8.3). And yet, the company's leadership kept attributing results to the sales structure and continuously demanding cost cuts in engineering, to which Guelton had to resist steadfastly time and time again. Learning by doing is messy.

By 2008, unit sales had increased 60 percent from their nadir in 2002, but the company was about to be hit badly by the 2009 Great Recession. For all the progress on fixing quality concerns, no "new" product came out of engineering to "save" the company. Having reached retirement age, Guelton continued to help as a sensei to his successor and the engineering manager as the three of them launched the new meter. This new meter was recognized as a superior no-drift meter (*drift* refers to the increasing quantities of fuel that meters miss as they age) by the market, and sales soared. By 2012 when Guelton stopped working with the business unit, sales had grown a further 30 percent compared to 2008. In typical Lean fashion, most of this growth had been absorbed by the Scottish factory without expansion. From 2009 to 2012, productivity increased 25 percent as work content fell by some 30 percent. Sales were up, productivity increased, capital use was increased, and structural products costs went down—a classic Lean outcome (Figure 8.4).

On the one hand, the product leaders had continued working hard at solving issues and adding features or local options one by one, while sticking to the 4 percent yearly selling price reduction goal. It was a messy,

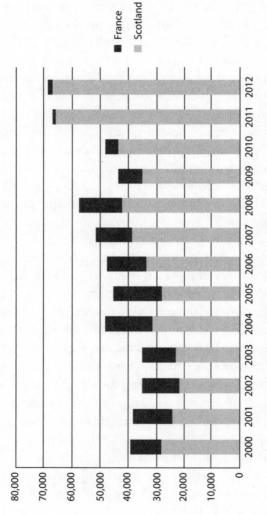

Figure 8.3 Sales Improvement That Followed Quality Improvement and the No-Drift Meter

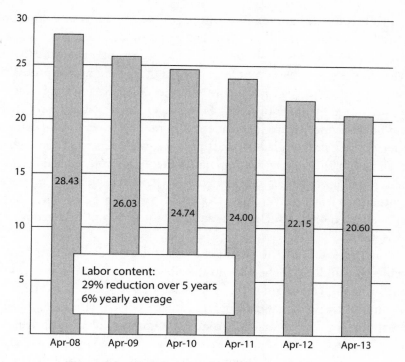

Figure 8.4 Work Contents: Labor Hours per Product

sometimes fraught process, but product value increased steadily. The new head of the reformed hydraulics department had come up with a better meter, and he was now ready to tackle the pump. Both the core functionalities of the product (measure and distribution) and the multitude of causes for friction from the customer were being addressed by the product leaders' intense collaboration with the functional specialty heads. It wasn't pretty project management, but it worked. The product evolved at several levels:

1. Model renewal, regularly set by the rhythm of the main trade show, by adding or changing features

2. Ongoing solving of quality issues

3. Spot customization to respond to specific customers' demands

4. Deep technological changes as and when offline innovations were fully developed and tested to entrust to customer products

Product leaders and engineering teams were, as a result, constantly focused on solving specific problems, on a one-by-one basis, and they were solving them in terms of physical performance or manufacturability, not just solving them on the computer screen. In the meantime, the production manager in the Scottish plant continued to doggedly improve flow and support kaizen by operator teams. Step by step, the collaboration between shop floor engineers, product leaders, and functional engineers delivered better products assembled on existing lines, with existing supply chains (when possible). The formal problem solving on joint issues led these different populations to get to know and understand each other better, and eventually to learn to truly work together. Additional customer benefits were delivered on a reducing cost basis, by squeezing the waste out of the entire system.

Engineers dedicated to product types and the collaboration between engineering and production led to the slow resolution of another intractable problem: creating flow lines for each of the products in the range. The unpredictable demand swings and huge work content variation from one option to the next made it completely impractical to have dedicated product lines—all dispensers were originally assembled by specialized area in the manufacturing hall. Progressively, nonetheless, as the link between options and work content was better understood, one flow line was created, and then another, until the plant identified value streams according to the products in the range. The next step would be then mixing products again in order to level the load on the line.

There is no end to the Lean journey because the aim of practicing Lean on the shop floor is not to get to Lean but to continue to learn how to further Lean the business. Lean thinking is about learning to take executive decisions to spur kaizen. Kaizen leads to improving the performance of technical processes by improving flow and right-first-time. Higher-performing technical processes both lower the total cost base of the enterprise and offer new opportunities for engineers to improve the products or services. In doing so, we can close the loop and pass on these value improvements to customers by enriching products and services. In turn, better value for money creates customer loyalty, which improves profitability.

This Lean engine is powerful, but it doesn't work on its own, and it requires constant management energy to keep it going. The magic lies in changing posture from telling others what they should do to improve to exploring with them what they think improving means in their own situation. Doing so effectively demands that managers learn how to steer this people-centric mechanism by managing individual (and then collective) learning curves.

CHAPTER 9

From Kaizen to Innovation

Solve current problems better with new solutions by managing learning curves through continuous, repeated kaizen.

How can small-step technical improvements lead to large-step technological breakthroughs? In fact, the question might be asked the other way around: how can breakthroughs not be the result of step-by-step progress? A common mindset among managers is that improvement to legacy technologies reinforces attachment to them and that true innovations emerge out of nowhere. They don't. Innovations are the result of individual competencies that progressively add up to organizational capabilities. Without capabilities, innovative ideas are only so much wishful thinking.

As Jacques discovered when he asked his engineering team to come up with a breakthrough product, making things is the result of a mesh of engineering knowledge and manufacturing know-how. Too big a leap, and reality fights back. Too small a leap, and engineers simply fiddle with technologies they're familiar with, seeking incremental change through new applications of their existing knowledge rather than tackling new, unfamiliar tech. Experiments come in two forms:

- *Assimilation:* Putting new information into the context of what is already known to extend the domain of what we know

- *Accommodation:* Changing the assumptions underlying what we know (or think we know) in order to accommodate the new information

Accommodating new technologies requires resilience—trying again and again until the new idea works. Conversely, attachment to legacy technologies is the result of abandoning experiments at the first setbacks. Kodak did not abandon the pursuit of digital technology because it didn't know how to make it work. It resisted crossing the chasm because management didn't want to invest time and effort in creating an internal competitor to the profitable film technology. It failed to tackle the most important challenge for any organization: make yourself obsolete instead of having someone else do it for you.

The current dominant narrative about innovation is *disruption and diffusion*: some genius has a brand-new idea, and with her friends in their garage, she proves it can work with a subpar product that succeeds in demonstrating the full potential of the new technology, which then attracts funding for a commercially viable version, which then takes markets by storm and then spreads even further as people learn to integrate the new appliance in their lives and coordinate its use with the other apps they're already working with, and so on. Disruption is seen as the sudden apparition of something new—the iconic moment when Steve Jobs unveiled the iPhone (no longer a phone, but a personal computer that also takes phone calls). Diffusion is supposed to spread along the "Gartner curve" of hype, as early adopters rave about the new gizmo, then expectations crash from the peak of irrational exuberance. Next we see slow progress out of the trough of disillusionment as mainstream users start adopting the now perfected product up the slope of enlightenment toward the plateau of productivity.

As the inventors of the theory of disruptive innovation themselves explain, this just-so story largely misses the point of disruption, which is the learning curve. Disruption is a process, not an event.[1]

No technology is born disruptive—it becomes so as its supporters learn to (1) improve the performance until it can compete viably with existing alternatives on the market and (2) figure out the new business model that makes the new technology attractive to customers and producers from a business point of view, not just because of the cool tech. The reality of innovation is that it is always built on slow, resilient, and gritty learning.

The traditional define → decide → drive → deal mental model largely accounts for seeing disruption as an event. In this way of thinking, the great leader steering the ship of the company defines the "innovation gaps" in his company (or has consultants do it for him), decides what to invest in, drives the innovation project until new products or services emerge, and then deals with the market reception, which is, statistically, overwhelmingly indifferent. For instance, a recent study of about 9,000 new products that achieved broad distribution at a U.S. retailer has shown that as little as 40 percent of them were still sold three years later.[2] The scope of the waste is staggering. Thinking innovation through the find → face → frame → form framework gets us to a very different vision of innovation.

First, we do not look for "innovation gaps" to fill but, rather, for customer problems to solve. When Toyota started developing hybrid technology in earnest, the technology itself was in fact well known in the industry, and it had been dismissed by most as unmarketable. Interestingly enough, the Toyota creators of the first Prius also believed the car would not sell, but they felt this was a problem they had to solve. Toyota had announced its Earth Charter in 1992, outlining goals to develop and market vehicles with the lowest emissions possible, and engineers had to face that challenge and deliver . . . something.

Second, we do not expect that the project—no matter how large or well funded—will deliver innovation by itself. Instead, we learn to frame the problem as a matter of alternatives. Toyota's exploration of the low-emission challenge included the hydrogen engine (now commercialized in the Mirai) and the fully electric car (they tried with the Rav4 in a joint venture with Tesla and pulled back from it), as well as hybrid, biofuel, and natural gas (Figure 9.1).

	Electricity EV	Hydrogen CV	Biofuel Internal Combustion Engine	Natural Gas Internal Combustion Engine
Well-to-wheel CO_1	Poor to excellent	Poor to excellent	Poor to excellent	Good
Supply volume	Excellent	Excellent	Poor	Good
Cruising range	Poor	Excellent	Excellent	Good
Fueling/charging time	Poor	Excellent	Excellent	Excellent
Dedicated infrastructure	Good	Poor	Excellent	Good

Figure 9.1 Characteristics of Alternative Fuels

Third, we understand that true innovation will emerge from forming solutions both with engineers and customers as we learn together to make it work, and we also understand that management's work is to somehow steer and support this learning curve. Legend has it that during the first presentation of the Prius to journalists, system engineers were in the back of the car keeping the software running. Managing a learning curve means realizing that not all problems are "closed" and not all problems have solutions—some remain "open": we don't know whether they have a solution or not. Only by crafting different ways of looking at the issues with others can we find a way through an open-problem landscape and learn cycle after cycle (Figure 9.2).

Each new cycle should deliver increased performance. It's never easy because at first, having to learn something from scratch, we struggle as we have to invest in the basics and the fundamentals. Then there's a fast improvement period, which is quite exhilarating, and finally a long, drawn-out stretch when every small gain in performance is achieved by many, many repeated cycles. This is the "mastery" part of the curve that distinguishes Olympic athletes from weekend joggers. This is where making the product truly fit to market is vital, and it requires grit and single-mindedness. Moving up this learning curve is as much a technical

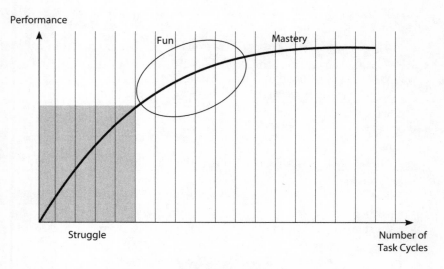

Figure 9.2　A Different Way to Look at Issues

issue (discovering new technical insights with every repeated cycle) as it is a human, motivational one (keep at it until breakthrough). Innovation doesn't happen ex nihilo. It's the result of work. Great discoveries might happen by accident, but they happen to those who look at their topic every day over decades.

The Lean theory of innovation is therefore fundamentally different from the superficial "disruption" narrative. The Lean starting point is the intent to solve a problem that customers have now, rather than looking for new things that a new technology could do for them. Once we've found a key problem we could solve better, the second step is to face the fact that we really need to do so and that none of the available technological alternatives allow us to do so. Incrementally using our legacy know-how will simply not get us to solve this problem in a reasonable time frame. Having faced the imperative to solve the problem with new ideas, we then frame the issue in terms of credible alternative starting points to crack the problem.

In reusable learning terms, we work with (1) a starting point and (2) a clear direction for improvement (product performance, quality, and cost). What then remains is to manage the small-step-by-small-step advances of the learning curve. At this stage, of course, proficiency with kaizen becomes a core organizational capability because engineers are familiar with the small-step approach and know how to form solutions progressively—and learn.

 Moving from kaizen to innovation means managing the learning curve. A learning curve is the representation of the relationship of experience to learning. Cumulative experience can either lead to steep learning or to no learning at all if the learners are convinced that each new experience only proves what they already know. The challenge is to lead incremental learning to breakthrough learning. The Lean leader manages the learning curve that links the kaizen to the product and process innovation change process on a point-by-point basis (Table 9.1).

 The core issue of innovation is, indeed, not just creativity but also having the capability to deliver on better quality and lower cost. The goal is not a gadget that does something cool but, rather, one that solves a problem for customers as effectively and efficiently as can be. Customers have different levels of tolerances for solutions. Some, the "early adopters," actually like new things simply because they're new, and they are quite willing to forgive

Gemba Kaizen	Technical Learning	Process Improvement	Product Improvement
Change point	Change point	Change point	Change point

Table 9.1   Managing the Learning Curve on a Point-by-Point Basis

quality and cost issues for the privilege of playing with something ahead of anyone else. Others, at the opposite end of the spectrum, will not switch from their current preferred way of solving their problem until the alternative is clearly superior both cost and quality-wise. From a new product development perspective, this means one needs to harness the initiative of the former to make the product evolve in order to satisfy the latter.

From a customer value perspective, an innovative product or service will do the following:

1. Help customers do better something they want to get done

2. In a way that hasn't been done before and is

3. Pleasing to use and cost-effective

4. And ultimately benefits society

Failing that, even the best ideas do not succeed as products (think of the Segway). Innovation is a hard taskmaster because it requires a deep understanding of customers' lifestyles and an equally deep understanding of technological evolutions and possibilities, as well as the production capability (for example, the sum of individual competencies) to deliver on promises. The problem, of course, is that people who have spent their lives becoming experts in what customers like and in a specific technology tend to have the greatest difficulties in seeing the benefits of an alternative approach. This is why Lean's approach to innovation is essentially about solving current problems better with new solutions and developing these new solutions from continuous, repeated kaizen.

How can this work in a high-tech environment? Proditec, whom we met in Chapter 2, is a specialist company that makes leading-edge machines for visual inspection of pharmaceutical tablets. The company serves a pressing need for its customers: FDA drug recalls due to quality problems have been increasing, and many prescription drugs are now in short supply. Tablet or capsule final inspection is a core challenge for drug manufacturers, and manual inspection is both labor intensive and costly. Proditec designs and sells machines that take a snapshot of the tablets as they stand on a fast-moving conveyor, analyzes this image, and ejects non-conforming tablets. This is demanding in terms of mechanics (control of the tablets' trajectory), vision (snapshots of small, fast-moving objects), and software ("seeing" the defects).

Although his sales were growing at a healthy pace after surviving the shock of the financial markets' drastic decline in 2009, Riboulet came to three sobering realizations after working at cleaning the window with his sensei. First, sales were continuing largely because approved projects that were put on hold just after the financial meltdown were now being concluded; this was occurring because much tighter investment controls were now being put in place in major pharmaceutical companies, which would make sales of capital-heavy machines much harder. Second, Riboulet saw that he had fewer and fewer repeat sales. He was indeed selling more machines, but never to the same customer. The company rationalized this by arguing that one such machine filled the need for inspection per site, but the CEO didn't buy this. Seeing the inspection needs at his customers' sites, he wondered why they did not purchase more machines, considering the potential gains. Third, new competitive entrants in Eastern Europe were catching up on the technological level of the current machines. Riboulet slowly grasped that while the company had been busy with developing special features to respond to customer demand, it was now lagging on core technology evolutions.

After an eye-opening study trip to Toyota in Japan, Riboulet continued to work with his sensei and progressively saw how his take-charge, define → decide → drive → deal leadership approach had led him to sponsor a sequence of patches to respond to customer problems with no overall vision of the impact on the product architecture and, unwittingly, generating a product drift (the product equivalent of "mission drift") that was progressively increasing the competitive gap with the field's leading competitors.

Day-to-day problem solving with his technical teams "cleaned the window," which gradually revealed key strategic challenges for Riboulet and his team to face:

1. *Quality challenge:* Products had too many stability issues in the field, which hampered customers in their use of the machines. By continuously customizing products for one customer or another, as well as fixing spot issues, without more clarity on the machine's modular architecture, engineering was creating a connectivity mess that needed to be sorted out to increase quality.

2. *Performance challenge:* Products had lost ground on key capabilities that required new technology developments to regain leadership over competitors, particularly new entrants, and to have something extra to propose to existing customers.

As these issues became clearer, the CEO realized that this would mean managing the learning curve of his technical department heads to keep them from falling back on trying to solve new problems with the old technologies they knew, as they had done all too often in the past. They would actually need to learn new tricks. After several years of experience with shop floor kaizen and point-by-point change, Riboulet began to see how this could apply equally well to his tech problems.

A key problem in managing learning curves in a tech environment is that you never know beforehand exactly where the solution is going to come from or what shape it will take. In fact, many disaster stories are born from motivated reasoning: getting fixated on a solution and building the argument for it regardless of the facts, which considerably slows down the learning process. Solving problems is not a matter of catching up and applying what others are doing but, rather, of exploration, testing, and mastering. Riboulet saw that he needed to manage a point-by-point learning curve for his vision head, software head, and human interface head.

The standard way to spot defective tablets was to use a low-angle ring light with neon tubes to create a shadow on the tablet surface. Cameras would detect the engraving edges, and the software would analyze them. This approach required about six hours of setting time at expert level for every new tablet inspected before every production run, and smaller defects were not always detected. To get his engineers to learn, Riboulet focused them on reducing the obvious waste to customers: the setting time (why do we impose this on customers?). No one knew how to do this, but each team head now had a clear target that implied teamwork across their specialties, as shown in Table 9.2.

Head of Vision Team	Head of Software Team	Head of Human Interface Team
Target: Stabilize lighting to maintain detection performance over time.	Target: Improve detection performances.	Target: Improve ease of use.
Point-by-point learning: • Target references for the light: adjust camera sensitivity in real time to compensate for changes in light variation. • Remove light variations in moving from neon tubes to LED lights with higher stability and duration life.	Point-by-point learning: • Instead of analyzing each tablet independently, learn a standard engraving image and store it. During the sorting phase, every tablet engraving is compared to the standard image. • Double the number of processing boards to get the right processing power, and explore the market for cheaper, more reliable boards.	Point-by-point learning: • Use the remaining processing power (from the processing board change) to reduce the number of parameters by a third for a more user-friendly setting.

Table 9.2 Innovation Targets for Inspecting the Tablets

The resulting efforts were a reduction in setting time by 60 percent and a far more reliable machine. However, small defects were still going undetected, and although many components have been challenged, the technology was so far essentially the same—improvement, but not innovation.

However, as a result of this work, Riboulet's technical teams better understood what was expected of them and how the company's capability for innovation rested on their own individual competence and the drive to continue to climb these learning curves. The next step proved quite stunning, as can be seen in Table 9.3.

The resulting machines could be set in a matter of minutes rather than hours, by a novice rather than an expert, which resulted in a huge performance gain for customers. Very small defects could now be detected—another bonus for customers. Quality improved as the robustness of the machine progressed because the teams working together learned to better understand the cross-impact of the functional elements through a clearer architecture and interface mastery.

Managing a learning curve means producing *knowledge* step by step. The natural tendency of all engineers is to solve their problem completely by adjusting all known variables. Engineers grasp complex problems by

Head of Vision Team	Head of Software Team	Head of Human Interface Team
Target: Stabilize lighting to maintain detection performance over time.	Target: Improve detection performances.	Target: Improve ease of use.
Point-by-point learning: • Target references for the light: adjust camera sensitivity in real time to compensate for changes in light variation. • Remove light variations in moving from neon tubes to LED lights with higher stability and duration life.	Point-by-point learning: • Instead of analyzing each tablet independently, learn a standard engraving image and store it. During the sorting phase, every tablet engraving is compared to the standard image. • Double the number of processing boards to get the right processing power, and explore the market for cheaper, more reliable boards.	Point-by-point learning: • Use the remaining processing power (from the processing board change) to reduce the number of parameters by a third for a more user-friendly setting.
• Replace camera by laser to get real 3D image coming from real surface height variation on the tablet surface—no longer rely on shadow images.	• Simplify the detection algorithms by using state-of-the-art shape engraving analysis.	• Continue to reduce the number of parameters by 80%.
Innovation: Use of Blu-ray laser 3D imaging	Innovation: Use of open source processing boards in an industrial environment	Innovation: Google-style flat design for the human interface

Table 9.3   Performance Gains Achieved for Inspecting the Tablets

one specific aspect, much as one lifts large objects by grasping their handle, and they then fix this aspect of the problem by moving the handle from the existing state to the desired state, often adjusting all other variables to the one they use as a handle. This approach, Riboulet discovered the hard way, is both dangerous (they'll find something for sure, but how likely is it to work in the real world) and unstable (because interfaces with other departments are not secured). By imposing a discipline of point-by-point change instead, the CEO led his engineers from their current knowledge state to the next proximal zone (Figure 9.3).

Without any method of capability development, innovation is no more than wishful thinking. And capability is ultimately no less than the sum

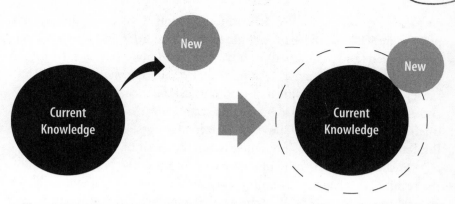

Figure 9.3 Moving from the Current Knowledge State to the Next Proximal Zone

of individual competencies. The secret to capability development lies in producing knowledge as well as work: fixing the problems is only half the job. Explaining the fix (and how and where it applies) gets the full points. Reusable learning is a process of moving from one state of knowledge to the next, knowledge that can be passed on from one person to the next, from one situation to the next. To be reusable, fixes and new learning must apply in a variety of conditions, not a single context-specific case. In the terminology of A3 problem solving, the problem is not resolved until the causal model is both clarified and validated.

As Riboulet discovered, helping people move up on their learning curve meant asking them to solve the same problem repeatedly in differing conditions. For instance, using open source processing boards was definitely new know-how for a company that had traditionally designed customized boards. This capability, however, did not arise from the first attempt. Only after multiple tries of solving the same problem again and again with slightly varying conditions did the engineers truly learn about open source boards and how to handle them—a know-how they can now reapply and pass on to other engineers. The rule of thumb is that a (large-scale) problem has to be solved 5 consecutive times simply to understand the problem and 10 to fully grasp the countermeasure.

The idea is not to learn how to solve one specific problem by changing everything, but, on the contrary, how to repeatedly learn to change one thing until knowledge is acquired—and then to understand how this can affect other elements of the system so that, typically, product and process co-evolve and deliver full-blown innovation. This vision of the creative process radically changes how engineers are managed and how products are designed (and redesigned). Innovation is no longer seen as an ex nihilo phenomenon that happens when we're lucky (and not when we're not) but, rather, as the result of giving a direction by asking the right questions (why should customers spend so much time setting our machines before a production run?) and driving repeated kaizen attempts, leaving room for the limited chaos—but chaos nonetheless—of the learning to learn.

Innovation is not some blue-sky wishful thinking. Nor is innovation the result of motivated thinking and command-and-control management. Innovation is a process of learning that emerges from the day-to-day improvement of technical know-how. Real innovation is about finding new ways to solve existing problems. Complex problems are rarely easy to solve, and the solution mostly involves both new techniques and new business models or social behaviors: the convergence of technical and social change *is* the innovation—it's a process. On the technical front, this process is sustained by companies that acquire new capabilities (the organizational ability to do stuff). These capabilities are built on individual competencies. As a fruit on a branch, a successful innovative product is the result of a mesh of new capabilities, themselves rooted in individual learning. Kaizen, step-by-step improvement, trains people to both learn and to sustain the energy of improvement. From a Lean perspective, kaizen is the fuel of the innovation process, with new products as its outputs.

Riboulet didn't solve his innovation problems by defining what his biggest innovation gaps were, pulling his best engineers into a Skunk Works room, getting them to design new solutions, and implementing them. He'd actually been doing this all along, and the complexity costs induced by this approach were crippling the company. On the contrary, he learned to focus on real, immediate, concrete customer issues to clear the window, then get his technical guys to face their greatest weak points in the day-to-day of their jobs, frame with them what kinds of solutions they sought to bring the products (and the company) forward, and then craft solutions step by step by managing the learning curve.

You can't organize for innovation—although you can definitely organize to stop innovation. Innovation comes out of the new ideas and new experiments people think of. It has to be a cognitive revolution to increase the flow of ideas and point toward the North Star to give a clear direction on the kinds of challenges we're trying to solve and the sorts of solutions we are seeking. Managing individual learning curves rather than controlling adherence to process is the true revolution. This is where Lean gets really exciting. And, as smart people get on board, fun as well. Moving ahead together is the greatest motivator.

CHAPTER 10

Change Your Mind

Create meaningful work by looking at the relationship between people and their work, and their work and customers' usage.

Progress is indeed the best motivation. In the unavoidable mix of daily successes and setbacks, feeling that you are making steps toward a meaningful goal keeps you going. By meaningful, we mean something that makes sense to you as an individual and as a person involved in a collective effort: having the opportunity to do what you do best every day, to make a larger impact. Meaningful work is its own reward. On the other hand, Taylorist bureaucracies managed by the numbers make work meaningless by taking people for granted, throwing endless frustrating obstacles in the way of doing good work, forcing people to override their personal better professional judgment for the sake of the system, and ultimately, disconnecting employees from their values and their supportive relationships.[1]

Lean thinking creates meaning by linking individual and team-level kaizen with the strategic challenges of the business as a whole. Doing so, however, requires a deep mental managerial shift in the way we *think* about jobs, in terms of how we look at people and work, and how we look at companies and markets.

Jacques had always prided himself in being a progressive boss. He was convinced that if employees felt good in their lives, they would feel good at work, so he had pioneered every new legal opportunity for more flexible time and more cooperative arrangements. And yet, throughout his 30 years' tenure as CEO, he was frequently surprised and frustrated to see that, overall, labor relations were not significantly better in his company than in so many others.

As he began practicing gemba walks to visit every workplace in the business systematically, he saw that employees were often left to deal with many unresolved issues such as hard work or unreliable equipment. He also saw that some of his middle managers who seemed fine in management meetings were disliked by their staff. He discovered that some of the individuals who were not perceived by the directors as having high potential were in fact highly respected by their teams. Finally, he realized that some of the flexibility practices he had championed had a deleterious impact on teamwork. For instance, operators could choose the time they started the day and the time they finished as long as they did the required daily hours. As a result some individuals would come in very early to finish early, and others would arrive after driving the kids to school and finish late. When Fiancette installed the pull system, it became apparent that teams were productive only when everyone was there together (no surprise), but Jacques also saw that the late people would blame the early people when something went wrong and vice versa.

Over time, he came to understand that his policy of adapting the company to individual schedules had the opposite effect to what he'd expected. He was not making employees more committed or loyal to their jobs. Instead, he was encouraging them to feel that their important life started after the job. As he started to see the results of kaizen efforts every week with his COO, he noticed a change: people were getting increasingly involved in their work and in achieving the production plans. They cared more. They were proud and pleased to show off the improvements they had made on their own with help from maintenance. So many managerial issues were revealed that Jacques and Fiancette had to make real changes, starting with a plan to improve the management skills of their frontline managers. Jacques had stumbled on the real secret to Lean thinking. Lean thinking is not about studying the work, nor is it about studying the people. It's about understanding the *relationship people have with their own work and management's* role in developing it.

Lean's promise is that aligning individual success and company success makes for a better-performing business model. By supporting individual employees in writing their own story and in helping you with your overall objectives for the business, you can change the story of the business and, by putting pressure on your competitors, the story of the industry as a whole. Becoming a market leader through challenging yourself (and forcing your competitors to catch up) is the key to sustainable and profitable growth, even in times of heightened disruption. Lean thinking is a structured method to learn how to do this.

Yet, considering the vast number of companies that have adopted Lean in some shape or form, a shocking few truly realize its promise. "Lack of leadership commitment" is the usual suspect, but to be honest, from the examples we have seen firsthand, leaders are committed and supportive of their Lean programs—but that isn't enough to make these programs succeed beyond the early days of gathering low-hanging fruit. As we look at the leaders who have indeed succeeded with Lean and stuck with it over decades, we are struck to see that they all share one thing in common: they have changed how they look at work.

Lean thinking doesn't focus exclusively on the study of work (Taylorism), nor on the study of people (as with motivation programs), nor indeed the study of financial management. Instead, Lean thinking focuses on looking specifically at the *relationship* employees have with their work. How do employees understand their work? Its purpose? How do they feel about it? How do they cope with problems that appear? How well do they collaborate with their colleagues? This is hard. As we look at any work situation, we have been trained to look at one of these:

- *The process:* For example, how well does it flow, where are the obstacles, and what is its cost?

- *The people:* For example, what is their attitude, are they competent, are they motivated, how experienced are they, and what are their personality traits?

But we rarely look at how the people think and feel about the job—the invisible cartoon bubble on the top of their heads that explains what they're going to do next.

This outlook shift is the secret to grasping Lean thinking. People are not machines. They are autonomous thinking, deciding, acting beings influenced by their emotional states and the context they find themselves in. At their best, people can achieve incredible things, be meticulous, helpful, supportive, dedicated, and creative—and fun to work with. At their worst, passive aggression and learned helplessness can drain the energy out of any work situation and screw up any task. The way they work is not set.

Lean tradition distinguishes true potential (what a person could achieve if always at her best) from normal performance (what really happens over the course of a day, week, or month). Lean thinking also understands that, as with an athlete, no one can improve this performance other than the person herself. You can't fix people. You can help them better understand what is happening to them, learn problem-solving strategies better, and become more resilient and mindful when coping with successes and setbacks. However, you can't do their thinking and learning for them.

That's why it's important to see how the traditional Lean tools are all about giving employees the *cognitive* skills to see their own work differently (Table 10.1).

Similarly, the "problems first" basic attitude to management is the key to change how people approach problems. Problems are the base material with which we build employees' relationship with their work. They represent a healthy challenge to respond productively to the reality of what we are doing. Human attention is, by nature, subject to habituation: after repeated experiences of the same situation, we stop paying attention, stop responding to any stimulus, and act out of habit. This is a natural form of learning that frees our minds to do something else, but it also leads to mindless reactions when the situation is not quite what we expect. Even when the problems are critically important, they have become so routine we act as if we no longer care.

Lean Tool	To Discover
Seven wastes	All the various unnecessary activities in getting the job done, such as correcting defects, producing work ahead of need, moving around, transporting parts, overworking them, storing them, or waiting for work
Standardized work	How work is performed compared to an ideal sequence to spot where actual work differs to what we know is the current best way to work
4Ms	Analyzing gaps in real work in comparison to standardized work by looking at how machines perform, how well we're trained to handle the work, how good are the materials (and information), and how effective is the current method to do the work
5Ss	How is the workplace set up to be able to follow the standardized work sequence easily, and what can hinder this: stuff out of place, tools put in the wrong place or not well maintained, or no routine to clean up the workplace after use
Single-piece flow	Focus on making jobs one by one to see the difficulties pertaining to this specific job rather than thinking generically in terms of a full batch
Spaghetti diagram	The complete path of assembly work (whether a product or a file through different departments) from station to station
Five "whys?"	The interplay of sequential causes that create a problem

Table 10.1 Giving Employees the Cognitive Skills to See Their Own Work Differently

Problems are unpleasant simply because they break the habit—something has changed, and the habitual reaction is either interrupted, or it doesn't lead to the planned result. Since this is a habit, an unconscious action, this obstacle leads to frustration and another attempt, with more attention, to getting around the barrier. On the other hand, another strong driver of human attention is curiosity. The mind is constantly, randomly inquisitive. Attention wanders because we're thinking of something else, exploring, whether in fancy or in fact. The trick to mindful work is to focus curiosity on the problems experienced with work. Problems are our basic material to form new ways of doing things—as well as new things to do.

Creating a work environment where problems are the building blocks of deeper learning and superior performance requires strong leadership. Separating work from people leads us to attribute problems to one of these causes:

- *Broken processes:* There's something wrong in the way the system works, which explains the problem as a logical result of how things are set up.

- *Careless people:* Incompetent employees are not doing their job or can't give five minutes' thought to the fact that the situation has presented a problem.

Both of those situations can occur, but in our experience, they do so very rarely. In general, things work OK. Problems pop up mostly because something in the environment has changed and neither the process nor the person are set up to deal with this specific case. By understanding that work processes are nothing more than what people do, and by looking at how employees relate to their work, problems appear in a different light. Typically, employees have been misled by their work environment in reacting habitually to a situation that merited a different response—one that too-rigid processes (made worse by computer systems) will not let them seek.

On the other hand, if people are encouraged to solve their own problems right now by their management and are given the opportunity to change their work processes with their colleagues, they will grow more attached to their jobs. The very act of caring for their work environment will deepen their relationship to their work, as well as their understanding of it.

In that sense, kaizen is Lean thinking's main object of study. Kaizen is where the relationship that people have with their work becomes clear and where you, as a manager, can most influence it by your own attitude (Table 10.2).

Step	Reasoning	Employees	Managers
Visual management to make intuitively clear what is versus what should be	Find	Notice the problem as opposed to letting habitual thinking ignore it	Challenge both the degree of visualization and why things are out of standard
Opportunity to improve performance	Face	Choose one aspect of the job to explore how to improve their performance	Ask: why this one? Clarify the line of sight between this aspect of performance and the business overall goals
Study current work method	Frame	Pick an analysis method to support the curiosity of delving into the details of how things really work versus how we think they work	Ask: why this analysis tool? Clarify the overall way to look at this problem and deepen the search for root cause
Come up with new ideas	Form	Loosen the grip of habit and think creatively about different ways of doing the job and dealing with the gaps seen in the analysis	Are as interested in ideas that don't work as in those that do—a failed experiment can hide the correct intuition and new thinking—keep them trying
Propose a plan for testing and approval	Form	Test ideas in practice and work with colleagues to get their input and commitment	Ask: have you checked with so-and-so? Facilitate meetings with either experts or key people to convince
Implement and measure the impact	Form	Make the changes in the work processes, with the team and support if needed, and check the impact	Are interested in the implementation process and its results, support it when necessary, and think of what other problems this reveals
Evaluate the new method	Form to find again . . .	Distinguish what has worked (and will be kept) and what hasn't and needs more work and make recommendations for procedure change	Support the procedure change, think of other problems that need to be solved for this change to stick, and consider other places where the same learning would apply

Table 10.2 Using Kaizen to Reveal the Relationship Employees Have with Their Work

This change in focus has profound, transformational consequences for the role of management. Traditionally, managers are supposed to handle the *work*, by organizing the activities of their departments and coming up with action plans, which come down to solving problems on paper and then breaking down the solution into components for subordinates to execute. Then they're supposed to manage *people*, which essentially comes down to motivating (inspiring, supporting, rewarding) and disciplining (controlling, evaluating, punishing) each person under their authority. People are merely instrumental tools to execute plans rather than dynamic pieces of the system.

Changing the focus of management to seeing how people think about their work and deepening their relationship with their job redefines the role to quite an extent:

- *Is the work environment conductive to doing good work?* Or is the friction of day-to-day obstacles to getting the job done such that people give up on doing the best they can?

- *Are teams stable and supportive?* Do people look forward to seeing their coworkers in the morning, and do they feel they can be themselves, drop the "company face," and discuss issues and take initiatives with their colleagues without risk of blame or criticism?

- *Is there a clear line of sight to the greater purpose and overall plan?* Beyond giving meaning to the job, a clear understanding of desired outcomes (as opposed to immediate output) enables autonomous decision-making, initiatives in unexpected conditions, and creative thinking for improvement that contributes to the overall result.

- *Can they learn and progress while doing their daily job?* Do people find opportunities to practice the skills they're interested in or new skills they want to acquire in an environment that recognizes their effort and hard work and tutors them into deepening their own mastery of their job?

- *Do leaders learn from local improvements?* And do they demonstrate to all how their efforts contribute to the common good? Is their contribution and effort recognized and fairly rewarded?

In practical terms, this change in focus requires "a plan per person": a diagnostic of where each person stands regarding her role, which areas she handles autonomously, and which is the next proximal area to develop, coupled with an assignment for her of a problem that will allow her to express her strengths while stretching her sense of responsibility (without breaking her by expecting too large a step). This kind of leadership is deeply respectful of people. It makes the best efforts to listen to everyone's point of view, develops everyone to the fullest of their natural abilities, and seeks opportunities, within day-to-day work, to experience the fun of creating new ways and of contributing to the improvement of the team and the company. Like coaching a sports team, the individual development of each athlete as well as the cohesion of the team are keys to success.

More radically, such an approach means changing one's decision-making pattern from optimizing the situation on paper and then staffing people as tools to "make it so," to making decisions that put individuals in the position of solving problems on their own—and supporting them in their learning experience (sometimes easy, sometimes a struggle). The key basis for a decision becomes whether it creates space for learning for a member of a team, or a team as a whole, as opposed to solving the problem oneself and using people to make the solution work.

To make this so, the Lean leader must in fact embrace the sense of loss of personal control. This shift is probably one of the most demanding changes in management practice involved in Lean thinking—which is why Lean managers so often ask questions and so seldom give answers. The Lean learning system, however, gives managers a concrete, methodical, and practical way to learn how to change their focus from command and control to instruct and improve. The four most important words in the Lean manager's vocabulary are, "What do you think?"

At the highest strategic level, the same deep perspective shift is also needed: from looking at markets and technologies with a static strategic mindset of constantly creating and then optimizing monopolies and monetizing resources to focusing on the *relationship with customers*. Businesses in the twentieth century were designed to *extract* value from their customers. The goal was to make money. The means were exploitations: hard selling to customers, hard productivity off workers' backs, hard cost pressures on suppliers. Markets were there to be conquered. Money was the single measure—everything could be expressed in terms of sales growth, standard costs, and profitability. Succeeding at this game meant protecting one's innovation and creating rigid processes to roll it out across the world in true Coca-Cola or McDonald's fashion. Leaders were supposed to find "cash cow" products that they could concentrate their resources on and convince new customers they really needed at the price most profitable to the company. As customers' incomes grew, so did their needs—there was always some new appliance or luxury to buy.

Successful businesses of the twenty-first century will be designed to *add* value to their customers. Things have changed. Consumers in developed countries already have everything, and their income is not growing. New markets, to which many companies have fled to find fresh growth opportunities, such as the Far East, are fast getting saturated as well. Customers must now be persuaded to replace existing products and services, not equip themselves with them. Switching costs are always lower.

Information is plentiful. Customers now need to be convinced to stay with the company's product or services. Extraction is no longer sustainable. Growth, in the new century, will be sustained by *adding* value to customers' lives, not extracting money from them. The key to success in the new game is to focus on retaining existing customers by constantly renewing the offer and solving problems for them so they can sustain the lifestyle they wish to have. This means greater quality, greater variety, and lower costs every day—the complete opposite of the previous strategies. Customers will renew their mobile phone because their chosen brand offers them a constant flow of apps they find useful—for free. The shoe is on the other foot now: it's a buyer's market, no longer a seller's one.

Lean thinking holds the key to a much deeper transformation than many believe. Toyota has developed organically as a system to deal with change by learning to learn, by focusing on the relationship the company maintains with its customers through the stream of products it offers. Lean is the method to develop this capability in your own business. Lean is not about making your current organization more efficient but fundamentally transforming how managers think—from the traditional define → decide → drive → deal cycle to Lean thinking's find → face → frame → form approach—in order to grow a business designed for constant renewal and change through continuous improvement. We're not looking at an optimization of the current way companies are structured and managed but a full-fledged revolution in management thinking. To understand how deep this transformation is, we need to take a step back and look at the bigger picture.

Our societies are built on a mishmash of technical, organizational, and political changes. For instance, back in the early nineteenth century, steam progressively became the dominant source of power (replacing wind and water) in fast-industrializing nations. In the same period, the division of labor and task specialization described by Adam Smith in a pin factory in 1776 created workshops where workers would perform a small, specialized, part of a job as opposed to one person crafting an entire product, dramatically increasing output. Steam-powered machines could then take over some operations, and the blend of steam power and division of labor made it possible to create centralized factories, drastically reducing the cost of making things, and to create huge consumer markets. As a result of industrialization, urban centers grew exponentially in the first decades of the nineteenth century, and the resulting upheaval brought great political changes and rapid democratization, establishing our current system of liberal democracies and welfare states—incredibly fast change at the societal level, but still relatively slow at the individual level (although one person would have to learn to accommodate one or two large-scale societal shifts within his lifetime).

Technical, organizational, or political breakthroughs do happen quickly in the historical record, but not so subjectively, taking at least a generation or two to become matter of fact.

A well-known organizational improvement was Henry Ford's famous moving assembly line. Work was now brought to workers with a conveyor rather than workers going to work where the product was. Several technical and organizational elements had to come together to make this possible. First, there was widespread availability of electricity. Previously, machines had been steam powered, which meant that they had to be aligned under a line shaft. Electricity-powered machines could be placed along the process. Second, parts had to be standardized so that they could be picked randomly from a container and assembled without the need for a fitter. Third, operator tasks had to be both specialized and standardized to make the work flow according to the conveyor's speed—which was made possible by Frederick Taylor's organizational innovation. Electricity was first used for lighting, and it took decades to retool factories from steam-powered line shafts to electricity-powered machines. It takes a generation . . . We're currently living through another such upheaval. We've all grown up with computers, but so far we've used computers to run companies designed for twentieth-century business. The Internet was invented in 1989, the year the Iron Curtain fell. Companies such as Amazon.com, Apple, or Google were the first to be designed around their web-based search engines. Amazon.com has created a logistics supply chain around its website, Apple's iPhone and iPad are portable platforms for apps, and Google is fitting wheels to its search engine. These technological platform changes come at a time of unprecedented globalization and market saturation. The upshot is that web-based companies are designed to provide ongoing free value to their customers in order to persuade them to repurchase. Whereas twentieth-century companies were designed to push black Ford Ts on every person in the world, twenty-first-century firms are designed for constant renewal to remain attractive to customers who can be tempted to change providers at the drop of a hat or a whim. It's a whole new ball game (Table 10.3).

The organizations we've grown up with were designed to equip the world with stable products. McDonald's, for instance, came about from, first, task specialization as the McDonald brothers concentrated on selling hamburgers because they'd realized that was where most of their profit came from, and then from Ray Kroc, as the seller of milkshake machines to the McDonald's hamburger restaurant, who decided to franchise these restaurants across the country. The parallel success of the automobile led the move to the suburbs, which created space for the franchise's expansion, and Kroc's obsessive search for standardization and automation enabled the golden arches franchise to maintain its quality and cost balance and expand all over the world.

The dominant model in this period was to patent an innovation to protect it, standardize the process, roll out to all markets by attacking them in military fashion through a blitz marketing campaign, and then cookie-cutter replication. Managers thought in terms of products lines, sold to customer segments, delivered through task-by-task specialized supply chains where costs and quality were secured by extreme standardization—and adopted IT systems to drive this through as they became ubiquitous. This worked superbly. The only downside, that companies like McDonald's struggle with to this day, is that it doesn't handle variety well. Supply chains are complex, processes are rigid, change is by nature a problem, and IT often confuses issues even further.

Traditional line hierarchies had the clear drawback of creating functional silos with poor information flows. Frederick Taylor came up with

Technical Innovation	Organizational Innovation	Company Design
Steam	Division of labor	Top-down hierarchy
Electricity	Standardization of processes	Staff-line functional structure
Digital	Continuous improvement	Value streams of teams

Table 10.3 Evolution of Technical and Organizational Innovation and Company Design

the notion that "one best way" could be defined by engineers and adopted as a standardized process. His assumption was that workers could not both carry out the work and think about their own work methods in the way an overseeing engineer could. His solution was widely adopted throughout the twentieth century, and staff departments were created to run line hierarchies generating the infamous matrices where one person had both a line boss (division) and a functional boss (such as sales, finance, logistics, quality, or Lean). Such organizations were obsessed with process standardization, and all too often, staff departments behaved as silos as well, solving their own problems from their perspective and burdening line managers with ever increasing constraints.

Toyota's reasoning started from a very different point of view. Toyota's leaders realized that as the company grew, it would develop what it called "big company disease": shifting focus away from customers and toward internal concerns—bureaucratic concerns that would trump employee realities in the workplace and complacency that would foster unnecessary investment and legacy choices. Rather than worry about having the perfect organization, Toyota leaders committed to keeping their focus on adding value for their customers and encouraging a healthy dose of paranoia of falling behind customer expectations and competitors' capabilities. Toyota developed a model based on the constant dynamics shown in Table 10.4.

This dynamic vision of value is supported by the ongoing practice of find, face, frame, and form in always seeking to better understand the relationship the company has with its customers and how this relationship can be improved and deepened. Trust drives customer loyalty, and loyalty supports profitable growth.[2] By linking kaizen in the workplace with value for customers, Toyota has pioneered a uniquely different enterprise model, fully adapted to today's business conditions. Alfred Sloan's big idea was

Value	Value Analysis	Value Engineering
Understanding customer experience and making sure to provide value according to customers' specific preferences to support their lifestyles	Improving products and services currently in production to increase customer value and understand current problems in the delivery process	Design new features and functions to provide more value to customers by solving current problems with innovative solutions and build future capabilities

Table 10.4   Toyota's Business Model Based on Constant Dynamics

that you didn't need to know the specifics of a business to run it, as long as the numbers were good. This ushered in a world of mediating relationships with work through financial accounts and ultimately treating people and their products as meaningless—black boxes to be bought, sold, and refinanced.

Lean thinking is a more powerful competitive model precisely because the relationships between the firm and its customers and between the employees and their work are at the very center of management focus. This is a dynamic relationship that can be deepened every day as more detailed problems are solved and that can evolve every day as the world changes—and people's expectations and needs with it.

CONCLUSION

Toward a Waste-Free Society

Lean strategies are a more powerful fit to the disruptive—and disrupted—world of the twenty-first century than the tired old manage-by-the-numbers strategies of the past century. First, the focus on orientation and team flexibility make Lean strategies more agile and better at adapting to rapidly changing circumstances. Second, Lean strategies are far less costly because they don't involve making huge gambles on the basis of "boss knows best" visions. The progressive capability-building approach of Lean strategies make it far less likely to throw good money after bad on bet-the-farm bets that don't pan out. The Lean strategy involves a revolutionary mindset change. For more than a quarter of a century, strategy has been shaped by five key questions captured by Michael Porter:

1. How do you respond to the bargaining power of customers?

2. How do you increase our bargaining power over suppliers?

3. How do you counter the threat of substitute products or services?

4. How do you deal with the threat of new entrants?

5. How do you better jockey for position among current competitors?

Businesses that frame strategy through this mindset think in terms of maximizing power and positioning. They treat the enterprise as a black box whose activities are a commodity, a constant rather than dynamic variable in the formula for growth. They seek growth through external factors, whether that is an obsession with their global footprint (which divisions to sell, which companies to buy—to acquire footholds in markets or technologies), a cold eye toward operational cost reduction (after all, if activities are commodities, there should be a way to achieve the same for cheaper), or a speculative approach to using financial engineering as a means of optimizing the pieces of their enterprises in markets that behave as much like casinos as like sources of capital.

To which we can only ask one question: how's that working for you? The overall outcome of this approach is questionable, to say the least. The durability of companies is more fragile than ever today. At the latest tally, the average lifespan of companies on the Standard & Poor's 500 Index has fallen from 60 years in 1960 to 25 years in 1980, and it is down to 18 years today. Although financial valuations remain high, EBITDAs (the measure of operational efficiency) continue to fall. Innovation is stagnant at best and from a managerial perspective the last 20 years have been nothing short of disastrous, with estimates of less than 30 percent of employees feeling engaged, 82 percent of people not trusting their boss, 50 percent quitting their job because of their managers and the feeling that 60 to 80 percent of leaders act destructively.[1]

In her powerful new book *Makers and Takers*, journalist Rana Foroohar cautions that the rise of financial activism as the source of an ever-growing share of corporate profits has in fact diverted resources, attention, and commitment from those companies that make things better through making better things.[2] This aligns with the Porter-based, mechanistic, profit-optimizing vision of strategy, where the winners are the financiers who thrive on corporate wheeling and dealing and make a profit on the market every time a company or a division is bought and sold, irrespective of the value actually created by the said company. Not surprisingly, this strategic model is concurrent with the rise of shareholder activism and the notion that the value of a company is defined by its share price rather than by the value it offers its customers, its long-term profitability, or the strength of its brands.

Despite this environment, Toyota has grown to dominate the automotive market by following a radically different approach—indeed, a "non-strategy" according to Wall Street analysts. Toyota's leaders chose to respond to five different questions:

1. How do you increase customer satisfaction to build brand loyalty?

2. How do you develop individual know-how to increase labor productivity?

3. How do you improve collaboration across functions (and other partners) to boost organizational productivity?

4. How do you encourage problem solving to better engage employees and grow human capital?

5. How do you support an environment conducive to mutual trust and developing great teams to nurture social capital?

Neither Toyota nor any company with a complete Lean strategy treats the enterprise and its activities as a black box. Its activities are seen instead as an organic, generative, dynamic source of growth and renewal. They are seen as the very source of fit to market by following customers narrowly and flexibly, of innovation through partnership with suppliers, and of putting relentless pressure on competitors by challenging themselves on key technical issues. Traditional strategy assumes that you can ideate the best strategic "plan" and then buy the operational "best practice" for execution. We, on the other hand, completely reject this distinction between strategy and execution: you cannot buy this quality transactionally. You must grow it, continuously.

The mainstream strategic model emphasizes the leader's grand vision and the organization's execution discipline. The best example that comes to mind is Jack Welch's ability to turn stodgy old GE into a "growth stock" by replacing 60 percent of the business (getting out of industry and refocusing on financial services), cutting head count by 40 percent, and making a fortune for himself in the process. GE has since had to find its way back to industry and adopted . . . Lean thinking to do so.

The Lean strategy, on the contrary, rests on radically different assumptions.

The first is that execution is not the result of enforcement by middle management but of the careful development of autonomy and flexibility of value-adding teams through continuous efforts at kaizen. Management's role is to support and sustain training and improvement so that the teams themselves find, step by step, better ways to work and support the organization's mission in satisfying customers.

Second, strategic direction is not just the result of the leader's bold vision but, rather, the outcome of patient discussion with frontline teams to find how high-level intent can be made to work in practice by developing everyday capabilities.

The Lean strategy rests on the Lean learning system to craft together a better way, every day, everywhere, with everyone.

This strategic learning occurs at three levels:

- Team-based agility makes it easier to pick up customer signals and respond faster to adapt continuous processes to customer real-life usages.

- Kaizen activities and managing learning curves creates a reflexive learning environment where development topics are tackled deliberately in order to reinvest gains from improvement into technical and teamwork learning.

- These two levels of learning activities build up a strategic capability for learning to learn: how to go to the market with experiments, and follow them up quickly if they work or backtrack without losses if they don't, but also the ability to face difficult issues and explore new domains to keep offering new, undiscovered value to customers.

How can this "learn to learn" strategic capability be acquired? The CEOs you've met in this journey have—just as they've all had to pivot their strategy in the wake of the Great Recession and the brutal market turbulence that ensued. This required them to change their minds and abandon the traditional management reasoning of define, decide, drive, deal:

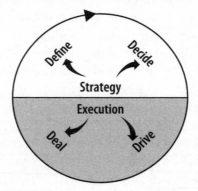

It forced them to accept the workplace-base, from the ground-up strategic thinking of find, face, frame, form:

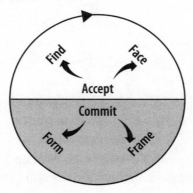

This, in turn, necessitated a deliberate commitment to learning on their part. Our 20-year study of lean transformation efforts has shown that CEOs who succeed with Lean all share three rare traits:

1. *They find a sensei:* After experimenting with improvement workshops and projects, at some point they look for and find a sensei with whom they can work.

2. *They accept the exercises the sensei prescribes:* Although some of the tasks seem counterintuitive or do not relate easily to what is currently perceived as urgent, they agree to explore and find out, and get involved in practical exercises to learn by doing.

3. *They commit explicitly to learning—their teams and themselves:* At some point, they look beyond immediate results from kaizen activities (which remain important as a sign of better response by the teams) and they look for learning (whether the experiment has succeeded or failed, what has this taught whom and what is the next step?)

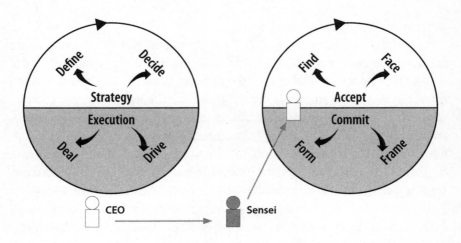

The need for this type of systematic and dynamic approach to strategy is becoming increasingly urgent. For two centuries Western societies have been educating their elites in abstract problem solving in which the optimal solutions omit external costs. Yet we are at a time when the true costs of making things can no longer be left out of the equation.

When faced with a world stripped of resources, in which there is limited access to capital and not much more than the amazing potential of each employee's mind, Toyota reinvented a frugal way to compete, based on a different way to think. The TPS model of Lean thinking was, to start with, to solve small problems as they arose, create abstract causal models, and return to concrete solutions until new insights appeared. Continuing this virtuous cycle over years and then decades helped generate one of the world's most resilient and productive organizations.

It also pointed to a better *system* of thinking and acting. This mindful way of solving problems recognized that shifting the burden of unresolved problems would always return as waste. It also recognized that its challenge would always be to solve the problem without passing on the burden to other people, be they operators, suppliers, or resource producers.

Daily progress offers a great source of daily motivation, even when it is hard to envision greater wins for people or companies. Improving every day with one's teammates creates a space of motivation for management and workers. They can come together to celebrate working well by striving to work better for customers and competing against competitors, by building customer loyalty capital, labor productivity, organizational productivity, human capital, and social capital rather than extracting more value from weaker partners.

This sense of progress and well-being can in fact help tackle even greater problems than the profound and yet trivial challenges of daily work. More people than ever seek the Western ideal of happiness through material consumption in the face of three dominant challenges: greater strain on the environment, increasingly saturated markets, and spreading structural inequalities. Each of these forces will touch us all in our daily lives in some form or other. Should we, as some suggest, abandon our way of life and return to . . . what? Or, as others do, ignore the problem and assume that mythical "free markets" will somehow fix things for the best?

We believe that Lean strategy offers a better way. By looking at how each of us, in the course of our working days, makes choices that generate waste at the same time as we create value, we can envision a better, more hopeful course: a waste-free society. One in which we (all of us) might be able to enjoy "prosperity without growth."[3]

This revolution starts with us. When faced with overwhelming global challenges, it's easy to feel powerless, keep our heads down, and just do as we're told. Adopting a Lean strategy, on the other hand, gives us a way to change the larger story by changing our own story. The Lean learning system teaches us how to think differently about everyday instances—upside down, so to speak, because it rubs where it encounters mainstream thinking. Just-in-time and jidoka are a suit that is a size too small, so it rubs and pinches and shows you exactly where you should lose weight, and it suggests the exercise program to do so. Lean thinking frees us to think for ourselves and to write our own stories.

Practicing Lean thinking gives us a compass that doesn't tell us what to do or where to go but, rather, tells us what is up and what is down and which direction our next step should take toward the North Star of a waste-free society. In changing our thinking, we change ourselves. In changing ourselves, we model a new kind of behavior aimed toward reconciliation: reconciling the business with its customers, reconciling people with their work, and reconciling the company with its outside partners. Practicing Lean thinking daily, in its two dimensions of deeper technical understanding and greater teamwork across functional barriers, also grows other perceptions of both our competence and our confidence that we will solve problems with them, not against them—the two pillars of trust. By modeling a determination to face challenges with courage, creativity, and cooperation, we tip the balance of conflicts and influence the spirit of the times. In doing so, we change the world by redefining what is possible when everyone works hard and mindfully together. This strategy creates a more resilient company (needed in today's economy), a more innovative company (in every definition, and, yes, essential given the way companies work in everything from digital to anything else), and a more resourceful company (better use of capital and resources and, yes, people, at a time when companies must do better with their people while creating less waste).

A Lean strategy is both personal (learn to learn) and global (learn to lead). In this, it offers hope that we can reframe issues that today seem impossible to tackle, and we can build the relationships we need to face against seemingly impossible odds and, in the end, prevail, step by step. To go fast, we must first go by ourselves, and then, to go far, we must go together. We can proudly look back at what we've accomplished as a society in the past and feel confident that if we learn to learn, we can face today's challenges and amaze ourselves with the solutions we'll come up with tomorrow.

NOTES

ACKNOWLEDGMENTS

1. Robert S. Kaplan and H. Thomas Johnson. *Relevance Lost: The Rise and Fall of Management Accounting*. Boston: Harvard Business School Press, 1987.

INTRODUCTION

1. See, for example, Erik Brynjolfsson and Andrew McAffee, *The Second Machine Age*, W. W. Norton, New York, 2014.

2. Takahiro Fujimoto, *The Evolution of Manufacturing Systems at Toyota*, Oxford University Press, New York, 2001.

3. James Womack and Daniel Jones, *Lean Thinking*, Simon & Schuster, New York, 1996.

CHAPTER 1

1. P. Hawken, A. Lovins, and L. H. Lovins, *Natural Capitalism*, Little, Brown, New York, 1999.

2. James Womack, Daniel Jones, and Daniel Roos, *The Machine That Changed the World*, Rawson Macmillan, New York, 1990.

3. Spelled out in Art Byrne, *The Lean Turnaround*, McGraw-Hill, New York, 2012, and *The Lean Turnaround Action Guide*, McGraw-Hill, New York, 2016.

4. See Pascal Dennis, *Getting the Right Things Done: A Leader's Guide to Planning and Execution*, Lean Enterprise Institute (LEI), Cambridge, MA, 2006.

CHAPTER 2

1. H. Neave, *The Deming Dimension*, SPC Press, Knoxville, TN, 1990.

2. J. Shook, "How to Change a Culture: Lessons from NUMMI," *MIT Sloan Management Review*, January 2010.

3. See Orest J. Fiume and Jean E. Cunningham, *Real Numbers: Management Accounting in a Lean Organization*, Managing Times Press, Durham, NC, 2003.

CHAPTER 3

1. E. Simpson, *War from the Ground Up*, Oxford University Press, New York, 2013.

2. Described in Stephen Bungay, *The Art of Action*, Nicholas Brealey, London, 2011.

3. D. Dinero, *Training Within Industry: The Foundation of Lean*, Productivity Press, New York, 2005.

4. Jeff Liker, *The Toyota Way*, McGraw-Hill, New York, 2004.

5. Jeff Liker and Gary Convis, *The Toyota Way to Lean Leadership*, McGraw-Hill, New York, 2012.

6. C. Christensen, R. Alton, C. Rising, and A. Waldeck, "The Big Idea: The New M&A Playbook," *Harvard Business Review*, March 2011.

CHAPTER 4

1. Teruyuki Minoura, *Toyota Special Report*, 2003.

2. A great chronicle of this can be found in *The Birth of Lean*, Koichi Shimokawa and Takahiro Fujimoto, eds., Lean Enterprise Institute, Cambridge, MA, 2009; and the original training materials in Toshiko Narusawa and John Shook, *Kaizen Express*, Lean Enterprise Institute, Cambridge, MA, 2009.

3. N. Shirozou and S. Moffett, "As Toyota Closes on GM, Quality Concerns Also Grow," *Wall Street Journal*, August 4, 2004.

4. E. Osono, N. Shimizu, and H. Takeuchi, *Extreme Toyota*, Wiley, New York, 2008.

5. http://www.toyota-global.com/company/vision_philosophy/toyota_production_system/origin_of_the_toyota_production_system.html.

6. See Toyota's recounting of this on its website, http://www.toyota-global.com/company/toyota_traditions/quality/mar_apr_2004.html.

7. https://www.youtube.com/watch?v=oKudR9wxO9M; https://www.youtube.com/watch?v=dbWnS127x14; and https://youtube/pB7GDtVmgPs.

8. R. Revans, *ABC of Action Learning*, Gower, New York, 2011.

9. I. Kato and A. Smalley, *Toyota Kaizen Methods*, Productivity Press, New York, 2011.

CHAPTER 5

1. T. Harada, *Management Lessons from Taiichi Ohno*, McGraw-Hill, New York, 2015.

CHAPTER 6

1. E. I. DuPont de Nemours & Co., Inc., *Guide to Venture Analysis*, 1971.

2. M. E. Raynor and M. Ahmed, "Three Rules for Making a Company Truly Great," *Harvard Business Review*, April 2013.

3. https://www.youtube.com/watch?v=lIzCjT7Znmc.

CHAPTER 7

1. Cynthia Laumuno and Enver Yucesan, *Lean Manufacturing at FCI (A): The Global Challenge*, INSEAD, *Harvard Business Review* Case Study, June 25, 2012.

2. Cynthia Laumuno and Enver Yucesan, *Lean Manufacturing at FCI (B): Deploying Lean at Nantong China*, INSEAD, *Harvard Business Review* Case Study, June 25, 2012.

CHAPTER 8

1. David Magee, *How Toyota Became #1*, Penguin, New York, 2007.

2. Eiji Toyoda, *Toyota: Fifty Years in Motion*, Kodansha International, Tokyo, 1985.

3. G. S. Vasilash, "Considering Sienna: 53,000 Miles in the Making," *Automotive Design & Production*, Gardner Publications, 2003.

4. Kim Reynolds, "First Test: 2011 Toyota Sienna LE, The New Best Minivan on the Market," *MotorTrend*, December 24, 2009.

CHAPTER 9

1. C. Christensen, M. Raynor, and R. MacDonald, "What Is Disruptive Innovation?" *Harvard Business Review*, December 2015.

2. D. Simester, "Why Great New Products Fail," *MIT Sloan Management Review*, March 15, 2016.

CHAPTER 10

1. C. Bailey and A. Maiden, "What Makes Work Meaningful—or Meaningless," *MIT Sloan Review*, Summer 2016.

2. F. Reicheld, "The One Number You Need to Grow," *Harvard Business Review*, December 2003.

CONCLUSION

1. Thomas Chamorro-Premuzic, "What Science Tells Us About Leadership Potential," *Harvard Business Review*, September 2016.

2. Rana Foroohar, *Makers and Takers: The Rise of Finance and the Fall of American Business*, Crown Business, New York, 2016.

3. Tim Jackson, *Prosperity Without Growth: Economics for a Finite Planet*, Earthscan, London, 2009.

INDEX

Note: page numbers followed by "f," "t," and "n" indicate figures, tables, and footnotes, respectively.

A3 thinking, x, 4–5, 216, 233. *See also* Problem solving
Accommodation, 223
Accounting. *See* Growth, finances, and accounting
Acquired companies and leading from the ground up, 65–68, 67t
Action learning, 105
Action plans vs. learning curves, 49
Agetsuma, Fumio, 204t
Ahmed, Mumtaz, 154
AIO, 100–101, 102–103
Alliance MIM, 121–127
Alternatives, 225, 225f
Ambition, 82–83
Andon boards, 86, 90
Archimedes, 73
Assimilation, 223
Atmosphere in teams, 121
Autonomous machines, 90
Autonomy
  confidence facing problems and, 89
  engagement and, 105
  individual problem solving and, 193t
  learning by doing and, 57
  meaning of, 88
  OK/no-OK judgments and, 88–89
  problem solving with standards and, 109
  pull systems and, 112
  separation of human work from machine work and, 89–90
  team members and, x, 100, 139
  training and, 131
visual management and, 137–138
work satisfaction and, 106

Ballé, Freddy, 15–16, 18–19, 31, 132, 141, 174, 183
Ballé, Michael, 6, 19n
Batching and waste, 47–48
Batch sizes, large, 96, 188–189
Best practices, changing the thinking on, 19
Big company disease, xx–xxii, xxiii–xxiv, xxivf, 175, 248
Bihr, JC, 121–127
Black box, 251, 253
"Blue ocean" strategies, xxi–xxii
Bordier, Laurent, 216
Boundaries in teams, 120
Bourgeois, Christian, 21
Bouthillon, John, 59–63
Boyd, Steve, 214
"Brown ocean" strategies, xxi–xxii
Built-in quality. *See* Jidoka
Bureaucratization, leading from the ground up and, 57–58
Byrne, Art, 7, 39, 143, 157, 159, 195

Cadence, 95, 189
Capability development. *See also* Organizing for learning
  detectability and, 86, 86t
  financial management vs. Lean thinking and, 27t
  form phase and, 49–50
  for innovation, 232–233
  "learn to learn" strategic capability, 253–255
  people-centric approach and, 64
  progressive approach, 251

Capability development (*Cont.*)
uncertainty, using Lean strategy for
learning capability to respond to,
164–166
CEO role and thinking differently, 23–24, 255
Chaize, Jacques, 1–2, 6, 23–24, 33–34, 50,
53–54, 66, 71–72, 91–92, 117–119, 195,
197, 223, 237–238
Challenging oneself as strategic intent, 142
Change. *See also* Improvement; Kaizen
hurdles to taking the next step, 129–130
identifiable arc of organic change,
127–128
as individual skill, 57
Socla change framework, 119, 119t
steps in Lean change engine, 128
Chief engineer systems and product models,
201–208, 203–206t, 215
Clerico, Fabiano and Furio, 166–174
Cognitive skills, 240t
Collaboration, intensification of, 59, 67–68,
123. *See also* Teams and teamwork
Competitive advantage
ambition and, 82
changing thinking and, 7, 13
from developing people, 21
knowledge to reduce cost and, 20
National Electric Code and, 160
problem-solving skills and, 162
strategy and, 9, 142
sustainable, 114, 197
Toyota and, 74, 80–82
Conditions
jidoka, 84–85, 86–90
just-in-time, 84–85, 90–93
Confidence, 89, 90, 132
Constant dynamics model, 248–249, 249t
Continuous flow, 92, 95–97
Core functionality of a product, 216–220
Cost accounting, 40, 47
Costs
cost base reduction by intensifying kaizen
(FCI case study), 174–187
cost planning, 160
design phase, unnecessary costs from,
19
installed cost, 161
investment cost, 79
learning for reducing, 20
local raising of costs and revealing waste,
139
people viewed as cost, 146

standards and, 109
target costing, 160
Culture of "problems first," 142, 240–241
Curiosity, 241
Customer concerns
after-sales complaints board, 35–36
customer gemba visits, 172
extracting vs. adding value, 244–245
innovation from customer perspective,
227–228
karakuri and, 102
process focus vs., xx–xxi
right and wrong from customers' point of
view, 88
safety, quality, cost, lead time, morale, and
energy efficiency in TPS, 83
varying priorities among customers,
168–169
"what do they really use?," 211
"what do they say they want?," 210–211
"who are our customers?," 210
Customer values investigation, 171t

Daily problem solving
Clerico brothers case study, 173
as frame, 108–110, 108t
innovation and, 229
performance problems, daily, 50, 138
Dané, Cyril, 100–101, 102–103
Define, decide, drive, deal cycle, 24–26, 25f, 27t,
29t, 224, 229, 254–255
Deming, W. Edwards, 29, 30
Design and engineering. *See* Engineering,
design, and accelerating gains
Design robustness, 78
Detectability, 86, 86t
Disruptive theory of innovation, 224–225
Division of labor, narrow, 155
Dojo training, 124, 125–126, 172
Drucker, Peter, 81
Dynamic virtuous cycles of Lean, 197, 197f

Earnings before interest, taxes, depreciation,
and amortization (EBITDA), 144, 174,
175f, 176f, 252
Economies of scale, 14, 155
Employee satisfaction, 105–106, 128, 237–244
End-to-end value stream improvement
projects, 139
Engagement of employees, 105
Engineering, design, and accelerating gains,
195–221

chief engineer systems and product models, 201–208, 203–206t
design robustness, 78
learning by doing for people-centric solutions (fuel dispenser case study), 209–220
people centricity and product design, 200–201
sustainable growth and, 196–199
takt time of product evolution, 202, 203t–206t, 207
Toyota and, 199–207
value formed by people-centric solutions, 207–209
Evolution of products and of technical processes, 199
Experiments
assimilation and accommodation, 223
find phase, 35–36
making things better, 31–32
measurement and, 38
repeated, to grow learning, 165
Socla case study, 187–193
targeted, 50
thinking differently and, 12–13, 17–18
at Toyota, ix

Face phase. *See* Find, face, frame, form (4F) phases
FCI group, 174–187
Fiancette, Frédéric, 1–2, 23, 53, 66–67, 71, 92, 117–119, 187–190, 195, 197, 198, 238
Financial management. *See* Growth, finances, and accounting
Find, face, frame, form (4F) phases
acquired company case study and, 67–68
capability development (form phase), 49–50
ground-up strategic thinking and, 254–255
improvement dimensions and pushback (frame phase), 42–49, 46t
improving to learn (find phase), 31–37
Lean thinking and, 28t
measurement (face phase), 38–42
role of sensei and, 166
traditional management vs., 27–29, 29t
Fiume, Orest "Orry," 6, 14, 39–41, 68, 143, 148–152, 156–157, 195
5S (sorting, straightening, sweeping, standardizing, sustaining), 60, 60–61n, 133, 240t

Flows
from clearing the window to improving flow of quality (Clerico brothers cases study), 166–174
complicated, 96
continuous flow, 92, 95–97
improving, to understand the situation, 31–32
one-piece flow, 95
sales and inventory turnover increases and, 161–162
of value, ideas, and work, 80
work routing flow, 134, 135f
Ford, Henry, 79, 211, 246
Ford Company, 99
Forecasts, 99–100
Form phase. *See* Find, face, frame, form (4F) phases
Foroohar, Rana, 252
4Ms (manpower, machines, materials, methods), 107, 240t
Frame phase. *See* Find, face, frame, form (4F) phases
Frames and tools, 71–115
ambition, 82–83
daily problem solving, 108–110, 108t
defined, 73
employee satisfaction and, 105–106
"encourage kaizen" as frame, 145–146
how Toyota chose to compete, 76–80
jidoka conditions, 84–85, 86–90
just-in-time conditions, 84–85, 90–93
kaizen as frame, 80, 110–112, 111t
kanban, 97–103, 101f
Lean learning system and, 71–73, 112–115, 113f
leveled plans, 97
regular pickup trains, 103–104
standards, 107
takt time, 93–97, 94t
Taylorism and management by objectives vs., 80–82
TPS as "Thinking People System," 73–76
visual management, 107–108
France, Lean practices in, 6
Frederick II the Great, 55
"From the ground up" as strategic concept, 54, 254–255. *See also* Leading from the ground up
Frontline managers
autonomy, developing, 106
eliminating obstacles, 106

Frontline managers (*Cont.*)
    frames for development, 106–107
    habit change and, 137, 187t
    kaizen, respect for people, and, 132
    Lean change engine and, 128
    leveled plans and, 97
    role and responsibilities of, 112
Fujimoto, Takahiro, xviii
Fumex, Matthias, 188–193

Gains, accelerating. *See* Engineering, design,
    and accelerating gains
Gates, Bill, 42
GE (General Electric), 253
Gemba
    customer gemba visits, 172
    leading from the ground up and, 53, 55
    at Socla, 24, 237
Genchi genbutsu, 202
General Electric (GE), 253
General Motors (GM), 81, 149
Goals
    ambition and, 82, 83
    behaving contrary to, 48
    changing thinking and, 50
    counterproductive and contradictory,
        81–82
    daily problem solving and, 173
    define, decide, drive, deal cycle and, 24–25,
        29t
    FCI case study, 176–177, 177t
    in find and face phases, 11
    of innovation, 227–228
    leading from the ground up and, 69
    learning cycle and large-scale goals, 39
    Toyota's low emissions goals, 225
    Wiremold stretch goals, 143, 150
Growth, finances, and accounting, 141–162
    financial managers, convincing, 146
    financial statements and "Plain English
        P&L," 40, 41, 44, 149–150, 151f, 158
    kaizen, encouraging, 143–146
    margin increases through built-in quality,
        153–154
    new product introduction from flexible
        investments, 159–161
    physical vs. financial metrics, 38–42
    return on assets (ROA), 154
    return on investment (ROI), 142–143,
        147–148, 152, 153f
    sales and inventory turnover increases,
        161–162
    standard cost accounting, 149–150, 155
    strategy and strategic intents, 142–143
    thinking differently and, 26–27, 27t
    total basis diminishing by intensity of
        kaizen, 155–159
    traditional financial management vs. Lean,
        146–150
    Wiremold case study, 143–144, 148–152,
        155–161, 158t
Growth, sustainable, 196–199
Guelton, Evrard, 163, 167, 209–217

Habits, 120, 121, 137, 187t, 240–241
Hansei (self-reflection), 30, 32, 126
Hasegawa, Tatsuo, 203t
Hawken, Paul, 3
Hayashi, Nampachi, 31
"Highest-paid person's opinion" (HIPPO),
    25–26
Honda, Takayasu, 205t
Hoshin planning system, 5
Human capital. *See* People-centric approach
Human work vs. machine work, 89–90
Hume, David, 165–166

Improvement
    directions and dimensions, in frame phase,
        42–49, 46t
    as discovery, 18–19
    end-to-end value stream improvement
        projects, 139
    kanban and, 100
    leadership attitudes, 58–59
    projects list approach, 2
    strategic principles, 58
    uneven pace of, 118
    waste-generating mechanisms as pushback,
        46–48
Improvement, continuous. *See also* Kaizen
    commitment to, 18
    FCI case study, 177, 179f
    Socla case study, 189, 190f
Incentives to learn, 49–50
Innovation, 225f
    alternatives, 225
    assimilation and accommodation, 223
    attachment to legacy technologies, 223–224
    capability development and, 232–233
    from customer perspective, 227–228
    disruption theory of, 224–225
    innovation gaps, 224–225, 234
    Lean theory of, 227

learning curves, managing, 226–227, 226f,
228f, 230, 231–232, 235
Proditec case study, 228–234, 231t, 232t
technical and organizational, evolution of,
246–248, 248t
Insecurities, 64
Installed cost, 161
Inventory. *See also* Just-in-time
Clerico brothers case study and doubling of
inventory turns, 169, 170f, 171f
improved inventory turns from increasing
quality and flow and reducing lead
times, 161–162
Toyota causes for poor delivery and high
inventories, 95–97
two ways of thinking about, 13–14
Investment cost, 79
Involvement of employees, 105

Jidoka (built-in quality)
Ehrenfeld on, 78n
FCI case study, 181–183
four basic elements of, 87
as frame, 84–85, 86–90
teams and, 136
at Toyota, 77–78
Jobs, Steve, 42, 224
Jones, Daniel, 2–3, 4, 6, 21, 45–46, 76, 148
Just-in-time
at Alliance MIM, 123, 126
employee satisfaction and, 105–106
end-to-end projects, 139
as frame, 73, 84–85, 90–93
intensifying supplier cooperation and, 145
MRP vs., 149
multiskill training and, 145
teams and, 136
at Toyota, 98–99
at Wiremold, 148–149

Kaizen. *See also* Improvement, continuous
accelerating from teams, 144–145
benefit of, 34
classic six steps of, 111, 111t
Clerico brothers case study, 173
cost base reduction by intensifying kaizen
(FCI case study), 174–187, 186f
defined, 32
"encourage kaizen" as frame, 145–146
events, 3, 4
facing deep problems as point of firsthand
kaizen, 69

financial performance and, 153–154
find phase and, 32–33
frames and, 80, 110–112
innovation and, 223–235
inventory turns and, 161–162
just-in-time conditions and, 85
Lean strategy and, 141, 143–144
learning by doing, 57–63
local raising of costs and revealing waste,
139
measurement and, 38
people–work relationship and, 242t
reflexive learning environment and, 254
Socla and, 117
teams, respect for people, and, 128–132
three main uses of, 50
total cost basis diminishing with intensity
of, 155–159
Kanban cards and system
as frame, 73, 97–103
rules of, 101–102
whiteboards, 101, 101f
Karakuri devices, 100–101, 102–103
Kato, Isao, 111
Key performance indicators (KPIs), 150, 176,
177t, 178f
Kodak, 223–224
KPIs (key performance indicators), 150, 176,
177t, 178f
Kroc, Ray, 247

Leadership
bureaucracy and, 57–58
define, decide, drive, deal vs. find, face,
frame, form, 29t, 229
employee satisfaction and, 129
engagement vs. strategy and execution, 57
"lack of leadership commitment," 239
people-centric approach and, 66
people–work relationship and, 238–244
personal transformation and, 24
in teams, 120–121
transformational change of posture, xxii
Leading from the ground up, 53–69
acquired company case study, 65–68, 67t
aim of, 55
attitudes, 58–59
to face real challenges, 53, 68–69
learning by doing, 57–63
meaning of, 54–57
people-centric solutions, looking for, 63–68
PO Construction case study, 59–63

"Lean" as verb, 28, 75
Lean Enterprise Institute (LEI), 6
Lean Global Network, 6
Lean strategy
    accomplishments of, 11, 11f
    accounting and finance decisions and, 141
    assumptions, failure to understand, 12–21
    assumptions, radical, 253
    "brown ocean" vs. "blue ocean" strategies,
        xxi–xxii
    defined, 8–11
    elements of, 163
    engineering work, structure of, 208–209
    as growth strategy, 159
    kaizen and, 141, 143–144
    "learn to learn" strategic capability,
        253–255
    Porter-based, mechanistic, profit-
        optimizing vision vs., 251–253
    response for every problem segment,
        208–209, 209f
    three strategic intents, 142–143
    Toyota's concrete method to pursue, 147
    Wiremold and, 143
Lean thinking. *See also* Thinking differently
    as action learning, 106
    big company disease and, xx–xxii
    deep transformation and, 245–246
    defined, 5–8
    early implementation efforts, 1–5
    five principles of, 7
    four deep questions, xxii–xxiii
    "outside in" vs. "inside out," 7–8
    reference points in a Lean thinking space,
        193t
    relationship to work and, 238–239
    as structured method to learn to learn, 164
    sustainable growth and, 196–199
    Taylorist "Lean" programs, 196
    three dynamic virtuous cycles of, 197, 197f
Lean Thinking (Womack and Jones), 2–3, 5,
    21, 148
Learning by doing
    connections across silos, 65
    gemba-based solutions and, 55
    leading from the ground up and, 57–63
    Lean learning system and, 114
    Lean thinking and, 31
    people-centric solutions and (fuel dispenser
        case study), 209–221
    Plan-Do-Check-Act (PDCA) method and,
        29

small mistakes and, 69
    traditional vs. Lean thinking and, 29–31
    Training Within Industry (TWI) and, 56
    workplace conditions for, 84
Learning curves, 49, 226–227, 226f, 228f, 230,
    231–232, 235
Learning organization, 72
Learning system for growing value, 163–193
    from clearing the window to improving
        flow of quality (Clerico brothers case
        study), 166–174
    management and learning systems,
        balancing, 15, 15f
    to reduce cost base by intensifying kaizen
        (FCI case study), 174–187
    repeated experiments to grow learning
        (Socla case study), 187–193
    uncertainty, using Lean strategy for
        learning capability to respond to,
        164–166
Learning systems, Lean
    frames and, 71–72
    mastering, 112–115, 113f
"Learn to learn" strategic capability, 253–255
Legacy technologies, attachment to, 223–224
Leveled plans, 97
Leveled pull principle, 191
Liker, Jeff, 59
Line managers
    FCI case study, 185
    line hierarchies and matrices, 248
    role and responsibilities of, 87–89
Line of sight, 100, 173, 242t, 243
Lovins, Amory, 3

Machines, autonomous, 90
Machine work vs. human work, 89–90
Magee, David, 199
Makers and Takers (Foroohar), 252
Management. *See also* Frontline managers;
        Leadership; Leading from the ground
        up; Line managers
    essential mission of a manager, 137
    management and learning systems,
        balancing, 15, 15f
    promoting managers on their ability to
        learn, 136–139
    relationship to work and, 238–239
    role, redefining, 243–244
Management, financial. *See* Growth, finances,
        and accounting
Management accounting, 148

Management by objectives, 81–82
Manpower, machines, materials, methods (4Ms), 107, 240t
Manufacturing resource planning (MRP), 14, 149, 156
Margin increases through built-in quality, 153–154
McDonald's, 247
Meaningful work, 237–244
Measurement
    face phase, 38–42
    financial management vs. Lean thinking and, 27t
    find, face, frame, form (4F) phases and, 28
    metrics at Wiremold, 150–152
Mentors, 130–131
Mérel, Yves, 163, 174, 180, 182–185, 189
Mergers and acquisitions and leading from the ground up, 65–68, 67t
Minoura, Teruyuki, 73–74
Mistakes, large vs. small, 69
Montaigne, 54
Mori, Kazuo, 202
MRP (manufacturing resource planning), 14, 149, 156

Nakamura, Kenya, 201
National Electric Code, 160
Natural capitalism, 2–3
New product development and introduction, 142–143, 159–161
Next step, anticipating, 130

Obeya rooms, 5
OEE (overall equipment effectiveness), 183
Ohno, Taiichi, 16, 31, 56, 73, 98–99, 103, 133, 164, 174, 201
OK/no-OK judgments, 88–89
Okudaira, Soichiro, 206t
100 percent checking rate, 182–183
One-piece flow, 95
Operations analysis, 186t
Organizing for learning, 117–140
    Alliance MIM case study, 121–127
    boundaries, leaders, habits, and atmosphere in teams, 120–121
    kaizen and respect for people, 128–132
    promoting managers on ability to learn, 136–139
    Socla case study, 117–119, 119t
    team leaders and, 132–134

value streams and stable flow, 134–136, 135f
Outcome ahead of output, 78–79
Outcomes measurement. See Measurement
Overall equipment effectiveness (OEE), 183

People-centric approach
    bottom-up vs., 65
    developing vs. devaluing human capital, xxi
    employee satisfaction, 105–106, 128, 237–244
    leadership and, 57
    learning by doing and (fuel dispenser case study), 209–221
    looking for people-centric solutions, 63–68
    "people centric," defined, 64
    people-free organizational designs vs., 56
    people-free solutions vs., 19, 63–64
    "soft" vs., 69
    team development and, 126
    value and, 207–209
    visual management and, 138
People-free thinking. See also Taylorism
    management by objectives, 81–82
    organizational design and, 56, 132
    people-centric approach vs., 19, 63–64
    people viewed as cost, 146
Pickup trains, regular, 103
"Plain English P&L," 40, 41, 44, 150, 151f
"A plan a person" diagnostic, 243–244
Plan-Do-Check-Act (PDCA) method, 24, 29–30, 189
PO Construction (POC), 59–63
Point optimization, 48
Porter, Michael, 251
Prévot, Eric, 53, 66–67, 71, 187–190, 195
Price and quality at Toyota, 79–80
Price recovery, 152
Problems, putting first, 58–59, 142, 240
Problem solving, 223–235
    daily, 50, 108–110, 108t, 138, 173, 229
    daily performance, 50, 138
    habits, changing, 187t
    innovation and, 233–234
    people–work relationship and, 241
    Plan-Do-Check-Act (PDCA) method and, 24, 29–30
Proditec
    deep problems, 44–45
    find phase and, 34–37
    innovation and, 228–234, 231t, 232t
    outcomes measurement, 41–42

Product development and introduction, new, 142–143, 159–161
Production analysis hourly board, 136
Production instruction cards, 98
Profit and profitability. *See also* Growth, finances, and accounting
    customer loyalty and, 82, 220, 248
    customer value and, 208, 252
    external factors vs. value and, xix
    FCI and, 174, 175f
    Foroohar on financial activity and, 252
    gemba and, 196
    kaizen and, 153
    as means vs. goal, xix
    "Plain English P&L" and, 150
    productivity and, 158–159
    strategy and, 8
    sustainable, xi–xii, 28, 79, 198–199
    target costing and, 160
    Toyota and, 5–6, 12–13, 75, 79–80, 199–200
    traditional financial management and, 26–27, 27t, 146
    Wiremold and, 144, 148–149, 160
Pull systems. *See also* Just-in-time
    at Alliance MIM, 125–126
    beyond logistics, 104
    as frame, 92
    frames and, 71
    kaizen and, 112
    leveled pull principle, 191
    MPR vs. JIT, 149
    regular pickup trains, 103–104
    at Socla, 191–192
Purpose, in frame phase, 42

QFD (quality function deployment), 159–160
Quality. *See also* Jidoka (built-in quality)
    from clearing the window to improving flow of quality (Clerico brothers cases study), 166–174
    engineers, nominally attributing quality responsibility to, 214–215
    innovation and, 230
    purchasing, integrating, 216
    "quality gates," 213
    at Toyota, 77–79
    tracking all quality issues (fuel dispenser case study), 212–213
Quality assurance, 86–87
Quality function deployment (QFD), 159–160

Raynor, Michael, 154
Regular pickup trains, 103
Regulatory environment, 212
Repellin, Lionel, 69
Responsibility, taking, 129
Return on assets (ROA), 154
Return on investment (ROI), 142–143, 147–148, 152, 153f
Reusable learning
    innovation and, 227, 233
    intensification of kaizen and, 185
    meaning of, 162
    reusable knowledge vs., 165–166
Rhythm, 94–95
Riboulet, Christophe, 34–37, 41, 44, 50, 229–234
ROA (return on assets), 154
ROI (return on investment), 142–143, 147–148, 152, 153f

Safety procedures and team leaders, 133
Saito, Akihito, 204–205t
Sasaki, Shirou, 203t
Scaffolding
    frames and, 74, 84
    people-centric approach and, 19
Schmidt, Eric, 25
Scientific Management, 56
Self-reflection (hansei), 30, 32, 126
Sensei consultants
    Alliance MIM and, 126
    on continuous flow, 127
    on expense today vs. tomorrow, 114
    kaizen events, 3
    learning to learn and, 164–166
    PO Construction and, 60
    Proditec and, 34–35, 44
    Socla and, 2, 23, 198
    successful CEOs and, 255
    thinking differently and, 17–18
    Toyota and, 16
Separation of human work from machine work, 89–90
Sequence of tasks, progression through, 88
Setback, overcoming, 129
Shewhart circle, 29
Shook, John, 31
Silo thinking, xxi
Simpson, Emile, 54
Single-minute exchange of die (SMED), 111
Single-piece flow, 240t

Sloan, Alfred, 81, 149, 248–249
Smalley, Art, 111
SMED (single-minute exchange of die),
    111
Smith, Adam, 246
Socla
    acquired company, 66–68, 67t
    decline of Lean at, 195
    financial crisis and, 1–2
    frames and, 71–72
    improvement to learn, 33–34
    just-in-time and, 91–92
    leading from the ground up, 53–54
    organizing for learning and framework for
        change, 117–119, 119t
    repeated experiments to grow learning,
        187–193
    thinking differently, 23–24
Sorting, in 5S, 60, 60–61n
Spaghetti diagram, 240t
Stability
    frames and, 71
    value streams and stable work routing flow,
        134–136, 135f
Standard cost accounting, 149–150, 155
Standardized work
    cognitive skills and, 240t
    constant training, 145
    daily problem solving and, 108, 109
    team leaders and, 133, 134
    TPS and, 73
Standardizing, in 5S, 60, 60–61n, 133
Standards
    daily problem solving and, 109–110
    as frame, 107
    jidoka and, 88
Stop-at-every-defect, 71, 78, 85
Stop-at-first-defect, 183
The story, changing, xvii–xx
Straightening, in 5S, 60, 60–61n
Strategy. *See* Lean strategy
Subcontractors, 60, 61
Suggestion systems
    Clerico brothers case study, 173
    daily problem solving and, 138
    flow of ideas and, 80
    Ford, 99, 200
    frontline managers and, 112
    jidoka and, 90
    kaizen and, 3, 32
    teams and, 119

    Toyota and, 18, 74, 99, 200
    TPS and, 81
Sustainable growth, 196–199
Sustainable profitability, xi–xii, 28, 79, 198–199
Sustaining, in 5S, 60, 60–61n
Sweeping, in 5S, 60, 60–61n
Systems approach vs. silo thinking, xxi

Takeuchi, Hirotaka, 75
Takt time
    calculating, 94–95, 94t
    as frame, 92
    of product evolution, 202–208
    rhythm vs. rate and, 93–94
    Socla, 188, 189
Target costing, 160
Taylor, Frederick, 56, 81, 149, 246, 247–248
Taylorism
    about, 56
    continuous flow and, 96
    "Lean" programs that are modern
        extensions of, 196
    meaningless work and, 237
    misinterpreting Toyota in terms of, 74–75
    mythical numbers in, 40
    narrow division of labor and economies of
        scale, 155
    non-thinking work, 81–82
    productivity and, 20
    traditional financial management and, 148
Teams and teamwork
    agility, team-based, 253
    boundaries, leaders, habits, and
        atmosphere, 120–121
    just-in-time conditions and, 85, 90–91
    kaizen efforts, 50, 144–145, 173
    manager-supported study of own work
        methods and improvement initiatives,
        138–139
    mission of value-adding team members,
        99–100
    people-centric development of teams, 126
    people with greatest learning-by-doing
        abilities and, 65
    production analysis hourly board and,
        136–137
    respect for people and, 128–132
    silo thinking vs., xxi
    small-step change as team norm, 130
    Socla and, 118–119
    team leaders, 132–134

Teams and teamwork (*Cont.*)
    time flexibility and, 238
    in Toyota sense, 91
    value streams and stable work routing flow,
        134–136, 135f
Tesco, 4
Thinking differently, 23–51. *See also* Lean
    thinking
    capability development (form phase),
        49–50
    CEO role and, 23–24
    define, decide, drive, deal cycle, 24–26, 25f,
        27t
    find, face, frame, form (4F) phases, 27–29,
        28t, 29t
    improvement dimensions and pushback
        (frame phase), 42–49, 46t
    improving to learn (find phase), 31–37
    measurement (face phase), 38–42
    PDCA cycle and, 24, 29–30
    traditional financial management thinking
        vs., 26–29, 27t, 29t
Tools, Lean. *See also* Frames and tools
    changing the thinking on, 15
    early implementation efforts and, 4–5
    as learning labs, 72
    as "tactics," 5
Total cost basis, 155–159
Total productive maintenance (TPM), 111
Toyoda, Akio, 63, 132
Toyoda, Eiji, 99, 164, 201
Toyoda, Kiichiro, 76, 91, 98
Toyota
    causes for poor delivery and high
        inventories, 95–97
    changing the story, xviii–xix
    chief engineer system and product models,
        201–208, 203–206t
    cleaner car revolution, 5–6
    concrete method to pursue Lean strategy,
        147
    constant dynamics model, 248–249, 249t
    constraints in 1950s and 1960s, 76–77
    cooperation vs. logistics, 91
    emissions and energy performance, 80
    as fast follower, 78
    flexible production lines, 74
    flows and, 8
    as imperfect, 75
    innovation at, 225
    jidoka and, 86
    kaizen, 110–112, 111t

    mission of value-adding team members,
        99–100
    as model, 3–4
    non-strategy of, 252–253
    PDCA and, 30
    profitability and, 5–6, 12–13, 75, 79–80,
        199–200
    quality, variety, and price, 77–80
    regular pickup trains, 103
    selling price strategy, 12–13
    takt time, 94
    team leader role, 133–134
Toyota Production System (TPS)
    better cars as secret to success, 199–200
    kanban, 98–100
    Lean thinking and, 5, 48
    learning system and European supplier
        case, 15–21
    as mental scaffolding structure, 74
    safety, quality, cost, lead time, morale, and
        energy efficiency, 83
    as system of frames or "Thinking People
        System," 73–76, 80–81, 114, 197
    Training Within Industry (TWI) and, 56
Toyota Production System leaflets, 99
Toyota Way, The (Liker), 59
TPAs (truck preparation areas), 180–181, 180t
TPM (total productive maintenance), 111
TPS. *See* Toyota Production System
Training, constant, 145
Training Within Industry (TWI), 56
Transformation, deep, 245–246
Truck preparation areas (TPAs), 180–181, 180t
Trust, mutual, 131, 132
TWI (Training Within Industry), 56

Uncertainty
    developing learning capability to respond
        to, 164–166
    exploring uncertain avenues, 129
    learning teams and, 49

Value. *See also* Learning system for growing
    value
    black box around construction of, xix
    customers and extracting vs. adding value,
        244–245
    flow of, 80
    loyal customers vs. share price, 147
    offering core and improved value in each
        generation, 207
    people-centric solutions and, 207–209

performance, quality, and cost-of-use
dimensions, 177, 180
"Value Stream Plain English P&L," 150, 151f
Value streams
end-to-end improvement projects, 139
of products performing a service for
customers, 202
seeing products as streams of value,
198–199
Socla, 189
stable work routing flow and, 134–136, 135f
Vareille, Pierre, 163, 174–177, 187
Variety, 79, 91
Visual control structures, 181
Visual management
FCI case study, 184–185
as frame, 107–108
manager support for, 137–138
organization and, 139–140
people–work relationship and, 242t
Volkswagen (VW), 5, 207

Waste. *See also* Inventory
changing the thinking about, 12–13, 13f
cognitive skills and, 240t
improvement, waste-generating
mechanisms as pushback against, 46–48
overfocus on, 2–3
Waste-free society, 251–257

Welch, Jack, 253
The window, clearing, 165, 166–174,
213–214, 229–230
Wiremold Company
acquisitions, 68, 155–156
competitors "chasing our tail lights,"
198–199
decline of Lean at, 195
financial management and strategy,
143–144, 148–152, 155–161, 158t
financial measures, 39–40, 40t
inventory and, 14
just-in-time at, 148–149
Lean thinking and, 5, 6
metrics at, 150–152
uneven pace of change, 118
Withdrawal cards, 98
Womack, Jim, 2–3, 4, 6, 21, 148
Work, meaningful, 237–244
Work conditions, 89, 106
Worker satisfaction, 105–106. *See also*
People-centric approach
Work routing flow, 134, 135f
World War II, 56

Yasui, Shinichi, 206t
Yokoten, 128
Yokya, Yuji, 202
Yoshida, Takeshi, 205t

ABOUT THE AUTHORS

Dr. Michael Ballé has been an executive coach for twenty years, cofounded the French Lean Institute, and has written five Lean books that have shaped international thinking and practice.

Daniel T. Jones is coauthor of the bestselling books that introduced Lean to the world (*The Machine That Changed the World, Lean Thinking,* and *Lean Solutions*) and is founder of the UK Lean Enterprise Academy and the Lean Global Network.

Jacques Chaize was CEO of Danfoss Water Controls, a leading French/Danish water valve specialist that served as a model of Lean practice. He cofounded the French Society for Organizational Learning.

Orest J. Fiume was Chief Financial Officer and a Director of The Wiremold Company, as well as a director emeritus of the Lean Enterprise Institute. He is the coauthor of *Real Numbers: Management Accounting in a Lean Organization,* and cofounded the Lean Accounting movement with others.